LIBRARY LESSONS
FOR GRADES 7–9
REVISED EDITION

by
Arden Druce

Illustrated by Carol Ditter Waters

The Scarecrow Press, Inc.
Lanham, Md. & London
1997

Please note: You are welcome to cut out and copy any pages which are worksheets. Permission to use other pages in this book must be sought through the publisher.

SCARECROW PRESS, INC.

Published in the United States of America
by Scarecrow Press, Inc.
4720 Boston Way
Lanham, Maryland 20706

4 Pleydell Gardens, Folkestone
Kent CT20 2DN, England

Copyright © 1997 by Arden Druce

British Cataloguing-in-Publication Information Available

Library of Congress Cataloging-in-Publication Data

Druce, Arden.
   Library lessons for grades 7–9 / by Arden Druce ; illustrated by Carol Ditter Waters.—Rev. ed.
        p. cm.—(School library media series ; no. 8)
   Includes index.
   ISBN 0-8108-3100-7 (cloth : alk. paper)
   1. Junior high school libraries—Activity programs—United States. 2. Library orientation for junion high school students—United States.   I. Waters, Carol Ditter.   II. Title.   III. Series
Z675.S3D794   1997
025.5678′223—dc20   95-46644
                                                                          CIP

ISBN 0-8108-3100-7 (cloth : alk. paper)

∞™The paper used in this publication meets the minimum requirements of American National Standard for Information Sciences—Permanence of Paper for Printed Library Materials, ANSI Z39.48–1984.
Manufactured in the United States of America.

CONTENTS

ACKNOWLEDGMENTS

Grateful acknowledgment is made to the following publishers for their contributions to this book:

The Associated Press for permission to reprint the article "Young prisoner's dad urges Singapore to cane him instead."

Barron's Educational Series, Inc., for permission to reprint an excerpt from *Profiles of American Colleges.*

Columbia University Press for permission to reprint a Key to Symbols page and to re-type and adapt excerpts from pages 495, 1517, 1796, and 2014 from *The Columbia Granger's Index to Poetry.*

Dynix for permission to reproduce material from their computer catalog.

Gale Research, Inc., for permission to reprint pages 173–175 from *Something About the Author.*

Hammond Incorporated for complimentary copies of *Essential Map Skills* and *The Intermediate World Atlas,* which were helpful in writing the lesson about atlases.

Little, Brown for permission to reprint page 603 from *Familiar Quotations.*

Marquis Who's Who for permission to enlarge and reprint the entry on Shirley Temple Black and for permission to reprint the Key to Information page from *Who's Who in America.*

Merriam-Webster, Inc., for permission to reproduce page 551 from *Webster's New Biographical Dictionary* and pages 224 and 799 from *Webster's New Geographical Dictionary.*

Random House, Inc., for permission to reproduce page 86 from *The Random House Thesaurus* and to paraphrase parts of an entry.

Star Tribune, The Minneapolis-St. Paul, for permission to reprint the feature story "Being Miss America is not an easy job" by Bruce Benidt.

The U.S. Bureau of the Census for use of the Education and Income statistical table.

The U.S. Department of Labor, Bureau of Labor Statistics, for the use of the article "Police, Detectives, and Special Agents" from *Occupational Outlook Handbook.*

USA Today for permission to reprint the cartoon by David Seavey and the editorial headlined "Let's crack down on abuse of steroids."

The H. W. Wilson Company for permission to reproduce excerpts from *Current Biography, Junior Book of Authors and Illustrators, Twentieth Century Authors,* and *Readers' Guide to Periodical Literature.*

The World Almanac and Book of Facts publishers for permission to reprint page 6 from *The World Almanac and Book of Facts* and for a complimentary copy of the filmstrip *How to Use an Almanac.*

World Book, Inc., for permission to reproduce pages 236, 250, and 276 from *The World Book Encyclopedia.*

INTRODUCTION

Library Lessons for Grades 7–9 is a complete library program. It covers library skills lessons, reference book lessons, and reference book reviews.

The library skills section consists of 19 lessons and 45 reproducibles.

The reference book section consists of 18 lessons plus a summary activity, a test, and 40 reproducibles. The lessons are arranged by subject. The instructor may want to teach these lessons according to specific needs or according to a grade level schedule. It is not necessary to have the books to teach the lessons. Reproducible sample pages from the books are included.

The section on reference book reviews contains 12 reviews ready for presentation.

Worksheet answers are found in the back of the manual.

If worksheet pages reprinted from various books and magazines need to be enlarged to be more readable, please enlarge them.

Each state, city, or school mandates the teaching of certain subjects at specific grade levels. To demonstrate the variance among schools, here are some responses to the grade level schedule:

"Biography and autobiography should be taught in the 7th grade." (Kentucky)

"Biography and autobiography should be taught in the 8th grade." (Alabama)

"Almanacs, atlases, and thesauri are mandated at the fifth grade level. Everything else on your list must be covered by the 7th grade." (Virginia)

For those who would like to have a sample grade level schedule, one is included on the next page. It can be used as presented, modified, or disregarded.

LESSONS BY SUGGESTED GRADE LEVELS

Seventh Grade

Library Orientation
Parts of a Book
Fiction
Dewey Decimal Classification
Nonfiction
Card Catalog
Computer Catalog
Biography and Autobiography
Types of Literature
Library of Congress
Encyclopedias
Atlases
Great Athletes (review)
Sports Almanac (review)

Eighth Grade

Library Orientation
Magazines
Readers' Guide
Newspapers
Vertical File
Almanacs
  The World Almanac
  Information Please Almanac
    (review). To be presented
    separately from the lesson
    about *The World Almanac*.
Biographical Reference Books
  Current Biography
  Webster's New Biographical
    Dictionary
  Who's Who in America
Career Reference Books
  (Social Sciences)
  Occupational Outlook
    Handbook
  Profiles of American
    Colleges
Anniversaries and Holidays
  (review)
Famous First Facts (review)
Abridged, Unabridged, Foreign
  Language, & Rhyming
    Dictionaries (review)

Ninth Grade

Library Orientation
Geographical Reference Books
  Webster's New Geographical
    Dictionary
  World Almanac of the U.S.A.
    (review)
  Lands & Peoples (review)
  World Almanac Infopedia
    (review)
Guinness Book of Records
  (review)
Literary Reference Books
  Familiar Quotations
  The Columbia Granger's
    Index to Poetry
  Junior Authors and
    Illustrators Series
  Something About the Author
  Twentieth Century Authors
  The Random House
    Thesaurus
  Young Reader's Companion
    (review)
  Books in Print (review)
Reference Book Roundup
Reference Book Test

The grade level schedule above is provided as a sample of how the lessons in this manual could be distributed. You may want to modify or disregard it.

PART 1

LIBRARY SKILLS LESSONS

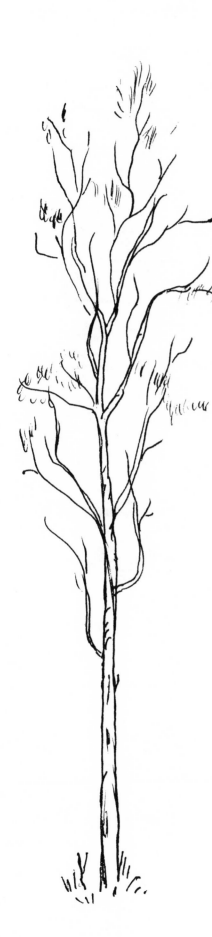

LIBRARY ORIENTATION

OBJECTIVES

1. To welcome students to the library
2. To discuss library rules and procedures
3. To point out the location of the card or automated catalog; the vertical file; the fiction, nonfiction, and reference sections; and any other materials, such as videos, microfilm, CDs and so forth

PREPARATIONS

Teacher:
1. Schedule a class library orientation visit with the librarian.
2. If your school doesn't have a librarian, find out what your school library's rules and procedures are, and present an orientation yourself. See the coverage below.

Librarian:
   Prepare a library orientation.

ORIENTATION

1. Welcome
2. Introduction of the librarian (and library staff, if desired)
3. Library hours
4. Students' responsibilities
   a. Quietness
   b. Care of books, videos, microfilm, etc.
      (1) How to turn pages (Hold a page at the top, right corner with the thumb and first finger. Slip your open hand behind the page and push it forward.)
      (2) Keeping books free from pencil marks; keeping computers free from moisture, etc.
      (3) The use of bookmarks (Bookmarks are thin and

1

flat. The turning down of page corners to mark your place is unacceptable.)

(4) How to care for videos, microfilm, CDs, etc.

(5) Returning books and other materials on time

(6) The returning of all library materials before moving

5. The location of the card or automated catalog; the vertical file; the fiction, nonfiction, and reference sections; and so forth

6. Audio-visual equipment, if any

7. Where an unwanted book is to be put (Should it be reshelved or be put on a table? If it's to be reshelved, tell students to shelve it right side up, in the correct place, with the spine facing out.)

8. The kinds and numbers of materials that may be checked out (books, pamphlets, current and back issues of magazines, videos, CDs, pictures, etc.)

9. The length of the loan period

10. How to check out books, magazines, pamphlets, videos, CDs

11. What to write on checkout cards

12. How to renew loans

13. Where to put books and other materials when returning them to the library

14. Overdues

15. Damaged books or other materials (Tell students not to repair library materials themselves.)

16. Lost books or other materials

17. Stealing (Why we don't. . . .)

18. Questions

Excuse students to browse and check out books or other materials.

PARTS OF A BOOK

LESSON 1A
(An alternative lesson. Choose Lesson 1A or 1B.)

In this lesson the instructor reviews or introduces parts of a book in a typical classroom presentation. In the alternative lesson (1B), the students learn about parts of a book by creating books of their own.

Lessons 1A and 1B contain special pages. If desired, these pages can be used with either lesson or as an additional lesson. Lesson 1A contains a study list, Worksheet 1, and a test, Worksheets 2a and 2b. Lesson 1B contains a page of resources and four pages of examples, Worksheets 4a–4d.

Lesson 1B contains a student instruction page (Create a Book, Worksheet 3), which is applicable only to 1B.

Select Lesson 1A or 1B to teach parts of a book. Alternative: Teach Lesson 1A one year, and teach Lesson 1B another year, as a review.

OBJECTIVES

1. To review basic parts of a book: title page, copyright page, table of contents, glossary, and index
2. To introduce or review lesser-known parts of a book: binding; endpapers; flyleaves; half-title page; frontispiece; dedication; acknowledgments; introduction, preface, or foreword; lists of maps and illustrations; text; appendix; bibliography
3. To review the meanings of these terms: title, author, illustrator, illustrations, publisher, place of publication, copyright

MATERIALS

1. A library book for each student. Use books students have checked out.
2. Library books for your use in illustrating the various parts of a book. Use the Resources page from Lesson 1B to simplify the collection of examples. Here is an or-

dered list of the parts you will want to present. (The parts in parentheses will be found in all books.)
   a. (Binding, spine, cover)
   b. (Endpapers) All hardbacks have endpapers, but few of them are illustrated. Try to present some beautiful endpapers for an example.
   c. (Flyleaves)
   d. Half-title page
   e. Frontispiece
   f. (Title page)
   g. (Copyright page)
   h. Dedication
   i. Acknowledgments
   j. Table of contents
   k. Introduction, preface, or foreword
   l. Illustrations
   m. List of maps or illustrations
   n. (Text)
   o. Appendix
   p. Bibliography
   q. Glossary
   r. Index
3. A paperback book
4. If extra drill is needed, students' textbooks that illustrate a table of contents, a glossary, and an index
5. A chalkboard, chalk, and eraser
6. Reproductions of the study list, Worksheet 1
7. Back-to-back reproductions of the two-page test, Worksheets 2a and 2b

PREPARATIONS

1. See that each student has a library book.
2. Use bookmarks to designate the examples you plan to present.
3. Write the following on the chalkboard:

The Call of the Wild
Kon-Tiki: Across the Pacific by Raft

LESSON

Students, hold up your library books. Good. Everyone has a book. Put everything else aside.

Who would like to tell us the name of your book?

Call on students who raise their hands.

The library book I have has a hardcover binding.

Hold up your hardbound book and point to the binding *around* it.

How many of you have hardcover bindings?

Does anyone have a paperback binding?

If so, have the book or books held up. If not, hold up your paperback. Explain that paperback bindings are made of paper, as their name indicates. Tell the students that books bound in paper are called paperbacks. Books with hardcovers are called hardbacks.

What information is on the front of your binding—on the cover? (probably the title and author)

Who would like to read the information on the cover of your book?

Call on one or more students. Comment on the kind of information on the cover of each book.

Hold up your example of illustrated endpapers.

My book has illustrated endpapers.

Show your book's front endpapers and back endpapers.

Endpapers cover the two inner sides of a hardbound book.

Often endpapers are just plain white. Does anyone have colored or illustrated endpapers?

If so, have the student or students hold up their books and show everyone the endpapers.

Flyleaves are the blank pages next to the endpapers. They are the first and last pages in a book.

Show the flyleaf in the front of your book and the one in the back.

This book has a half-title page: a page on which only the title appears.

Show your half-title page.

How many of you have books with half-title pages?

Tell the students to hold their half-title pages up. Check to make sure that each is actually a half-title page.

Hold up your example of a frontispiece.

This book has a frontispiece.

A frontispiece is a picture, chart, or map facing the title page.

If your book has a frontispiece, hold it up.

Check.

This book has a title page.

   Point to the title page.

How many of you have title pages?

What is the first thing on your title page? (the title)

What is a title? (the name of a book)

Point to the title of your book, and hold your book up so I can see it.

   Check to see if the students are pointing to their titles.

Who wants to read the title of your book?

   Call on students who raise their hands.

Look at the two titles on the board.

   Point to the titles.

The first title is *The Call of the Wild*. The second title is *Kon-Tiki. Kon-Tiki* has a subtitle: *Across the Pacific by Raft*. A subtitle clarifies a title. Notice the colon. A colon is a signal that what follows is a subtitle.

Does your book have a subtitle?

   If someone responds, ask the student to read the title first and then the subtitle.

What information is given next on the title page? (the author)

What is an author? (a person who writes a book or other literary work)

Point to the author of your book, and hold your book up so I can see it.

   Check each book.

My book lists an illustrator. What is an illustrator? (a person who creates illustrations)

What are illustrations? (pictures, designs, diagrams)

Who has a book that lists an illustrator?

If your book lists an illustrator, point to the illustrator's name, and hold your book up so I can see it.

   Check each book.

Does your title page say "illustrations by" or does it say "drawings by"? What does it say in reference to the illustrator?

Call on those who raise their hands.

My book was published by _____.

Point to the publisher's name, as you hold the book up so the students can see it.

What is a publisher? (a person or a company that has a book printed and sells it)

Point to the publisher of your book, and hold your book up so I can see it.

Check each book.

Who wants to read the name of your publisher?

Call on students.

The place of publication is listed under the name of the publisher.

Hold your book up so the students can see it. Point to the publisher and then to the place of publication.

Point to the place of publication, and hold your books up so I can see them.

Check each book.

My book was published in _____. Where was yours published?

Call on students.

On the back of the title page, you'll find the copyright. Turn the page.

Locate the copyright notice, which will be designated by the word Copyright or a circled © and the year.

Point to the copyright date, and hold your book up so I can see it.

Check each book.

What is a copyright? (an exclusive right to a literary work)

Who would like to read the latest copyright date listed in your book?

Call on students.

If you are reading a fiction, poetry, or fairy-tale book, it doesn't matter what the copyright date is. However, if you are reading a science, geography, or history book and you need current information, check the copyright date to make sure you have a recent book.

This book has a dedication. The author has dedicated the book to _____. The dedication reads: _____.

Do any of your books have dedications?

    If so, call on students to read their dedications.

When an author or publisher is indebted to others for contributions to a book, he or she acknowledges that fact.

Here is a page of acknowledgments.

    Hold up your book, and show the acknowledgments. Read a few lines.

Do any of your books have acknowledgments?

    If so, have the students hold their books up.

This book has a table of contents.

    Show your table of contents.

How many of you have tables of contents?

Hold up your tables of contents so I can see them.

The word *contents* is sometimes used instead of *table of contents*. *Contents* and *table of contents* mean the same thing.

What information does a table of contents contain? (a list of a book's chapters or stories and the pages on which they can be found)

How are the chapters or stories arranged? (in the order they appear in the book)

    If drill is needed, have students take out a specific textbook and turn to the table of contents. Ask questions like these: On what page does Chapter 2 start? On what page does it end?

    Have the students put their textbooks away and take out their library books again.

This book has an introduction. The introduction tells why the author has written the book and what he or she has tried to do.

There are two terms which are interchangeable with the term *introduction*. They are *preface* and *foreword*. *Introduction, preface,* and *foreword* mean the same thing.

Do any of you have an introduction, preface, or foreword in your library book?

    If so, have the students hold their books up.

My book has illustrations.

Show some illustrations.

What are illustrations? (pictures, designs, diagrams)

How many of you have illustrations in your books?

Turn to an illustration, hold up your book, and show me.

Check.

This book has a list of maps/illustrations and their page numbers.

Show the list.

Do any of you have a list of maps or illustrations?

If so, have the students hold their books up so everyone can see them.

The text is the main part of the book. The text of my book starts on page _____ and ends on page _____.

Hold up your book. One finger and thumb should be around an edge of the text.

On what page does your text start? On what page does it end?

Call on those who raise their hands.

This book has an appendix. An appendix is additional material at the end of a book.

Describe your book's appendix. Show it to the students.

Does your book have an appendix?

Call on students. Ask them to describe the contents of their books' appendixes.

This book has a bibliography. What is a bibliography? (a list of sources of information on a particular subject or a list of literary works)

Some bibliographies are found at the end of chapters, others are found in the back of books.

Do any of your books have a bibliography?

If so, have the students hold their books up.

This book has a glossary.

Show your glossary to the students.

What is a glossary? (a list and explanation of the difficult or technical words in a book)

Where are glossaries located? (in the back of books)

Who has a glossary?

Have students with glossaries hold them up.

If students aren't very familiar with glossaries, have them open a specific textbook to the glossary. Ask questions like these: How are glossaries arranged? What is the meaning of the word _____?

This book has an index.

Hold up your book.

See if your book has an index. Raise you hand if it does.

If your students aren't very familiar with indexes, have them take out a specific textbook and locate the index. Ask questions like these: On which page will you find information about _____? On which page will you find an illustration of _____?

What is an index? (a list of a book's subjects, arranged alphabetically with page references)

If the alphabetical arrangement of indexes wasn't mentioned, elicit that information.

Nonfiction books usually have more of the parts we've discussed than fiction books have.

Put your books away.

Review definitions of each part of a book. Either present definitions orally now and let students name the parts described, or wait until two or three minutes before the bell and present definitions. In the latter situation, reward students who answer correctly by letting them line up first. See Worksheet 1 for a list of parts of a book and their definitions.

When convenient, distribute copies of Worksheet 1. Tell students to study the page. Explain that they will be tested on definitions. Specify on which day the test will be given. For the test, use Worksheets 2a and 2b.

SUGGESTION

If your students need further practice in mastering the basic parts of a book (title page, table of contents, glossary, and index), use a textbook to drill on each of these parts. Follow the procedure presented in this lesson.

LESSON OUTLINE

Present these parts of a book in the order listed.

1. Binding, spine, cover (Hardback and paperback)
2. Endpapers

 3. Flyleaves
 4. Half-title page
 5. Frontispiece
 6. Title page (Title, author, illustrator, publisher, place of publication)
 7. Copyright page (copyright)
 8. Dedication
 9. Acknowledgments
10. Table of contents
11. Introduction, preface, or foreword
12. Illustrations
13. List of maps or illustrations
14. Text
15. Appendix
16. Bibliography (Two kinds. Two locations.)
17. Glossary
18. Index

PARTS OF A BOOK STUDY LIST

1. binding—the hardbound or paperback cover of a book
2. endpapers—the paper spread over the two inner sides of a hardbound book
3. flyleaves—the blank pages next to the endpapers. They are the first and last pages in a book.
4. half-title page—a page in a book that contains only the book's title
5. frontispiece—a picture, chart, or map facing the title page
6. title page—the page in a book which contains the book's title, author, illustrator, publisher, and place of publication
7. copyright page—the back side of the title page. The copyright date appears on this page.
8. dedication page—the page on which the author names the person or persons to whom he or she is dedicating the book
9. acknowledgments—a list of those to whom the author or publisher acknowledges indebtedness for contributions to the book
10. table of contents—a list of a book's chapters or stories, in their order of appearance, with page numbers
11. introduction, preface, or foreword—a page or pages which state why the author has written the book and what he or she has tried to do
12. illustrations—pictures, designs, or diagrams used to decorate or explain a book
13. list of maps or illustrations—a list of a book's illustrative material
14. text or body—the main part of a book
15. appendix—additional material at the back of a book
16. bibliography—a list of sources of information on a particular subject or a list of literary works
17. glossary—a list and explanation of difficult or technical terms contained in a book
18. index—an alphabetical list of the subjects in a book, including the page numbers where the subjects can be found

Not all books have all of the parts listed above, nor are the parts always in the order listed.

VOCABULARY

1. author—a person who writes a book or other literary work
2. title—the name of a book
3. illustrator—a person who creates illustrations
4. publisher—a person or company that has a book printed and offers it for sale
5. place of publication—the place where a book was published
6. copyright—the exclusive right to a literary work

PARTS OF A BOOK TEST

Fill in the blanks with the answers listed on the back of this paper.

1. The hardback or paperback cover of a book _____

2. An alphabetical list of the subjects discussed in a book, including page numbers_____

3. The paper spread over the two inner sides of a hardbound book _____

4. A picture, chart, or map facing the title page _____

5. A list and explanation of the difficult or technical words in a book _____

6. A list of sources of information on a particular subject _____

7. A list of those to whom the author or publisher acknowledges indebtedness for con-

    tributions to a book _____

8. The page in a book which contains the title, author, illustrator, publisher, and place of

    publication _____

9. Additional material at the end of a book _____

10. A list of stories or chapters in a book, in the order of appearance, with page numbers

    _____

11. The main part of a book _____

12. A page which states why the author has written the book and what he or she has tried

    to do _____

13. A page that contains only the book's title _____

14. Pictures, designs, or diagrams used to decorate or explain a book_____

15. An inscription in a book dedicating it to a person or cause _____

16. The blank pages next to the endpapers _____

17. The exclusive right to a literary work _____

18. A person who writes a book _____

19. A person or company that has a book printed and then offers it for sale _____

20. A person who creates illustrations _____

21. The place where a book is published _____

22. The name of a book _____

ANSWERS

title page	copyright	place of publication
illustrations	endpapers	illustrator
text	introduction	index
dedication	binding	bibliography
author	title	publisher
acknowledgments	half-title page	frontispiece
glossary	flyleaves	
table of contents	appendix	

LESSON 1B
(An alternative lesson. Choose Lesson 1A or 1B.)

NOTE

In this lesson, students learn about parts of a book by creating books of their own. In the alternative lesson (1A), students learn about parts of a book in a typical classroom presentation.

Lessons 1A and 1B contain special pages. If desired, these pages can be used with either lesson or as an additional lesson. Lesson 1A contains a study list, Worksheet 1, and a test, Worksheets 2a and 2b. Lesson 1B contains a page of resources and four pages of examples, Worksheets 4a–4d.

Lesson 1B contains a student instruction page (Create a Book, Worksheet 3), which is applicable only to 1B.

Select Lesson 1A or 1B to teach parts of a book. Alternative: Teach Lesson 1A one year and teach Lesson 1B another year, as a review.

OBJECTIVES

1. To review basic parts of a book: title page, copyright page, table of contents, glossary, and index
2. To introduce or review lesser-known parts of a book: binding; endpapers; flyleaves; half-title page; frontispiece; dedication; acknowledgments; introduction, preface, or foreword; lists of maps and illustrations; text; appendix; bibliography
3. To review the meanings of these terms: title, author, illustrator, illustrations, publisher, place of publication
4. To have students utilize the information they learn by creating books of their own

MATERIALS

1. Students' textbooks that illustrate as many parts of a book as possible
2. Examples of any parts of a book that aren't found in the students' textbooks. See Resources at the end of this lesson for some suggestions.
3. A paperback book

15

4. A chalkboard, chalk, and eraser
5. Paper for the students' books. See Suggestions at the end of this lesson.
6. Reproductions of the instruction page, Worksheet 3
7. Reproductions of the four pages which illustrate and define parts of a book, Worksheets 4a–4d

PREPARATIONS

1. Select one of the students' textbooks to illustrate as many parts of a book as possible. Obtain a copy for your use. Use bookmarks to designate the different book parts listed under Objectives above. On the Resource page, at the end of this lesson, designate which parts of a book are contained in the textbook.
2. Examples of those parts of a book not contained in the textbook need to be found. See Resources, at the end of this lesson, for suggestions.

LESSON

Have you ever wanted to write a book?

Experts say that you should write about something you know.

If you were to write a book, what would you write about?

Would you write about sports, pets, holidays, music, art, television?

Let's find out what it's like to write a book. You won't need to write a whole book; a few pages will be enough.

I'll review all of the parts of a book so you'll be sure to understand each one. You won't need to take notes. I'll give you a list with examples and descriptions after we finish.

Hold up a paperback book.

This book, as you know, is a paperback book. Its binding is made of paper.

Designate the binding: the front and back cover and the spine.

Hold up a copy of the textbook you've chosen to illustrate parts of a book.

This is a hardback book. Hardback books are usually bound in cloth-covered cardboard.

Point to the spine.

Who knows what information is usually printed on the spine? (the author, title, and publisher)

Your book won't have a hard cover like this book, so you won't need to be concerned with the spine.

What information is usually found on the front of a book's binding—on the cover? (the title and author)

What is a title? (the name of a book)

What is an author? (a person who writes a book or other literary work)

Open a book that has illustrated endpapers.

Some books have illustrated endpapers. Endpapers are the papers spread over the two inner side of hardbound books.

Show the endpapers at the front and at the back of your book.

Most books have plain, unillustrated endpapers.

Let's pretend that your book will ultimately be published in hardback and that you want illustrated endpapers. In reality, publishers provide endpapers, but, in this case, you may. The endpapers don't have to be fancy. You may draw pictures or designs.

Show some flyleaves: the blank pages next to the endpapers. (They are the first and last pages in the book.) Tell the students that to save paper, they won't include flyleaves in their books.

Show a half-title page.

What information is found on a half-title page? (the title)

You will need to include a half-title page in your book.

As I said, you will receive detailed, illustrated instructions about what to include in your book; however, this review should be helpful.

Hold up an example of a frontispiece.

A frontispiece is a picture, chart, or map which faces the title page. You are to include a frontispiece in your book.

Take out your _____ textbooks and turn to the title page.

What information do you find? (title, author, illustrator, publisher, place of publication)

If an illustrator isn't included, tell the students that most illustrated books list the illustrator's name on the title page.

Note the order of the title, author, illustrator, publisher, and place of publication. That is the usual order, and the one you should follow.

If your students aren't already familiar with each of the parts listed on a title page, you may want to name each part, one by one, and have students point to the part in their books. Check each student after each part is mentioned.

What do we call a person who writes books? (an author)

What do we call a person who puts writings from various sources together to make a book? (a compiler or editor)

What do we call a person who translates a book from one language into another? (a translator)

Many books are illustrated. What does that mean? (The books have pictures, designs, or diagrams.)

What do we call a person who creates illustrations? (an illustrator)

You may illustrate your own book or you may get a friend to illustrate it.

What is the first thing you'll put on your title page? (the title)

Let's say your title is *Jokes: How to Write Them.*

   Write that title on the board.

Technically speaking, *Jokes* is the title. *How to Write Them* is the subtitle. A subtitle clarifies a title: makes it clear, explains it. In this example, the subtitle is very important. Without it we might think the book contained a collection of jokes. The subtitle lets us know exactly what the book is about. It's about writing jokes.

Your title may or may not have a subtitle.

What comes next on the title page? (the author)

You are the author.

   Write the following on the board under the title: by _____.

   Record the name of a student after "by."

If someone else illustrates your book, you'll write "illustrated by" and the person's name.

   Write the following on the board: illustrated by

   Add a fictitious name. (If you write the name of the class artist, he or she may get swamped with requests for art.)

You don't have to say "illustrated by." You can say "pictures by," "decorations by," "photographs by," or any appropriate designation.

Most of you will do your own illustrations. In that case, you will probably say, "written and illustrated by" and your name.

Erase the references to the author and illustrator, and write: written and illustrated by _____.

Add a student's name.

What comes next? (the publisher)

What is a publisher? (the person or company that has a book printed and sells it)

Sometimes publishers use their own names. If Mr. Little and Mr. Brown own a publishing company, they may name it Little, Brown. Some publishers name their companies something imaginative like Lone Tree Publishers. Create a name for the publisher of your book.

Elicit the name of a publisher from the class and write it on the board.

What comes next? (the place of publication)

Record the name of the city where your publishing company is located. If you name a large city, like New York or Los Angeles, you won't need to add the state. However, if you use the name of a lesser-known city, you will need to add the state to make the location clear.

Elicit a place of publication from the students, and write it under the publisher's name.

The next page of your book is the copyright page. It is found on the back of the title page.

Turn to the copyright page in your textbook.

Find the copyright notice.

Write this on the board: Copyright © 1994

Substitute the current year for 1994.

What is a copyright? (the exclusive right to a literary work)

Why is the copyright date important to readers? (If a reader wants current information, he or she needs to use a book that was written recently. A recent copyright date is especially important in science, geography, and history books. The copyright date for fiction, poetry, and so forth is of no concern.)

Under current copyright law, a book is automatically copyrighted the minute it is written. However, most writers register their books and get official copyrights. In case of infringements, the stealing of parts of their books, or in case of lawsuits, officially registered copyrights are a better protection than copyrights that aren't registered.

Copyright protection lasts for the life of the author plus 50 years for works written on or after January 1, 1978.

To get a copyright, one fills out the proper form and sends it with a $20 fee and a copy of his or her unpublished work to the Register of Copyrights, Library of Congress, Washington, D.C. If the book has been published, two copies must be sent to the Copyright Office.

Add the following, jokingly.

It won't be necessary for you to pay the $20 fee to copyright the book you're going to write. An unofficial copyright will be sufficient.

Some authors dedicate their books to someone, probably to a friend or relative. The author may write a simple dedication like this: For my mother. Or like this: For my friend Robert Jones.

Some authors write long dedications, such as this one: Dedicated to all of those who have labored and are laboring for a better world.

If you have an example of a dedication, read it.

Your dedication can be simple or complex. Only one thing appears on the dedication page, and that is the dedication.

Some books have a page for acknowledgments. Such a page lists those to whom the author or publisher acknowledges indebtedness for contributions to the book.

If you have an example, read a few lines.

Find the table of contents in your textbook.

What is a table of contents? (a list of the chapters or stories in a book, including the page numbers on which they will be found)

How are the chapters or stories arranged? (in the order that they appear)

Are the contents in your textbook listed in the order of appearance? (yes)

Instead of the term *table of contents,* you can use the term *contents,* if you like. *Table of contents* and *contents* mean the same thing.

Ask a few questions about the textbook's table of contents, such as: On which page does Chapter 3 start? On which page does it end?

Give as much practice as is needed.

Many books have an introduction. An introduction tells why the author has written the book and what he has tried to do.

The words introduction, preface, and foreword all mean the same thing. They are interchangeable.

Some books which contain maps or illustrations list them and give the page numbers where they can be found.

Show an example.

The text of the book is next. The text is the main part of the book. Sometimes it's called the body.

Put your fingers around the edges of the text and hold your book up.

You are to write one page of text for your book.

The appendix is made up of additional material. It's found at the back of the book. The additional material can be any kind of supplementary information: charts, tables, supporting articles.

Show examples, if possible.

Some books include bibliographies. What is a bibliography? (a list of sources of information about a particular subject or a list of literary works)

If no one responds, define bibliography.

Some bibliographies are listed at the end of chapters, other are listed at the back of books.

Show examples, if you have some.

The way in which bibliographic material is presented is quite technical. For our purposes, use the simple form illustrated in the materials I'll distribute.

If you prefer to have the students use another bibliographic form, tell them.

Next we have the glossary.

Have the students turn to their textbook's glossary, if there is one.

What is a glossary? (a list of a book's difficult or technical words and their meanings)

In what order are the words arranged? (alphabetical)

If your textbook has an index, have the students turn to it.

What is an index? (a list of a book's subjects with page references)

In what order are the subjects arranged? (alphabetical)

Ask some questions about the entries? Example: On what page will you find some information about _____?

I'm going to distribute some directions that will explain how to prepare your books. I'll also give examples and descriptions of each page you are to include. Paper for your book will be distributed.

Distribute reproductions of the instruction page, Worksheet 3, the four illustrated Parts of a Book Examples, Worksheets 4a–4d, and the blank, stapled paper the students will use to make their books.

You may want to look at some books in the library to examine dedication pages, endpapers, and so forth.

Tell the students when they will be given time to work on their books.

Announce the date the assignment will be due.

Look at Worksheet 4d, Item 13, Appendix.

The illustration lists the three articles included in the book's appendix. The three articles themselves, not the list, are the appendix.

Look at Item 16, Index.

This particular index subdivides subjects. It isn't necessary to make this type of index. You can make a simpler one. Refer to some library books or your textbooks if you need help in writing an index.

Add any instructions that may be needed.

Students love awards. If you can think of an award for the best book, or for the best two or three books, tell the students. The award can be something intangible, such as a special privilege.

When grading the students' books, note parts to share with the class. Examples: interesting text, an inspiring dedication, beautiful endpapers, an unusual name for a publisher, and so forth.

SUGGESTIONS

1. The following are methods of preparing pages for the students' books. Choose one, if desired.
   a. Use nine pages of 8½" by 11" paper. You may want to use unlined paper for the first three pages and for the last page. The other five pages can be lined. This will provide a total of 18 pages (nine pages used on both sides). Staple at the side. These pages will allow for a *front and back* "binding," *two* endpapers, plus the other 14 parts described on Worksheets 4a–4d.
   b. If you want to save paper, make your books half size. Use five sheets of 8½" by 11" paper folded in the middle to create books 5½" wide by 8½" long. This will provide 20 pages (10 pages after folding, 20 pages if both sides of the 10 pages are used). Staple at the side. Tell the students to include a *front and back* "binding," *two* endpapers and the other 14 parts described on Worksheets 4a–4d. Explain that two pages

after the index will be blank and can be designated "Notes." The last inside page will be for endpaper. Books this size will save paper; however, you'll probably need to use all lined or all unlined paper.

   c. If an 8½" wide by 5" long book isn't objectionable, cut 8½" by 11" paper in half. You will need nine half-pages for each book. The first three pages and the last page can be unlined. The other five pages can be lined. This will provide a total of 18 pages (nine pages used on both sides). Staple at the side. These pages will allow for a *front and back* "binding," *two* endpapers, plus the other 14 parts described on Worksheets 4a–4d.

If you prefer to keep the project very simple, use all lined or all unlined paper.

You might try each of the above with different classes, and see which one works best for you.

2. You may want to set up a learning center to display volumes which illustrate various parts of a book.

LESSON OUTLINE

Present these parts of a book in the order listed. Item number three, flyleaves, which you should present, will not be included in the books students will create.

1. Binding, spine, cover
2. Endpapers
3. Flyleaves (not included in the books students will create)
4. Half-title page
5. Frontispiece
6. Title page
7. Copyright page
8. Dedication
9. Acknowledgments
10. Table of contents
11. Introduction, preface, or foreword
12. Lists of maps and illustrations
13. Text
14. Appendix
15. Bibliography
16. Glossary
17. Index

RESOURCES

The following chart has been made to simplify the collection of examples for this lesson.

   Textbook A. Choose a textbook that illustrates as many parts of a book as possible. Determine which examples it illustrates, and put an X in each of the appropriate squares in the column designated Textbook A. For future reference, record the book's title on the line provided at the bottom of the page.

If you use any of the books listed below, check to make sure your editions have the parts checked. Editions vary.

Several blank lines are provided on which you can enter book titles from your library. If you take time to find choice examples and enter them on the chart, you'll have them for future reference.

To cover all parts of a book, you'll need both fiction and nonfiction examples.

PARTS OF A BOOK	Textbook A	Black Stallion	Born Free	Johnny Tremain	Old Yeller	Rascal							
Endpapers (illustrated)				X		X							
Half-title page		X	X		X	X							
Frontispiece			X	X	X	X							
Title page		X	X	X		X							
Dedication		X		X	X	X							
Acknowledgments			X										
Table of contents		X	X	X		X							
Introduction			X										
Lists of maps/illus.		X											
Appendix													
Bibliography													
Glossary													
Index													
OTHER PARTS													
Other books by the author		X		X	X	X							
Two-page title page													

The title of Textbook A is _____

CREATE A BOOK

1. You are to create a book about a *nonfiction* subject of your choice.
2. Your book should include each of the sixteen parts listed on Worksheets 4a–4d. Regarding endpapers (Worksheet 4a, #2), make two, which will give you seventeen pages to prepare. The eighteenth page will be the back "binding."
3. Choose a subject that is of interest to you.
4. In choosing, ask yourself if the subject will lend itself well to the creation of a table of contents, glossary, and index. If not, choose a subject that will.
5. The introduction may be short.
6. Write one page of text.
7. As a rule, have at least three entries for each of the following pages:
   Acknowledgments
   Table of contents
   List of maps or illustrations
   Bibliography
   Glossary
   Index

8. Illustrate the endpapers in the front and back of your book. You may make simple drawings with circles, stars, and so forth, or you may draw pictures.
9. Make the order of your book's pages correspond to the order of the examples. (In actual practice, the order may vary slightly.)
10. Before turning your book in, check each of the instructions above to see if you have followed them.

   The lengths designated above are guidelines for your book. They do not represent the lengths of books in general.

Name _____ Date _____

PARTS OF A BOOK: EXAMPLES

Country Cookbook
by
Lynn Wallace

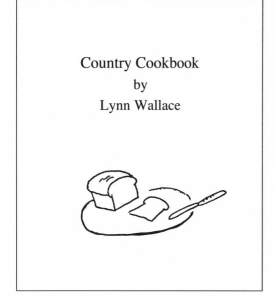

1. Binding
The hardback or paperback cover of a book

2. Endpapers
The paper spread over the two inner sides of a hardback book

Country Cookbook

3. Half-Title Page
A page in a book that contains the book's title

4. Frontispiece
A picture, chart, or map facing the title page

```
┌─────────────────────────┐   ┌─────────────────────────┐
│                         │   │                         │
│  Country Cookbook       │   │                         │
│     written             │   │                         │
│       and               │   │                         │
│    illustrated          │   │                         │
│        by               │   │                         │
│   Lynn Wallace          │   │                         │
│                         │   │                         │
│                         │   │                         │
│  Lone Tree Publishers   │   │                         │
│     New York            │   │                         │
│                         │   │   Copyright © 1994      │
│                         │   │                         │
└─────────────────────────┘   └─────────────────────────┘
```

5. Title Page

The page in a book which names the title, author, illustrator, publisher, and place of publication

6. Copyright Page

The back side of the title page. The copyright date appears on this page.

```
┌─────────────────────────┐   ┌─────────────────────────┐
│                         │   │   Acknowledgments       │
│                         │   │                         │
│                         │   │ I am especially grateful to the │
│                         │   │  following people for their │
│                         │   │  contributions to this book: │
│                         │   │                         │
│ For my friend Anne Jones│   │     Jane Riley          │
│                         │   │     Brad Stewart        │
│                         │   │     Betty Scott         │
│                         │   │                         │
│                         │   │                         │
│                         │   │                         │
│                         │   │                         │
└─────────────────────────┘   └─────────────────────────┘
```

7. Dedication Page

The page on which the author names the person or persons to whom he or she is dedicating the book

8. Acknowledgments

A list of those to whom the author or publisher acknowledges indebtedness for contributions to the book

Worksheet 4b

Contents

9. Table of Contents
A list of the chapters or stories in a book, in the order of appearance, with page references

Introduction

As a child growing up in rural New England, I often watched my mother spend many happy hours creating recipes. As a result, I began to create recipes, too.

Over the years my collection has grown and grown. In my old age, I seek a safe home for my collection. I offer it to you with warm wishes.

10. Introduction
The introduction, preface, or foreword states why the author has written the book

List of Illustrations

11. List of Maps or Illustrations
A list of a book's maps or illustrations, with page references

Banana Ice Cream

Peel and slice one banana. Spread the slices out in a plastic container. Freeze overnight. Put four strawberries and the banana slices in a blender. Blend until soft and smooth.

Serves one.

12. Text
The main part of the book

Appendix

13. Appendix

Additional material at the end of a book. (The three articles themselves are the appendix, not the list.)

Bibliography

Allen, Bob. *The Cookie Cookbook.* Chicago: Johnson & Smith, 1993.

Bronson, Cathy. *Soups and Salads.* New York: Unicorn Press, 1994.

Cates, John. *Outdoor Cooking.* Los Angeles: ABC Publishers, 1994.

14. Bibliography

A list of sources of information about a particular subject

Glossary

Legumes: Plants of the pea family — peas, beans, lentils

Pasta: Spaghetti, macaroni, ravioli

Sauté: Fry quickly and turn many times in a small amount of fat

15. Glossary

A list of the book's difficult or technical words and their meanings

Index

16. Index

A list of the book's subjects and the pages on which they can be found

FICTION

NOTE

If you have a school library, teach the entire lesson. Part of the lesson may be taught in the classroom, if desired.

If you don't have a school library, teach up to where you find instructions to end the lesson.

OBJECTIVES

1. To discuss the meaning and arrangement of fiction
2. To present the following fiction classifications: E, F, Fic, SC, YA, J
3. To discuss the fact that the words "a," "an," and "the" are disregarded as first words of titles
4. To check mastery with a follow-up worksheet
5. To give students practice in locating fiction books

MATERIALS

1. Several fiction books to present to the class. For some ideas, see Recommended Reading, Worksheets 6a–6b.
2. Nine sentence strips. See Preparations, #2. Alternative: Write the sentence strip information on the board.
3. If you plan to use sentence strips, you will need a flannel board.
4. A chalkboard, chalk, and eraser
5. Reproductions of the follow-up page, Worksheet 5
6. If desired, back-to-back reproductions of Recommended Reading, Worksheets 6a–6b
7. If and when desired, back-to-back reproductions of Young Readers' Favorite Books, Worksheets 7a–7b
8. If needed, reproductions of the book report form, Worksheet 8
9. Schools with libraries. 20 slips of paper, 3" by 5"

PREPARATIONS

1. Copy the example below on the board.

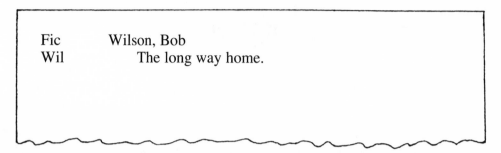

Fic   Wilson, Bob
Wil   The long way home.

2. Make the following sets of sentence strips. Alternative: Write the sentence strip information on the board.

Set 1

1	James	Smoky the Cow Horse	(3)
2	Farley	Black Stallion	(1)
3	Gipson	Old Yeller	(2)

Set 2

1	O'Hara, Mary	Thunderhead	(3)
2	O'Hara, Bob	Sudden Storm	(1)
3	O'Hara, Mary	My Friend Flicka	(2)

Set 3

1	Smith, Bert	A Trumpet for Joe	(3)
2	Santos, Joe	An Evening in Madrid	(1)
3	Smith, Bert	The Canoe Trip	(2)

After the sentence strips are lettered, paste several pieces of sandpaper or felt on the back sides. Write the set and strip number on the back of each one. Place the strips on the flannel board in the order numbered at the left. Students should rearrange the strips according to the order designated in parentheses.

3. The following picture illustrates shelf arrangement. If you have a library, explain this arrangement as you point to the shelves. To illustrate shelf arrangement in the classroom, point to a bookcase or put the following drawing on the board, and point to it.

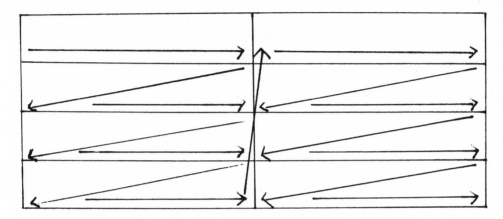

4. Schools with libraries
   a. Reserve a 30–45 minute library period. If you plan to rotate groups on different days, instead of on the same day, reserve two periods a week apart.
   b. Have a student compile a list of 20 fiction books and their authors' names from the library shelves. If possible, the authors' names should start with different letters of the alphabet so the books will be spread throughout the fiction section.
   c. Copy each of the 20 titles with their authors onto a separate 3" by 5" slip of paper in card catalog format. See the example under Preparations, #1. (In titles, capitalize only first words and proper nouns. Put either "F" or "Fic" and the first three letters of the authors' last names in the left corners of the slips.)

LESSON

I am going to present several fiction books.

Hold the books up, one at a time, and give their titles and authors.

What is fiction? (literary works about imaginary characters and events; books that are made up, untrue)

How is fiction arranged on the shelf? (by the authors' last names)

Walk over to the fiction shelves. (If you don't have a school library, use a bookcase to illustrate the following. Otherwise, use the illustration suggested in Preparations, #3.)

The books by authors whose last names start with the letter "A" are shelved first in the fiction section. The authors whose last names start with the letter "B" come next, and so forth.

Point with your hand while you explain the following.

The shelves are arranged like lines on a page. You read the first line, the second line, the third line, the fourth line, and so forth until you come to the bottom line. Then you go to the top of "the next page" and read the first line, the second line, and so forth.

Put the first set of sentence strips on the flannel board. Alternative: Point to the board where you've written the sentence strip information.

I've put three sentence strips on the flannel board. Each strip has the name of an author and a title of one of the author's books. Who can put the strips in order?

Call on someone.

After the student finishes, point to the first letter of the authors' names.

F, G, J. These books are in order by the authors' last names.

Although we say that fiction is shelved by the authors' last names, the authors' first names are considered secondarily. If you have two authors named Brown, Betty Brown's book will come before Stephen Brown's book. Betty comes before Stephen alphabetically.

Put the second set of sentence strips on the flannel board.

Who can put these in order?

Call on someone.

All three last names are the same, therefore, we have to consider the first names. Bob comes alphabetically before Mary. So Bob O'Hara's book comes first. Next we have two books by Mary O'Hara. The two books should be alphabetized by title. *My Friend Flicka* comes alphabetically before *Thunderhead*.

Who remembers which three words are disregarded if they are first words in a title? (a, an, the)

If no one remembers, tell the students.

Nearly every title in the library starts with "a," "an," or "the." If those three were considered as first words of titles, nearly every title would start with the letters "a" or "t." To prevent this, we disregard "a," "an," and "the" as first words in titles.

Put the third set of sentence strips on the flannel board.

Who can put these in shelf order?

Call on someone.

Fiction books are put in order by the authors' last names. Santos comes before Smith, therefore, Santos's book will be first. You didn't need to look at the titles at all. Next you have two books by Bert Smith. To decide which comes first, you look at the titles. Disregard "a," "an," and "the" as first words.

Cover "A" and "The" in the two titles.

Canoe comes alphabetically before Trumpet.

In some libraries, young people's fiction is divided into three groups: easy fiction, fiction, and story collections.

Write this on the board: E

The letter "E" on the spine of a book, on catalog cards, or on the computer screen, means the book referred to is easy fiction.

Fiction that isn't classified as easy is referred to simply as fiction.

Erase the "E."

Write the following on the board, and point to each item as you explain it.

F	Fic	
Smi	Smi	Smi

School libraries usually classify fiction in one of three ways: with an "F" for fiction, with "Fic" for fiction, or with one, two, or three letters of the author's last name.

Point to the board again, as you continue.

These are three ways of classifying the same fiction book.

Erase the fiction examples above.

Write on the board:	J	YA
	Smi	Smi

Public libraries usually classify young people's fiction with the letter "J" for Juvenile or with the letters "YA" for Young Adult.

Point to the board.

In public libraries, books for young people are shelved separately from books for adults.

Some libraries separate collections of stories from other fiction books. These libraries put the letters "SC," for Story Collection, on the books' spines, on catalog cards, and in the computer.

Write this on the board: SC

Point to it.

If a library doesn't separate story collections, the books will be classified and shelved like fiction.

Public libraries often shelve mysteries and westerns apart from the other fiction books.

Let's see how much you remember about fiction. I'm going to distribute a paper for you to do. Don't start work until I explain the paper.

Distribute Worksheet 5, and explain it. After the students finish, let them grade their own papers as you read and discuss the answers.

Collect the papers.

If you don't have a school library, end the lesson here.

Decide whether you have time to let two groups locate fiction books today.

Everyone is going to locate two fiction books. Half of you will locate them now and the other half will locate them after the first group finishes/during the next library visit.

I'm going to distribute a slip of paper to those who will look for books first. The paper lists one of the books you are to find. Look at the example I've put on the board.

Point to the example.

Fic	Wilson, Bob
Wil	The long way home.

What is the title of the book? (The long way home)

Note that the words long way home aren't capitalized. Librarians capitalize only first words and proper nouns in titles.

Who is the author of the book? (Bob Wilson)

What does "Fic" mean? (fiction)

What does "Wil" stand for? (It stands for Wilson, the author's last name.)

Where would you look for this book? (in fiction)

Would you start looking at the beginning of fiction? (no)

You would start looking near the end of fiction, wouldn't you?

When you find the book that's listed on your slip of paper, touch the book with one hand and raise your other hand. Don't remove the book from the shelf. I'll check to see if you have found the right book. If you have, I'll take your slip of paper and give you another. You will then repeat the process with the second slip of paper. Everyone is to find two books. Afterwards, you may browse or check some books out.

What does browse mean? (to look through a book or library in a leisurely way)

Divide the class into two groups.

We'll have two groups. The _____ group will locate books first. While that group is look-ing for books, the other group may browse or check books out.

Only those with slips of paper are to be in the fiction section. Everyone else should browse elsewhere.

I'm going to distribute one slip of paper to each student in group _____. As soon as you receive your slip, go look for your book.

After distributing the slips, excuse the other group to browse.

When a student with a slip finds a book, check to make sure it is the correct one. If it is, give the student a second slip.

If you plan to rotate the groups today, do so after the first group has finished locating books. If you plan to rotate the groups next week, at that time prior to the activity, review the location procedure.

FOLLOW-UP

1. If you desire, distribute Recommended Reading, Worksheets 6a–6b. You may offer the list merely as suggested reading, or you may want to require the reading of one of the books. If desired, reproduce and distribute the book report form, Worksheet 8.
2. You may want to distribute copies of Young Readers' Favorite Books, Worksheets 7a–7b. The list may be used to recommend titles for book reports, free reading, and so forth.
3. Put six fiction books, preferably library books, in a learning center. Choose books by authors whose last names start with the same letter. Example:

Abbot
Allen
Anderson
Armer
Astor

Disarrange them. One student at a time can put the books in correct order and check his or her work against an answer card. The student should disarrange the books when finished so that they will be ready for the next student.

NOTES

You will be surprised at how many students don't know how books are arranged in a section. Teach them that books are arranged like lines in a book.

You will also be surprised at how many students haven't had experience locating a book on the shelves.

Students at the junior high level, as well as at the elementary level, enjoy using flannel board strips and enjoy locating books.

FICTION

Answer these questions.

1. What is fiction? _____

2. How is it arranged? _____

3. What does "Fic" stand for? _____

4. E? _____

5. SC? _____

6. Which words are disregarded as first words of titles? _____

7. What do "J" and "YA" stand for?_____

Put these fiction books in order on the lines provided.

1. Sutton   *Whispers*   _____ _____

   Sanders   *Night Train*   _____ _____

   Sanchez   *Surprise Visit* _____ _____

2. Brown, Ed *An Island Afar* _____ _____

   Brown, Ed *The Bridge*   _____ _____

   Jones, Pat *A Trip East*   _____ _____

3. Jones, Ann *Sisters*   _____ _____

   Jones, Bill *New Car*   _____ _____

   Jones, Ann *The Crossing* _____ _____

RECOMMENDED READING

Contemporary classics (Classics—literature of the highest excellence, characterized by enduring qualities. Contemporary—of our times.)

Fiction

Author	*Title*
Armstrong, William H.	*Sounder*
Bagnold, Enid	*National Velvet*
Bonham, Frank	*Durango Street*
Bradbury, Ray	*The Martian Chronicles* (and other books by Bradbury)
Burnford, Sheila	*Incredible Journey*
Cavanna, Betty	*Going on Sixteen*
Cleary, Beverly	*Fifteen*
	Jean and Johnny
Cunningham, Julia	*Dorp Dead*
Daly, Maureen	*Seventeenth Summer*
Du Jardin, Rosamond	*Boy Trouble*
Farley, Walter	*The Black Stallion*
Forbes, Esther	*Johnny Tremain*
George, Jean Craighead	*Julie of the Wolves*
	My Side of the Mountain
Gipson, Fred	*Old Yeller*
Heinlein, Robert A.	*Citizen of the Galaxy* (and other books by Heinlein)
Holm, Anne	*North to Freedom*
Hunt, Irene	*Up a Road Slowly*
James, Will	*Smoky, the Cow Horse*
Keith, Harold	*Rifles for Watie*
Kjelgaard, James A.	*Big Red*
Knight, Eric	*Lassie Come Home*
L'Engle, Madeleine	*A Wrinkle in Time*
Lewis, Elizabeth Foreman	*Young Fu of the Upper Yangtze*
Morey, Walt	*Gentle Ben*
Neville, Emily	*It's Like This, Cat*
O'Dell, Scott	*Island of the Blue Dolphins*
O'Hara, Mary	*My Friend Flicka*
	Thunderhead
Rawlings, Marjorie Kinnan	*The Yearling*
Rawls, Wilson	*Where the Red Fern Grows*
Schaefer, Jack	*Shane*
Sewell, Anna	*Black Beauty*
Speare, Elizabeth George	*The Bronze Bow*
	Calico Captive
	The Witch of Blackbird Pond
Steinbeck, John	*The Red Pony*
Terhune, Albert Payson	*Lad: A Dog*
Thomas, Allison	*Benji*

Author	Title
Tolkien, J. R. R.	*The Hobbit* (and other books by Tolkien)
Tunis, John R.	*World Series* (and other books by Tunis)
Ullman, James R.	*Banner in the Sky*
Wells, H. G.	*The War of the Worlds* (and other books by Wells)
Wibberley, Leonard	*John Treegate's Musket*
Wilder, Laura Ingalls	*The Long Winter* (and other books by Wilder)

Nonfiction

Frank, Anne	*The Diary of a Young Girl*
	The Diary of Anne Frank
Heyerdahl, Thor	*Kon Tiki: Across the Pacific by Raft*
Keller, Helen	*The Story of My Life*
Lathan, Jean Lee	*Carry on, Mr. Bowditch*
North, Sterling	*Rascal*
Washington, Booker T.	*Up from Slavery*

YOUNG READERS' FAVORITE BOOKS

Recommended books for young readers usually represent the choices of librarians, teachers, or parents. One notable exception is from California where a selection of favorite books is made annually by the vote of young readers. The books winning the most votes receive the California Young Reader Medal. Here is a list of The Middle School/Junior High winners and nominees. (The award for this level was begun in 1980, but was not included in the voting in 1981.)

1994	*Winner*	*There's a Girl in My Hammerlock,* by Jerry Spinelli
	Nominees	*Face to Face,* by Marion Dane Bauer
		Voices After Midnight, by Richard Peck

1993	*Winner*	*Something Upstairs,* by Avi
	Nominees	*Mouse Rap,* by Walter Dean Myers
		Dealing with Dragons, by Patricia Wrede

1992	*Winner*	*Sniper,* by Theodore Taylor
	Nominees	*The Facts and Fictions of Minna Pratt,* by Patricia MacLachlan
		The Secret of Gumbo Grove, by Eleanor Tate

1991	*Winner*	*December Stillness,* by Mary Downing Hahn
	Nominees	*On My Honor,* by Marion Dane Bauer
		Black Star, Bright Dawn, by Scott O'Dell

1990	*Winner*	*The Other Side of Dark,* by Joan Lowery Nixon
	Nominees	*Hatchet,* by Gary Paulsen
		Return to Bitter Creek, by Doris Buchanan Smith

1989	*Winner*	*The Stalker,* by Joan Lowery Nixon
	Nominees	*Sizzle and Splat,* by Ronald Kidd
		After the Dancing Days, by Margaret Rostkowski

1988	*Winner*	*The Root Cellar,* by Janet Lunn
	Nominees	*The Fighting Ground,* by Avi
		Come Sing, Jimmy Jo, by Katherine Paterson

1987	*Winner*	*You Shouldn't Have to Say Goodbye,* by Patricia Hermes
	Nominees	*Someone is Hiding on Alcatraz Island,* by Eve Bunting
		Dragon's Blood, by Jane Yolen

1986	*Winner*	*Girl with the Silver Eyes,* by Willo Davis Roberts
	Nominees	*Who Killed Sack Annie?,* by Dana Brookins
		A Solitary Blue, by Cynthia Voigt

1985	*Winner*	*Taking Terri Mueller,* by Norma Fox Mazer
	Nominees	*The Animal, The Vegetable and John D. Jones,* by Betsy Byars
		Dicey's Song, by Cynthia Voigt

Worksheet 7a

1984	*Winner*	*There's a Bat in Bunk Five,* by Paula Danziger
	Nominees	*The Lemon Meringue Dog,* by Walt Morey
		Alan Mendelsohn, the Boy from Mars, by Daniel M. Pinkwater

1983	*Winner*	*Tiger Eyes,* by Judy Blume
	Nominees	*Can You Sue Your Parents for Malpractice?,* by Paula Danziger
		The Young Landlords, by Walter Dean Myers

1982	*Winner*	*Hail, Hail, Camp Timberwood,* by Ellen Conford
	Nominees	*The Pistachio Prescription,* by Paula Danziger
		Tex, by S. E. Hinton
		The Mark of Conte, by Sonia Levitin
		Ghosts I Have Been, by Richard Peck

1980	*Winner*	*The Pinballs,* by Betsy Byars
	Nominees	*Dragonsong,* by Anne McCaffrey
		Bridge to Terabithia, by Katherine Paterson
		Roll of Thunder, Hear My Cry, by Mildred D. Taylor
		Dragonwings, by Laurence Yep

Name_____ Date _____

BOOK REPORT

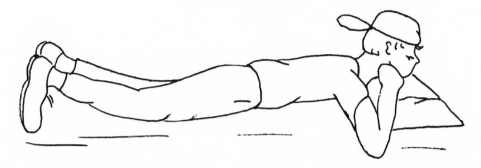

Title_____

Author_____

Main character _____

Summary_____

_____

_____

_____

_____

What was your favorite part? _____

_____

_____

_____

_____

Why did you choose this book? _____

_____

_____

On a scale of 1 to 10, with 10 being the highest number, what rating do you give this book?

_____

DEWEY DECIMAL CLASSIFICATION

OBJECTIVES

1. To present the Dewey Decimal Classification
2. To give students practice in using the Dewey system

MATERIALS

1. Back-to-back reproductions of two Dewey Decimal Classification pages, Worksheets 9 and 10
2. Reproductions of the follow-up paper, Worksheet 11

LESSON

At one time library books were shelved according to when they were acquired. The first book a library purchased would be put first on a shelf, the second book purchased would be put second on a shelf, and so forth.

In 1876 Melvil Dewey, a twenty-five-year-old librarian, devised a new system of classifying books. In his system, the Dewey Decimal Classification, books were grouped together by subject. For example, all of the books about sports were grouped together. If a library patron wanted a sports book, he or she wouldn't have to look all over the library. With the Dewey system all of the sports books would be found in one place.

Melvil Dewey assigned a number to every subject. For example, 796 is the number for sports books. Baseball is found under 796.357. Football is found under 796.332.

In the Dewey Decimal Classification all knowledge is divided into ten main categories.

I'm going to distribute a back-to-back paper which outlines the Dewey system.

Distribute back-to-back reproductions of Worksheets 9 and 10.

Look at Worksheet 9. At the top you see the ten main classifications of the Dewey system.

Read the ten main classifications to the students or have them read them silently to themselves.

Each of the ten main classes can be subdivided. Let's consider History, 900, for an exam-

45

ple. Look at number two: Subclassifications of History. Note that 900 is divided by tens first: 900, 910, 920, 930, 940, 950, 960, 970, 980, 990.

Read Subclassifications of History to the students or have them read them silently to themselves.

What are the numbers for the history of North America? (970–979)

Let's see how the numbers 970–979 can be subdivided. Look at number three on your paper. It's titled Subclassifications of History of North America.

Read the subdivisions to the students or have them read them silently to themselves.

What is the number for the history of the United States? (973)

If you need a book about United States history, you can go to the library and look under 973, can't you?

United States history can be subdivided into historical periods. Look at number four on your paper. Notice that 973 has been subdivided with the use of decimals.

Read the subdivisions to the students or have them read them silently to themselves.

If you want a book about the Civil War, what number would you look under? (973.7—Read as follows: nine seventy-three point seven.)

In each of the ten main classes there are 100 numbers. For example, in the 900s, there are numbers 901, 902, 903, and so forth up to 999. Each of those numbers can be subdivided with decimals.

Turn your papers over.

This page lists the ten main classifications of the Dewey system, and it subdivides the classifications by tens. The first three classifications have been abridged.

What does abridged mean? (shortened)

Look back at Worksheet 9. Look under number one: Main Classifications. I'm going to read some titles of books. See if you can tell me the general classification number for each of them. For example, if I ask for the number for a book titled *Wild Animals of America,* you'll say 500. Five hundred isn't the precise number; it's a general number. Books about animals are found in the 500s.

What is the general classification for each of these titles?

The Rainbow Book of Art? (700)
What the Great Religions Believe? (200)
A Planet Called Earth? (500)
Abraham Lincoln? (900)
Betty Crocker's Cookbook? (600)
An Inheritance of Poetry? (800)

Encyclopaedia Britannica? (000)
A Treasury of American Folklore? (300)
Cassell's Spanish Dictionary? (400)
Philosophy Throughout the Years? (100)

Most school and public libraries use the Dewey Decimal Classification.

I'm going to distribute a worksheet for you to do. Refer to the main classifications on Worksheet 9 for the answers.

Distribute Worksheet 11.

Have the students correct their own papers as you read and discuss the answers.

If you are going to let the students keep the back-to-back classification reproductions, Worksheets 9 and 10, announce this fact.

DEWEY DECIMAL MAIN AND SUBCLASSIFICATIONS

1. Main Classifications

000-099	General works (encyclopedias, yearbooks)
100-199	Philosophy (psychology, ethics, paranormal phenomena)
200-299	Religion (religion, mythology)
300-399	Social sciences (government, careers, folklore)
400-499	Language (dictionaries, other languages)
500-599	Pure science (math, astronomy, plants, animals)
600-699	Applied science (airplanes, cars, gardening, cooking)
700-799	The arts (art, photography, music, theater, sports)
800-899	Literature (poetry, plays, essays)
900-999	History (history, geography, travel, biography)

2. Subclassifications of History

900-909	World history
910-919	Geography and travel
920-929	Biography
930-939	Ancient history
940-949	History of Europe
950-959	History of Asia
960-969	History of Africa
970-979	History of North America
980-989	History of South America
990-999	History of Oceania and polar regions

3. Subclassifications of History of North America

971	History of Canada
972	History of Mexico and the Caribbean
973	History of the United States
974	History of northeastern states
975	History of southeastern states
976	History of south central states
977	History of north central states
978	History of western states
979	History of far western states

4. Subclassifications of U. S. History

973.1	Discovery and exploration to 1607
973.2	Colonial period, 1607–1775
973.3	Revolution and confederation, 1775–1789
973.4	Constitutional period, 1789–1809
973.5	Early 19th century, 1809–1845
973.6	Middle 19th century, 1845–1861
973.7	Civil War, 1861–1865
973.8	Later 19th century, 1865–1901
973.9	20th century, 1901 to the present

DEWEY DECIMAL CLASSIFICATION (ABRIDGED)

000	*General works*
020	Library science
030	General encyclopedias
070	Journalism and newspapers
100	*Philosophy*
130	Paranormal phenomena
150	Psychology
160	Logic
200	*Religion*
220	Bible
290	Other religions
300	*Social sciences*
310	Statistics
320	Political science
330	Economics
340	Law
350	Public administration
360	Social welfare
370	Education
380	Commerce
390	Customs and folklore
400	*Language*
410	Science of language
420	English (dictionaries)
430	German
440	French
450	Italian
460	Spanish & Portuguese
470	Latin
480	Classical & modern Greek
490	Other languages
500	*Pure sciences*
510	Mathematics
520	Astronomy
530	Physics
540	Chemistry
550	Earth sciences
560	Paleontology
570	Anthropology and biology
580	Botany (plants)
590	Zoology (animals)

600	*Applied sciences*
610	Medical sciences
620	Engineering (airplanes, cars)
630	Agriculture (gardening)
640	Home economics (cookbooks)
650	Business
660	Chemical technology
670	Manufactures
680	Miscellaneous manufactures
690	Building construction
700	*The arts*
710	Civic & landscape art
720	Architecture
730	Sculpture
740	Drawing
750	Painting
760	Graphic arts
770	Photography
780	Music
790	Recreation (sports)
800	*Literature*
810	American literature
820	English literature
830	German literature
840	French literature
850	Italian literature
860	Spanish & Portuguese literature
870	Latin literature
880	Classical & modern Greek lit.
890	Literature of other languages
900	*History and geography*
910	Geography, travel
920	Biography
930	History of ancient world
940	History of Europe
950	History of Asia
960	History of Africa
970	History of North America
980	History of South America
990	History of other areas

Worksheet 10

Name _____ Date _____

CLASSIFICATION PRACTICE

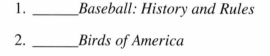

Write the general Dewey classification number for each of these titles.

Example: *900 Let's Travel to Japan*

1. _____*Baseball: History and Rules*

2. _____*Birds of America*

3. _____*Mark Twain: A Writer's Life*

4. _____*The Bible*

5. _____*Philosophy for Today*

6. _____*Cars that Made History*

7. _____*The World Book Encyclopedia*

8. _____*Poems for Young People*

9. _____*United States Government*

10. _____*Webster's Intermediate Dictionary*

11. _____*Compton's Encyclopedia*

12. _____*Reptiles and Amphibians*

13. _____*Best Plays of 1994*

14. _____*How to Draw Animals*

15. _____*History of the World*

16. _____*Greek Mythology*

17. _____*Careers for You*

18. _____*French for Beginners*

19. _____*World War II Airplanes*

20. _____*The Psychology of Survival*

Worksheet 11   **50**

NONFICTION

NOTE

If you have a school library, teach the entire lesson.
If you don't have a school library, teach up to where you find instructions to end the lesson.

OBJECTIVES

1. To discuss the meaning and arrangement of nonfiction
2. To present class and call numbers
3. To teach students how call numbers with decimals are arranged
4. To discuss the meaning and arrangement of reference books
5. To check mastery with a follow-up worksheet
6. To give practice in the location of nonfiction books

MATERIALS

1. Three nonfiction books: a history book, a sports book, and a biography
2. A chalkboard, chalk, and eraser
3. Reproductions of the follow-up paper, Worksheet 12
4. Schools with libraries. 20 slips of paper, 3″ by 5″

PREPARATIONS

1. Copy the example below on the board.

549	Mitchell, Brian
Mit	Rocks and minerals.

2. School with libraries
   a. Reserve a 30–45 minute library period.
   b. Have a student compile a list of 20 nonfiction books from the library shelves. The list should include titles, authors, and call numbers. The books listed should be spread throughout nonfiction.
   c. Copy the information about each of the 20 books onto separate slips of paper in card catalog format. See the example above. (Capitalize only first words and proper names in titles.)

LESSON

I have several books I want to present to you.

　Hold up a history book, and read its title.

This is a nonfiction book.

　Hold up a sports book, and read its title.

This, too, is a nonfiction book.

　Hold up a biography, and read its title.

This biography is also nonfiction.

What is nonfiction? (literary works that are true; books that are true)

We classify nonfiction as true even though fairy tales, jokes, and myths, which are found in the nonfiction section, aren't true.

As a broad statement, we say nonfiction books are true.

How are nonfiction books arranged on the shelves? (by numbers)

What do the numbers represent? (the books' subjects)

Reference books are nonfiction; however, they are shelved separately.

What are some of the characteristics of reference books? (Reference books are not designed to be read from cover to cover. One refers to them for quick information. They can't be checked out of the library. Often expensive books are put in the reference section.)

Here's an example of a reference call number:

　Write on the board:　R
　　　　　　　　　　　973
　　　　　　　　　　　Smi

What does the "R" stand for? (reference)

What does the 973 stand for? (the subject)

What does "Smi" stand for? (S-m-i are the first three letters of the author's last name.)

The *nonfiction* section starts with the number 000 (zero hundred) and goes through 999 (nine ninety-nine). The *reference* section starts with the number 000 and goes through 999. In other words, nonfiction and reference are classified the same. To differentiate between the two, an "R" is placed above the call number of reference books. Nonfiction and reference books are shelved separately.

Nonfiction is arranged primarily—first—by numbers. It is arranged secondarily by authors' last names. Here's an example:

Write on the board: 973
Atk

973
Bur

973
Cas

All three of the books represented here are classified 973. They are all about United States history. To make the location of specific books easy, the books are arranged secondarily by the authors' last names.

If 000 through 999 were the only numbers available, classification of nonfiction books would be very limited.

With the Dewey Decimal Classification, every number can be subdivided indefinitely. Here's an example:

Write on the board: 973

The number 973 (nine seventy-three) stands for United States history. By adding a decimal and another number, one can increase the numbers available for classifying.

Point to the number 973 on the board.

Add a decimal and a seven. (973.7)

The 973 means United States history.

Cup your hands around the 973.

The decimal seven subdivides United States history to a specific period of history: the Civil War period.

Cup your hands around the decimal seven.

The number can be further subdivided by adding more numbers to the right of the decimal.

You won't need to learn the numbers in the Dewey system, but you will need to understand how numbers are arranged on the shelves.

Write on the board: 629.13
629.2

The number 629.13 (six twenty-nine point thirteen) stands for aviation. If you are interested in finding some books about airplanes, look under 629.13.

The number 629.2 (six twenty-nine point two) is the number for automobiles. If you want to find some books about cars, look under 629.2.

Unless you understand how the books with decimals are arranged, you may not be able to locate what you're looking for.

If you were looking for 629.2 and didn't understand decimals, you might give up before you found it.

    Point to 629.13.

You might find 629.13 and think that you had already passed where 629.2 should have been. You might think all of the books about cars were checked out. Actually, you wouldn't have looked far enough.

The number 629.2 comes after 629.13. It's larger than 629.13.

    Cup your hands around the two 629s on the board.

The number 629 is the same in both of these numbers, so let's forget it and look only at the numbers after the decimals.

There are two ways to determine which number is larger.

You can compare the first numbers after the decimal.

    Cup your hands around the numbers designated by parentheses:
        629.(1)3
        629.(2)

One comes before two.

Another way to determine which number comes first is to have an equal number of numerals after the decimal. In 629.13, there are two numbers after the decimal. In 629.2, there is only one number after the decimal. If we add a zero to 629.2, we will have an equal number of numerals after the decimal.

    Add a zero to 629.2. (629.20)

Now we can compare. Which is smaller? 629.13 or 629.20? (629.13)

Let's look at another example.

    Write on the board: 796.23
                          796.7

These are in order. The smaller number is first. How do you know? (If you add a zero after the seven, thereby having an equal number of numerals after the decimal, you will see that twenty-three is smaller than 70. You can also compare the first numbers after the decimal: 2 and 7. Two is smaller.)

Add a zero to 796.7.   (796.70)

Let's do one more example.

Write on the board: 598.40
                        Tho

                        598.7
                        Atw

Which of these comes first? (598.40)

Cup your hands around the numbers in parentheses: 598.(4)0
                                                  598.(7)

If I compare the first numbers after the decimals, four and seven, I can readily see which is smaller.

Add a zero to point seven. (598.70)

If I add a zero to point seven, I can compare point 40 to point 70. Point 40 is smaller.

We didn't look at the three letters of the authors' last names. We didn't need to. Nonfiction is arranged primarily by numbers. If two or more numbers are identical, consider the authors' names.

Write on the board: 811
                        Ste

                        811
                        Ard

In this case, since the numbers are the same, we will have to look at the letters of the authors' last names to determine which book comes first.

Write on the board: 811
                        Ard

                        811
                        Ste

This is the correct order. The classification numbers are the same. We have to look at the authors' names to determine which book comes first. The author whose last name starts with the letter "A" comes before the author whose last name starts with "S."

Write "incorrect" above the first example and "correct" above the second one.

incorrect	correct
811	811
Ste	Ard
811	811
Ard	Ste

Give students time to study the two examples.

Erase both.

Write this on the board: 917.3

Nonfiction is divided into classes. A class number is the number for a particular subject. Think of the word *class* as being short for classification. The number 917.3 is the classification number for United States geography.

Add the letter "B" to the example: 917.3
                                          B

If I add one, two, or three letters from the author's last name, I've changed a class number to a call number.

Write these examples on the board.

917.3   917.3   917.3
  B   Br   Bro

Call numbers give *all* the information about a book's location.

If you ask a librarian to help you find a book, you will need to tell him or her the book's call number. If you look for a book on the shelf yourself, you will also need to know the call number.

It's easy to distinguish between a class number and a call number. The call number is the number with *all* of the information.

Write this on the board: c(all)

The word *call* has all in it.

After I write some numbers on the board, I'll ask you to tell me if they are class numbers or call numbers.

Write the following on the board. (Don't write the answers, which are in parentheses.)

621 (class number)

398 (call number)
Sta

796 (call number)
Bro

811 (class number)

Call on students to classify each of the practice items.

Let's see how much you remember about nonfiction. I'm going to distribute a paper for you to do. Don't start work until I explain it.

Distribute Worksheet 12, and explain it. After the students finish, let them grade their own papers as you read and discuss the answers.

Collect the papers.

If you don't have a school library, end the lesson here.

Decide whether you have time to have two groups locate nonfiction books today. If not, modify the lesson, and have one group look for books today and the other group look for books during the next visit.

Everyone will locate two nonfiction books. Half of you will locate them now and the other half will locate them after the first group finishes/during the next library visit.

I'm going to distribute a slip of paper to those who'll look for books first. The paper lists one of the books you are to find. Look at the example I've written on the board.

Point to the example:

```
549    Mitchell, Brian
Mit        Rocks and minerals.
```

What is the title of the book? (*Rocks and minerals*)

Notice that one of the important words in the title, minerals, isn't capitalized. Librarians capitalize only first words and proper nouns in titles.

Who's the author of the book? (Brian Mitchell)

What is 549 Mit? (the call number)

The number 549 is the Dewey classification number for rocks and minerals.

What does "Mit" stand for? (the author's last name)

Where would you look for this book? (in nonfiction)

Would you start looking in the 000 (zero hundreds)? (no)

You would start looking in the middle of nonfiction, wouldn't you?

When you find the book listed on your slip of paper, touch the book with one hand and raise your other hand. Don't remove the book from the shelf. I'll check to see if you've found the right book. If you have, I'll take your slip of paper and give you another. You will then repeat the process with the second slip of paper. Everyone is to find two books. After you have found two books and have been checked, you may browse or check books out.

We'll divide into two groups. The _____ group will locate books first. When that group is looking for books, the other group may browse or check books out.

I'm going to distribute one slip of paper to each person in the group that is going to look for books today. As soon as you receive your slip, go look for your book.

Only those with slips of paper are to be in the nonfiction section. Everyone else should browse elsewhere.

After the slips are distributed, excuse the other group to browse.

If you plan to rotate the groups today, do so after the first group has finished locating books.

If you plan to rotate the groups next week, at that time review the location procedure prior to the activity.

FOLLOW-UP

1. You may want to have students locate books again. If so, mix fiction and nonfiction slips of paper. When a student hands you a fiction slip, hand him or her a nonfiction slip. If the student hands you a nonfiction slip, hand him or her a fiction slip.
2. Here's an idea for a learning center. Put five or six nonfiction library books with closely related numbers on a table. Some of the numbers should include decimals. One student at a time can put the books in the correct order and check his or her work against an answer card. When finished, the student should disarrange the books so that they will be ready for the next person.

Here's an example:

598
Zoe

598.14
Smi

598.2
Joh

598.3
Bur

599
And

The numbers above are in order.

Disarrange books when putting them on a table.

NONFICTION

1. Write the following numbers under the correct headings.

	Class Numbers	Call Numbers
a. 926.3	_____	_____
b. 623 A	_____	_____
c. 423 Smi	_____	_____
d. 021	_____	_____

2. Write these numbers in order on the lines provided.

a. 623.8	_____	b. 973.7	_____
623.15	_____	973	_____
623	_____	973.14	_____
623.2	_____	973.2	_____
623.73	_____	972	_____

3. Is nonfiction true or untrue?

4. How is nonfiction shelved?

5. *True* or *False*

   a. _____ Reference books are nonfiction.

   b. _____ They can't be checked out.

   c. _____ They aren't meant to be read from cover to cover.

   d. _____ They are fiction.

   e. _____ Expensive books are usually put in the reference section.

THE CARD CATALOG

LESSON 1: Catalog Labels; Guide Cards

OBJECTIVES

1. To discuss the use of labels on card catalog drawers
2. To discuss the three basic kinds of catalog cards
3. To introduce illustrator and series cards
4. To review the fact that the words "a," "an," and "the" are disregarded as first words of titles
5. To discuss the use of guide cards
6. To check mastery with a follow-up worksheet

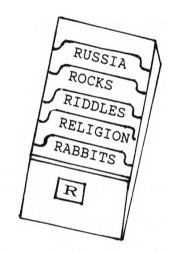

MATERIALS

1. Three catalog cards, file cards, or slips of paper
2. A hardbound and a paperback book
3. Optional. A card catalog drawer
4. A chalkboard, chalk, and eraser
5. Back-to-back reproductions of the guide card and card catalog follow-up papers, Worksheets 13 and 14

PREPARATIONS

1. Copy Worksheet 14's card catalog on the board. Alternative: Distribute back-to-back reproductions of Worksheets 13 and 14, and let students refer to the card catalog at the top of Worksheet 14 when needed.
2. Copy the catalog drawer at the top of this page on the board.

LESSON

What's the purpose of a card catalog? (to index a library's holdings)

That's right. (Pause) The card catalog indexes a library's collection. It tells you if the library has a particular item, and if it has, it tells you where to find it. A library may index its books in one section of the card catalog and its other materials such as videos, CDs, etc. in another section.

Hold up a hardbound book.

All hardbound books are indexed in the card catalog.

Hold up a paperback book.

Paperbacks are not usually indexed.

Do you have to know a book's author to be able to locate a book in a library? (no)

What three things might you know about a book that would enable you to find it? (the author, title, or subject)

The librarian anticipates that library patrons will know the author, title, or subject of a book for which they're searching. Therefore, the librarian usually makes three cards for each book: one for the author, one for the title, and one for the subject.

Hold up three catalog cards, file cards, or slips of paper.

Although three catalog cards for a book are basic, some books may have more. If the illustrations in a book are important, the librarian may make a card for the illustrator.

If a book covers numerous subjects, more than one subject card may be made.

Most catalog cards are made by catalogers, librarians who make catalog cards. Individual libraries buy most of their catalog cards already prepared.

Some books are part of a series. For example, *Frankenstein, Dracula,* and *Creature from the Black Lagoon* are all part of Ian Thorne's Monsters Series. Books in a series have a similarity of subject. The Enchantment of the World Series features books about different countries. Sometimes a special card is made for a book which is part of a series. Such a card is called a series card.

How are cards arranged in the card catalog? (alphabetically)

If you didn't copy Worksheet 14's card catalog on the board, distribute back-to-back reproductions of Worksheets 13 and 14 now.

Look at the card catalog pictured on the board/Worksheet 14.

In which drawer would you look for a book about baseball? (A–B)

Weather? (W–Z)

Horses? (F–H)

Author cards are filed under the authors' last names. The authors' first names are considered secondarily.

In which drawer would you look for a book by John Tunis? (T–V)

Enid Bagnold? (A–B)

Jack London? (L–M)

Title cards are filed under the first words of titles.

Write the following on the board: a, an, the

Point to the words.

The words "a," "an," and "the" are disregarded as first words of titles. Nearly every title starts with one of those articles. If "a," "an," and "the" were considered, most titles would appear in the "a" or "t" section of the card or computer catalog or on book lists. By disregarding "a," "an," and "the," titles fall within the whole alphabet.

In which drawer of the card catalog would you look for these titles?

Tell Me Everything? (T–V)

An Introduction to Watercolor? (I–K)

Animal Rights? (A–B)

The Silent Storm? (Q–S)

A Weekend with Leonardo da Vinci? (W–Z)

If you are going to look for an author in the card catalog, will you look under the author's first or last name? (last name)

If you are going to look up a title, which word will you look under? (the first word, unless it's "a," "an," or "the")

Title cards couldn't be filed under the third or fourth words. Millions of people would get confused as to which word to look under. The rule has to be simple. More importantly, some titles have only one word. Titles are filed under their first words, unless those words are "a," "an," or "the."

What's the purpose of the card catalog? (to index a library's book collection)

What do you need to know about a book to be able to locate it in the card catalog? (the author, title, or subject)

Which books are not listed in the card catalog? (paperbacks)

How many catalog cards do most books have? (three)

Can you name two cards besides the author, title, and subject card that a book might have? (an illustrator card, a series card)

The label on a drawer of catalog cards tells you which cards are filed in that drawer.

Inside the drawers, guide cards help you locate the card for which you are looking.

If you have a catalog drawer, show it to the students. Refer to the guide cards.

Point to the catalog drawer you've drawn on the board.

Guide cards stand higher than catalog cards.

There are hundreds of cards in a catalog drawer. To make it easier for you to locate the card you want, the drawer is subdivided by guide cards. Use the guide cards as an alphabetical help. Don't waste time by looking through hundreds of cards.

Important subjects are often listed on guide cards. If you are looking for an important subject, you may be able to find it listed on a guide card.

Guide cards help us alphabetically and they give us quick help in locating important subjects.

The guide cards in the sample drawer on the board are RABBITS, RELIGION, RIDDLES, ROCKS, and RUSSIA.

Which cards would you look between to find robots? (RIDDLES/ROCKS)

Reptiles? (RELIGION/RIDDLES)

Railroads? (RABBITS/RELIGION)

A book about Babe Ruth? (after RUSSIA)

The book *Racing Cars that Made History?* (RABBITS/RELIGION)

If you haven't distributed back-to-back reproductions of Worksheets 13 and 14, do so now.

Look at Worksheet 14. We're going to do this page together orally. Later you'll fill in the answers in writing.

The worksheet says, "Do you know the author, title, or subject for the books below? In which drawer will a card for each of the following be found?"

Look at the first practice item: books about magic. What do you know about the book—the author, the title, or the subject? (subject)

In which drawer will the subject be found? (L–M)

Continue through all of the items.

For your convenience, the answers are on the next page.

1. subject (L–M)
2. title (I–K)
3. author (A–B)
4. subject (Q–S)
5. title (I–K)
6. author (C–E)
7. subject (Q–S)
8. title (W–Z)
9. author (N–P)
10. subject (T–V)

Look at practice item 2. Why are the words *Kings and Queens* in italics? (They're the title of a book.)

In practice item 5, why is *It's Like This, Cat* in italics? (It's the title of the book.)

In practice item 8, why is *Western Lawmen* in italics? (It's the title of the book.)

According to standard rules, book titles are always underlined or printed in italics. This rule is not observed on catalog cards.

Take out your pencils and do both sides of the worksheet.

You may want to have students check their own papers so you can discuss difficult items with them.

Name _____ Date _____

GUIDE CARDS

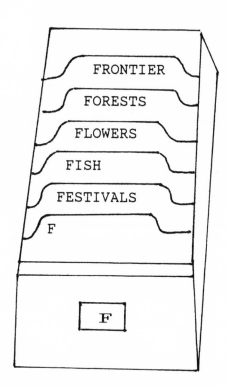

Between which guide cards will you find these?

1. Books about fireflies   _____   _____

2. The book *Fifteen*   _____   _____

3. Books about fashion   _____   _____

4. Books by Eugene Field   _____   _____

5. Books about football   _____   _____

6. The book *Foghorns*   _____   _____

7. Books about France   _____   _____

8. Books by Rae Foley   _____   _____

9. The book *Flying Saucers*   _____   _____

10. Books by Aileen Fisher   _____   _____

THE CARD CATALOG

A – B	I – K	Q – S
C – E	L – M	T – V
F – H	N – P	W – Z

Do you know the author, title, or subject for the books below? In which drawer will a card for each of the following be found?

	Kind of Card	*Drawer*
1. Books about magic	_____	_____
2. The book *Kings and Queens*	_____	_____
3. A book by Joy Adamson	_____	_____
4. Books about soccer	_____	_____
5. The book *It's Like This, Cat*	_____	_____
6. A book by Arthur Clarke	_____	_____
7. Books about rabbits	_____	_____
8. The book *Western Lawmen*	_____	_____
9. A book by Howard Pease	_____	_____
10. Books about Texas	_____	_____

LESSON 2: Catalog Cards

OBJECTIVES

1. To discuss the card catalog
2. To present the following cards: author, title, subject, illustrator, subject analytic, annotated, "see," "see also," fiction, nonfiction
3. To present the abbreviation "unp"
4. To present a tracing
5. To test mastery with a follow-up worksheet

MATERIALS

1. A chalkboard, chalk, and eraser
2. Back-to-back reproductions of Worksheets 15 and 16
3. Reproductions of Worksheet 17
4. Back-to-back reproductions of Worksheets 18a and 18b

PREPARATION

Copy the following catalog card on the chalkboard. Leave room at the top for one additional line of writing.

796.357 Joh	Johnson, Brad
	Baseball for boys and girls; illustrated by Gary Smith. New York: Bronson Publishing Company, 1994.
	298 p. illus.

LESSON

What's the purpose of the card catalog? (to index a library's book collection; to tell you if a library has a particular book, and if it has, to tell you where to find it)

How is the card catalog arranged? (alphabetically)

What three things can you know about a book that will enable you to find it in the library? (author, title, subject)

If a student gives only one answer, elicit the other two answers from the class.

If you're looking for an author in the card catalog, should you look under the author's first or last name? (last name)

If you're looking for a title, which word of the title should you look under? (first)

There are three words we disregard as first words of a title. What are they? (a, an, the)

Let's look at the catalog card I've put on the board.

If the card you've put on the board has a ragged edge, explain that the ragged edge means that you've shortened the card.

What's the title of the book? (*Baseball for boys and girls*)

What is a title? (the name of a book)

Note that only the first word in the title is capitalized. Librarians capitalize only first words and proper nouns in titles.

What is the call number? (796.357 Joh)

What does "Joh" stand for? (the author's last name)

Who illustrated the book? (Gary Smith)

What do we call a person who illustrates a book? (an illustrator)

What's an illustration? (a picture, design, or diagram)

Where was the book published? (New York)

Who is the publisher? (Bronson Publishing Company)

What is a publisher? (a person or company that has a book printed and offers it for sale)

What is the copyright date? (1994)

How many pages are in the book? (298)

Erase 298 p., and in its place write: unp.

Some book pages aren't numbered. In such cases, "unp" for unpaged is recorded on the catalog cards.

Erase "unp" and put "298 p." back.

The information in the left corner of the card tells you where to find the book. Where would you look for this book? (796.357 Joh)

The first line tells you whether a card is an author card, a title card, or a subject card.

Is this an author card, title card, or subject card? (author card)

How do you know? (the author's name is on the first line)

Write the title on the board above the author's name. (The title now appears twice.)

What kind of card is this now? (a title card)

Erase the title that you have just written on the board, and put the subject BASEBALL in its place. Be sure to print the subject in full capitals.

What kind of card is this now? (subject card)

How do you know? (The first line is capitalized.)

Subjects are always fully capitalized on catalog cards. That's the librarian's way of warning you that you are not looking at a title card, you are looking at a subject card. If a line is totally in capitals, it's a subject.

Each book in a library usually has at least three catalog cards.

I'm going to distribute a paper which shows some examples.

Distribute back-to-back reproductions of Worksheets 15 and 16.

Look at Worksheet 15.

This page pictures a set of catalog cards.

The librarian will file the author card for students who may look for the book under the author's name. The title card will be filed for the students who may look for the book under the title. The subject card will be filed for students who won't have a particular author or title in mind, but who will be looking for a fiction book about the United States Revolution.

If the card catalog has a drawer for every letter of the alphabet in which drawer will the first card be filed? (F)

The second card? (J)

The third card? (U)

Which card is a title card? (the second card)

Which card is an author card? (the first card)

Which card is a subject card? (the third card)

How do you know the third card is a subject card? (Every letter of the first line is capitalized.)

Who is the author of the book? (Esther Forbes)

What is the title? (*Johnny Tremain*)

Is the book fiction or nonfiction? (fiction)

How do you know? (The card says "Fic." There isn't a number.)

What does "For" stand for? (Forbes)

How many pages are in the book? (256 pages)

Who is the illustrator? (Lynd Ward)

What is the copyright date? (1943)

Who is the publisher? (Houghton Mifflin)

Are there any pictures? (yes)

How do you know? (The card says "illustrated by Lynd Ward," and it says "illus.")

Turn your worksheet over.

The three cards pictured are for three different books.

Study the first card, and see if you can tell me what kind of card it is. (an illustrator card)

Remind students that when a book's illustrations are important, a card may be filed for the illustrator.

How do you know the first card is an illustrator card? ("Illus." appears on the first line after Susan Smith's name. Also the card says "pictures by Susan Smith," which further confirms the fact that Susan Smith is the illustrator.)

Look at the second card.

How is this card different? (It says that information about the subject, BABE RUTH, can be found on pages 227–235.)

This subject card is only for a part of a book. It's called a subject analytic card.

Who wants to read the book's title? (*Great lives* or *Great lives: sports*)

Great lives is the main title. The part after the colon, *sports,* is a subtitle. The subtitle lets us know that the biographies included in the book are limited to great people in the field of sports.

The book is a compilation of the biographies of many sports figures. If you need information about Babe Ruth, you can find a few pages about him in this book.

Look at the third card.

What's different about it? (The card includes a description of the story.)

The description at the bottom of the card is called an annotation. It helps you decide whether you might be interested in the book.

Some catalog cards have annotations, others don't.

Distribute reproductions of Worksheet 17.

Look at Worksheet 17.

The first two cards at the top of the page are called cross reference cards.

The first one is a "see" card: s-e-e. A "see" card refers you from a heading that isn't being used to one that is. The heading MODEL CARS isn't being used. Look under AUTOMOBILES—MODELS instead.

The next card is a "see also" card. A "see also" card refers you to additional material. You'll find some books listed under SECRET WRITING. If you want additional information, look under CIPHERS and under CRYPTOGRAPHY.

Look at the third card.

What kind of card is it? (a subject card)

How do you know? (Every letter on the first line is capitalized.)

What is the subject? (DOGS)

What is the title of the book? (*The complete dog book*)

What's the call number? (636.7 Ame. Read: six thirty-six point seven A-m-e.)

What is the class number? (636.7)

What does A-m-e under the number stand for? (the first three letters of the author's last name)

What's the author's name? (The American Kennel Club)

How many pages are in the book? (832)

What does the letter "p" after 832 stand for? (pages)

Where was the book published? (New York)

Who published the book? (Howell Book House)

What's the copyright date? (1992)

Is this book fiction or nonfiction? (nonfiction)

If the book hadn't been designated nonfiction, how would you have known? (Nonfiction books have numbers in the left corners of their catalog cards.)

Look at the last card on the page.

What is the title of the book? (*Old Yeller*)

What is the subject? (DOGS—FICTION)

What kind of card is this—author, title, or subject? (subject)

How do you know? (Every letter in the first line is capitalized.)

Who is the author? (Fred Gipson)

What does "Fic" stand for? (fiction)

What do the letters "Gip" under "Fic" stand for? (Gipson)

How many pages are in the book? (158 pages)

Who published the book? (Harper)

Where was the book published? (New York)

Is this book fiction or nonfiction? (fiction)

If the letters, "Fic" and the words fiction weren't on the page, how would you know? (The book doesn't have a number. Nonfiction has numbers; fiction doesn't.)

Look at the bottom of the card. That information is for the librarian's use. It's call a tracing.

Some public libraries have divided catalogs. Instead of having author, title, and subject cards filed together, they separate subject cards. If you start looking for a book by author or title, you must look in the author/title catalog drawers. If you want to look up a subject, you have to look in the separate subject catalog drawers.

Some libraries have book catalogs or computer catalogs instead of card catalogs.

> Distribute back-to-back reproductions of Worksheets 18a and 18b.

Take out your pencils and complete Worksheets 18a and 18b. If you need help, raise your hand.

> You may want to have the students correct their own papers, so you can discuss the practice items as you check them.

> Have students pass Worksheets 15, 16, and 17 in. If you want students to pass Worksheets 18a and 18b in, have them passed in separately.

Fic   Forbes, Esther
For   Johnny Tremain; illustrated by Lynd Ward.
          Boston, Houghton Mifflin Company, 1943.
              256p.   illus.

Johnny Tremain

Fic   Forbes, Esther
For   Johnny Tremain; illustrated by Lynd Ward.
          Boston, Houghton Mifflin Company, 1943.
              256p.   illus.

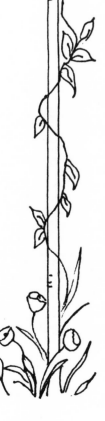

UNITED STATES—HISTORY—REVOLUTION—FICTION

Fic   Forbes, Esther
For   Johnny Tremain; illustrated by Lynd Ward.
          Boston, Houghton Mifflin Company, 1943.
              256p.   illus.

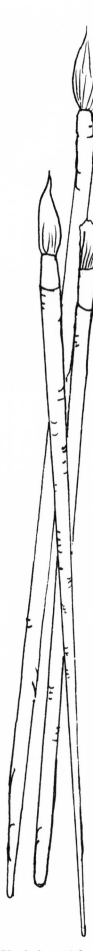

Smith, Susan, illus.

Fic Thompson, Robert
Tho   The last parade; pictures by Susan Smith. New York: Grant Publishing Company, c1994.
    132p.   illus.

RUTH, BABE, pages 227–235

920 Sullivan, George
Sul   Great lives: sports. New York: Scribner, 1988.
    273p.   illus.

Fic Burnford, Sheila Every
Bur   The incredible journey; illus. by Carl Burger. Boston: Little, Brown, c1961.

    A cat and two dogs travel 250 miles across the Canadian wilderness to their former home.

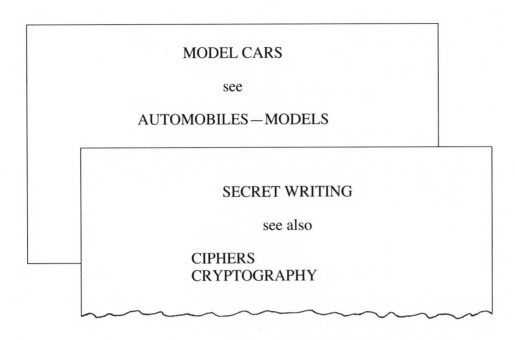

MODEL CARS

see

AUTOMOBILES—MODELS

SECRET WRITING

see also

CIPHERS
CRYPTOGRAPHY

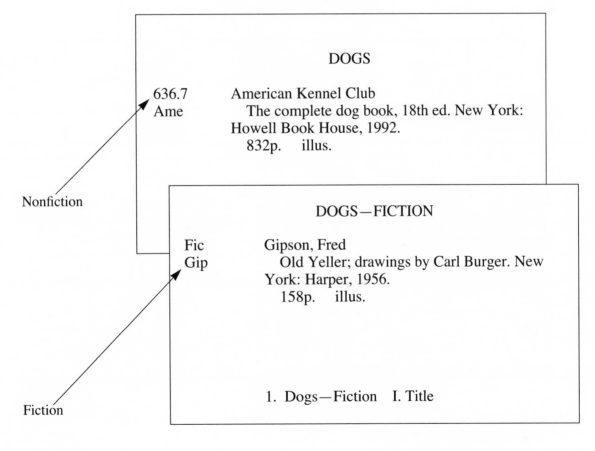

DOGS

636.7   American Kennel Club
Ame   The complete dog book, 18th ed. New York:
             Howell Book House, 1992.
                 832p.   illus.

Nonfiction

DOGS—FICTION

Fic   Gipson, Fred
Gip   Old Yeller; drawings by Carl Burger. New
             York: Harper, 1956.
                 158p.   illus.

             1. Dogs—Fiction   I. Title

Fiction

CATALOG CARDS

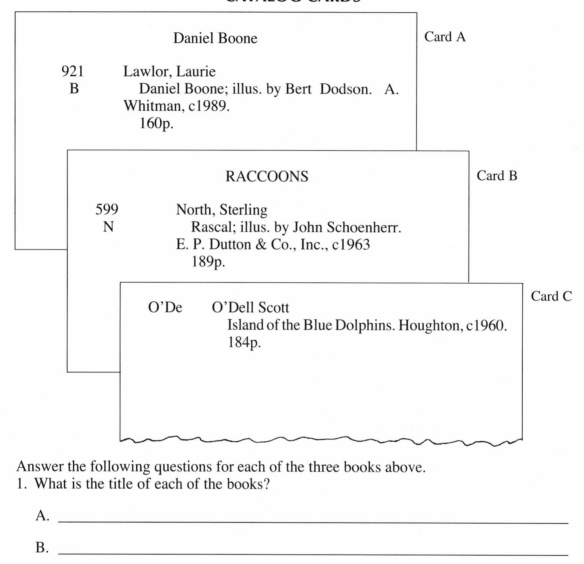

Card A

Daniel Boone

921   Lawlor, Laurie
B   Daniel Boone; illus. by Bert Dodson.   A.
          Whitman, c1989.
              160p.

Card B

RACCOONS

599   North, Sterling
N   Rascal; illus. by John Schoenherr.
          E. P. Dutton & Co., Inc., c1963
              189p.

Card C

O'De   O'Dell Scott
              Island of the Blue Dolphins. Houghton, c1960.
              184p.

Answer the following questions for each of the three books above.
1. What is the title of each of the books?

  A. _____

  B. _____

  C. _____

2. What is the author's last name?

  A. _____ B. _____ C. _____

3. What is the call number?

  A. _____ B. _____ C. _____

4. Who is the publisher?

   A. _____ B. _____ C. _____

5. Who is the illustrator?

   A. _____ B. _____ C. _____

6. How many pages are there?

   A. _____ B. _____ C. _____

7. What is the copyright date?

   A. _____ B. _____ C. _____

8. What kind of card is each?

   A. _____ B. _____ C. _____

LESSON 3: How Catalog Cards Are Filed

OBJECTIVES

1. To teach students the order in which the cards are filed
2. To check mastery with a follow-up worksheet

MATERIALS

1. A chalkboard (large, if possible), chalk, and eraser
2. Reproductions of Worksheet 19

PREPARATIONS

Copy the following on the board. Don't include the answers, which are in parentheses.

Set 1

____ *The American West* (1)
____ *A Tale of Two Cities* (4)
____ *The Greeks* (3)
____ *An Egyptian Adventure* (2)

Set 2

____ *100 Story Poems* (5)
____ *Secret Armies* (7)
____ *St. Patrick's Day* (6)
____ *Mr. Revere and I* (3)
____ *Moccasin Trail* (4)
____ *Dogs and More Dogs* (2)
____ *Dr. Dolittle* (1)

Set 3

____ McDonald (2)
____ MacArthur (1)
____ McNeer (5)
____ MacMillan (4)
____ McGovern (3)

Set 4

____ BRONZE AGE (3)
____ SIGN LANGUAGE (5)
____ BOSTON TEA PARTY (2)
____ SCIENCE FICTION (4)
____ BLACK HOLES (1)

Set 5

U.S.—HISTORY—REVOLUTION
U.S.—HISTORY—REVOLUTION. FICTION
U.S.—HISTORY—CIVIL WAR
U.S.—HISTORY—CIVIL WAR. FICTION

LESSON

Who remembers how catalog cards are arranged? (in alphabetical order)

Which three words in titles are disregarded as first words? (a, an, the)

Write this on the board: *6 on Easy Street*

Where would you look for this book in the card catalog? (under *Six on Easy Street)*

After a student answers, write "Six" above the number 6.

When you look in the card catalog for a number, spell it out.

Write this: *101 Dalmatians*

Where would you look for this? (Spell 101 out and look under *One Hundred and One Dalmatians.*)

Write *One Hundred and One* above the number 101.

Numbers must be spelled out.

Write this: *St. Francis of Assisi*

Where would you find this book? (under Saint Francis of Assisi)

Words that are abbreviated are filed as if they were spelled out. To find this book you should look in the card catalog alphabetically under S-a-i-n-t. However, the word will be printed St.

Write Saint above St. in the title.

Write: Dr. Seuss

Dr. is abbreviated. When you look for Dr., you must spell it out: D-o-c-t-o-r. The word will be printed Dr.

Write Doctor above Dr.

Write this: *Mr. Popper's Penguins*

Where would you find this book? (under *Mister Popper's Penguins*)

Mr. will be filed alphabetically under M-i-s-t-e-r.

Write Mister above Mr. in the title.

The word Mrs. is an exception. It is filed exactly as it appears.

Spelling out numbers and abbreviations has been standard practice for many years. Some libraries may change their method of filing abbreviated words. Start by spelling an abbreviation out. If you don't find what you're looking for, look under the word's abbreviation.

In these examples I've written numbers and abbreviations out. In actual practice, we just spell them out mentally.

Write the following on the board: McDonald
MacDonald

Some people whose last names start with Mc, for example, McDonald, spell Mc: M-c. Other spell Mc: M-a-c.

Point while you explain.

In the card catalog, Mc is always filed as if it were spelled "Mac."

Add Bob and Steve to McDonald and MacDonald, so that the board now reads:

McDonald, Bob
MacDonald, Steve

We always think of Mc as having the letter "a" in it, so the two McDonalds are the same. Since the last names are identical, we have to alphabetize by the first names. Bob comes before Steve.

Some subjects consist of more than one word: Here's an example.

Write on the board: BURIED TREASURE

Do you know which word to look under in the card catalog? (BURIED)

Always look under the first word.

Write on the board: SKIN AND SCUBA DIVING

Which word would you look under? (SKIN)

Write on the board: RHODE ISLAND

Which word would you look under? (RHODE)

Look at the practice items on the board. Why do you think the items in Sets 1 and 2 are underlined? (They're titles.)

Who would like to number Set 1 in order?

Call on someone.

Discuss what the student did. If the student didn't cross off the words "a," "an," and "the," do so. Show the students how easy it is to alphabetize the four items when "a," "an," and "the" are disposed of.

Who'd like to number Set 2 in order?

Call on someone.

Discuss the fact that 100 should be spelled out, that St. (S-a-i-n-t) comes before Secret, that Mr. (M-i-s-t-e-r) comes before Moccasin, that Dr. (D-o-c-t-o-r) comes before Dogs.

Who'd like to number Set 3?

Call on someone.

When the student is finished, put your hand over all the Macs, leaving this:

> Donald
> Arthur
> Neer
> Millan
> Govern

Explain how easy it is to number these. (All of the Macs/Mcs are the same, so they can be disregarded.)

Set 4 is composed of subjects of two or more words. Who can number Set 4 in order?

Call on someone.

Look for subjects under their first words.

We say that the card catalog is arranged alphabetically. There is one exception to that rule. Subject cards for historical periods are arranged chronologically.

What does chronologically mean? (according to time, according to when something happened)

To find a subject card for a historical period, start by looking under the name of the country. If you're interested in a particular period of United States history, look under U.S. HISTORY and then the period, such as U.S. HISTORY—REVOLUTION.

You'll find many cards under U.S. HISTORY. They'll be arranged chronologically.

Look at Set 5, which lists a few historical periods.

Does Revolution come alphabetically before Civil War? (no)

The Revolution came before the Civil War chronologically. It came before the Civil War in time.

There are three ways to locate subject cards for historical periods. Some libraries file a card at the beginning of historical periods, which lists all of the periods chronologically. By referring to this card, you can locate a particular period. If you know your history well, you'll be able to locate what you want. As a last resort, you can thumb through all of the historical periods until you come to the one for which you are looking.

If you are interested in French history, you should look under FRANCE—HISTORY. For Chinese history, you'd look under CHINA—HISTORY, and so forth.

I'm going to distribute a worksheet. Complete both sides.

Distribute reproductions of Worksheet 19.

It's very effective to correct and discuss papers individually as each student finishes.

CATALOG CARD ARRANGEMENT

Number the following catalog cards in order.

Set 1

_____ *An Early Spring*
_____ *The Victory*
_____ *Sherlock Holmes*
_____ *A Time to Remember*

Set 2

_____ BOY SCOUTS
_____ MOUNTAIN LIFE
_____ BIRD WATCHING
_____ SEA HORSES

Set 3

_____ *St. Lawrence River*
_____ *Mr. Justice Holmes*
_____ *Solar System*
_____ *Dr. Elizabeth*
_____ *1984*
_____ *Don Quixote*
_____ *Moby Dick*

Set 4

_____ MacGuire
_____ McFarland
_____ McDowell
_____ MacCall
_____ McAllister
_____ McKay
_____ McBride

Answer these questions.

1. What three things might you know about a book that would enable you to locate it in the card catalog?

   _____

2. How are subject cards for historical periods filed?

   _____

3. Which three words are disregarded as first words in a title?

   _____

LESSON 4: Practice in Using the Card Catalog and in Locating Books

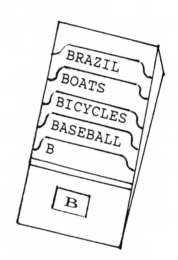

NOTE

Schools without libraries can adapt parts of the lesson.

OBJECTIVES

1. To give practice in using guide cards
2. To give practice in locating catalog cards and the books they represent

MATERIALS

1. A card catalog
2. A chalkboard, chalk, and eraser
3. Reproductions of Worksheet 20, cut in half. Make enough half sheets so each student will have one.

PREPARATIONS

1. Copy the catalog drawer above on the board.
2. Next on the board, copy the following catalog card.

```
629.2   William, West
  Wil      Classic cars; illus. by David Allen. Sheldon Publishing
         Company, 1994.
             276p. illus.
```

3. Copy this sample worksheet on the board.

Subject ___*Alaska*_____
Author _____
Title _____
Call number _____

4. Prepare enough copies of Worksheet 20 for half of your students. On each worksheet list one subject from a different drawer of the card catalog. Try to avoid using subjects that are on guide cards.

Make duplicate worksheets for the other half of your class. Put them away until needed.

Teacher. Before going to the library, present the review in the classroom. Only the activity needs to be conducted in the library.

LESSON

Tell the students that during their library visit today half of them will be using the card catalog to locate books on specific subjects. The other half of the class will browse and check out books or other materials. The groups will rotate at the next library visit.

If your library's catalog isn't big enough for half of the class to be using drawers at the same time, modify the lesson so that location of catalog cards and books is scheduled for three library visits, instead of two.

Let's start today's library lesson with a quick review.

What's the purpose of the card catalog? (to index the library's book collection; to tell you if a library has a particular book, and, if so, to tell you where it's located)

Look at the catalog drawer and guide cards I've drawn on the board.

What's the purpose of guide cards? (to provide alphabetical help in locating cards)

Between which cards will you find a book by Ray Bradbury? (BOATS / BRAZIL)

A book about birds? (BICYCLES / BOATS)

A book by Zachary Ball? (B / BASEBALL)

A book about bats? (BASEBALL / BICYCLES)

The book *Bronze Bow*? (after BRAZIL)

If necessary write *Bronze Bow* on the board.

Which would be the faster way to locate cards on bears: look through all of the cards in the drawer or look between the guide cards BASEBALL and BICYCLES? (Look between the guide cards.)

Look at the catalog card on the board.

Is this an author, title, or subject card? (author)

What is the title of the book? (*Classic cars*)

Who is the author? (West Williams)

How many pages are in the book? (276 pages)

Are there illustrations? (yes)

How do you know? (The card says illus. by David Allen. It also says illus.)

What's the copyright date? (1994)

Who is the publisher? (Sheldon Publishing Company)

What's the call number? (629.2 Wil)

What's the purpose of the call number? (to tell you where the book is shelved)

What do the three letters under the number represent? (the first three letters of the author's last name)

Is this book fiction or nonfiction? (nonfiction)

I'm going to give a worksheet to half of you. It'll look like this.

   Point to the board.

I've written a subject at the top of each paper. In this case, the subject is Alaska. If you receive this paper, you'll get the "A" drawer of the card catalog and find a nonfiction book about Alaska.

How will you know if a book is fiction or nonfiction? (Nonfiction books have numbers.)

On the paper, fill in the author, title, and call number. Then go to the shelves and find the book. Don't remove it. Touch it with one hand, and raise your other hand. I'll check you. If you've found the book listed on your paper, you may then browse or check out books or other materials.

Each worksheet has a different subject.

Half of the class will do the assignment today and the other half will do it during the next library visit.

   Announce who will do the assignment today.

Teacher. Take the class to the library.

Librarian. Continue the lesson.

Teacher and librarian. Pass out papers to those who will be doing the assignment.

Tell the students that due to the nature of this particular assignment, they should take the catalog drawers to the tables.

Excuse a few students at a time to get catalog drawers. After the assignment group has started to work, excuse the other group.

Circulate among the assignment group. See if each student is using guide cards. Check students who have located the books listed on their papers.

Next week, after a review, rotate groups.

FOLLOW-UP

If you feel there is a need for further practice, try one or more of these variations.

1. Have students locate a *fiction* book about a specific *subject*. Prepare enough copies of Worksheet 20 for half of your students. On each worksheet list a fiction subject from a different drawer of the card catalog. Here is an example of a fiction subject: DOGS—FICTION. Notice that subjects are in full capitals. Make duplicate copies of the worksheets for the other half of your class.

   Tell students they are to locate a fiction book for the subject listed on their papers. Remind them that fiction books don't have numbers.

   Students should write the author, title, and author's letters on Worksheet 20 and then locate the book.

2. Have students locate a fiction or nonfiction book by *title*. Instead of writing a subject on each worksheet, write a title on the title line. Try to choose each title from a different drawer in the card catalog. Students can write the author, and the call number/author's letters on Worksheet 20 and then find the book on the shelf. The subject line will be blank.

3. Have students locate a fiction or nonfiction book by *author*. Instead of writing a subject or title on each worksheet, write an author on the author line. Try to choose each author from a different drawer in the card catalog. Students can write the title and call number/author's letters on Worksheet 20 and then find the book on the shelf. The subject line will be blank.

Name _____ Date _____

PRACTICE IN USING THE CARD CATALOG AND IN LOCATING BOOKS

Subject _____

Author _____

Title _____

Call number for nonfiction _____

Author's letters for fiction _____

Worksheet 20

Name _____ Date _____

PRACTICE IN USING THE CARD CATALOG AND IN LOCATING BOOKS

Subject _____

Author _____

Title _____

Call number for nonfiction _____

Author's letters for fiction _____

THE COMPUTER CATALOG

Dynix Computer Catalog. Ameritech Library Services. Provo, Utah, 1983–.

An automated catalog containing information about the book and other collections of libraries participating in a particular network. Other information, such as library events, patrons' library records, etc., may also be programmed into the computer.

OBJECTIVES

1. To introduce a computer catalog
2. To familiarize students with automated catalog searches

MATERIALS

1. Back-to-back reproductions of a computer catalog keyboard, Worksheet 21, and patron record screens, Worksheet 26.
2. Back-to-back reproductions of Worksheets 22 and 23, and Worksheets 24 and 25.
   Staple these two pages together, in order.

PREPARATIONS

1. Find out if your local public library has a computer catalog.
2. If you are not already familiar with the automated catalog, study this lesson. Then practice on an automated catalog until you feel comfortable with it.
3. *Teachers.* Find out if your school library has an automated catalog.

LESSON

Libraries have recorded information about their book and other collections in several different kinds of catalogs: card catalogs, book catalogs, and computer catalogs. Today we're going to consider computer catalogs.

Our local public library has/doesn't have a computer catalog. Our school library has a computer catalog/a card catalog.

The terms computer catalog and automated catalog are synonymous. They mean the same thing.

Various libraries in neighboring areas join together to form a network in which their books and/or other collections are entered on one computer base. This allows participating libraries to know where specific books and materials are located and whether they are currently available.

The particular network we're considering today also allows a librarian access to holdings of five other states and can indirectly access all the other states. If the book you need is located in another state, this access is helpful. It allows the librarian to get the book for you through interlibrary loan.

Some libraries or individuals may have Gopher software on the Internet. This gives them access to the catalogs of hundreds of libraries all over the world.

There are numerous brands of computer catalogs. As far as I know, all of them are self-teaching. By that I mean that the catalogs themselves instruct you as to their use.

Today we'll consider a Dynix Computer Catalog. When you learn how to use it, you should be able to transfer your knowledge to any brand of automated catalog.

How many of you know how to use computers?

How many know how to type?

How many know how to use calculators?

Do any of you know how to use a computer catalog?

I'm going to distribute a page which illustrates the keyboard of a Dynix Computer Catalog.

Distribute back-to-back reproductions of Worksheets 21 and 26.

How is this keyboard like a typewriter keyboard? (The letters of the alphabet and the numbers above them are the same as those on a typewriter keyboard.)

Why do you think the letters and the numbers above them were placed in the same position as those on a typewriter? (The identical placement makes it easy for those familiar with typewriter keys to use the automated catalog keyboard.)

How is the keyboard different from a typewriter keyboard? (A typewriter keyboard doesn't have the keys F1–Help, the number keys on the right, and blank keys. Also the punctuation keys are somewhat different.)

At present, the keys F1–F12 are not programmed on this computer. They may be programmed later.

The number keys on the right are arranged like those on the key pad of a calculator. They are particularly for people who are familiar with calculator keys.

There are two main instructions one gives to the computer we are considering today. The first is "Start Over." When you sit down at an automated catalog, if the screen is not picturing the beginning of a cycle, you can command "Start Over" to get to the beginning. You do that by pressing "S" and "O" or by pressing the key labeled "Start Over." You may be in the middle of a search yourself and want to start over; if so, you press the "S" and the "O" or the key labeled "Start Over."

The other key that is used a great deal is "Return."

Find the two return keys. You may press either one when you want to go to the next screen.

We are going to do a title search. Let's presume that the person who used the computer before us didn't finish, and the screen is not showing the beginning of a cycle. Start over either by pressing the "S" and the "O" keys or by pressing the key labeled "Start Over."

I'm going to distribute some pages which illustrate a title search. We will go through a search together, step-by-step.

   Distribute Worksheets 22, 23, 24, and 25.

Look at Worksheet 22a. This is the first screen of a cycle.

Follow as I read:

11 FEB 95 COTTONWOOD PUBLIC LIBRARY 10:38 am
Welcome to the Computer Catalog
Please choose a number from the menu and press [RETURN]

The menu means the ten items listed.

   1. TITLE—Alphabetical (BROWSE)
If you choose BROWSE, you'll see all the titles that start like the one you are looking for. This is often the best choice in looking for a title.

   2. TITLE—Any word(s) (KEYWORD)
If you know only one word of the title, you can search by keying it into the computer. However, much of the time it will be insufficient, and a second word will be required.

   3. AUTHOR—Alphabetical (BROWSE)
If you enter the name of the author of the book for which you're looking, you'll get a list of all his/her books listed in this computer. This is often the best of the author choices.

   4. AUTHOR—Any word(s) (KEYWORD)
You may need more than one word. For example, a name such as Smith might have 150 listings. A first name may be required. If you have the author's first name, use number 3 on the menu, instead of number 4.

   5. SUBJECT—Alphabetical (BROWSE)
If you type the subject "dogs" into the computer, you may get 171 titles. Do you really want to have to select from that many titles?

6. SUBJECT—Any word(s) (KEYWORD)
Instead of entering a large subject like "dogs," if you enter something more specific like "guide dogs," you won't have as many titles to consider.

7. SERIES—Alphabetical (BROWSE)
To see a list of books in a specific series, type the series name. For example, if you want to know which titles are in the Monster Series, press 7 and type the word "monster."

8. Contents—(if available)
At the Cottonwood Library, contents aren't programmed into the computer. You might see if your library has programmed #8.

9. Your library record
If you want to know about your library record, you can press 9. We'll consider this more fully later.

10. Quit searching. This command stops your search.

You've been told at the top of the screen, "Please choose a number from the menu and press [RETURN]." Now you're told the same thing again, but in different words: "Enter your selection (1–10) and press <Return>."

Let's select number 1, title search. On your keyboard, press either of the number ones. Then press the return key, which will take you to the next screen.

Notice that two commands are listed at the bottom of the screen: "?" meaning Help, and BB meaning Bulletin Board. By pressing a "?" you'll get a screen of helpful ideas, if that key is programmed. Bulletin Board refers to the library's bulletin board. If you press BB, library activities will appear on your screen.

The commands on each screen are for that screen alone.

Worksheet 22b pictures the next screen you'll see on the computer.

Follow along as I read it.

11 FEB 95 COTTONWOOD PUBLIC LIBRARY 10:39 am
TITLE—Alphabetical (BROWSE)
That lines tells us that we have chosen to search under title. To be specific, we have chosen an alphabetical browse selection.

Now we're given some examples. We can enter a complete title, such as *Gone with the Wind,* or we can shorten a title, such as *From Here to. . . .*

After we read the examples, we are told to enter the title for which we want to search. For practice, let's enter the title *Big Red.* On your keyboard, type B-i-g. Then press the long blank bar at the bottom of the keyboard to space between words. Next type R-e-d. It doesn't matter whether you capitalize words or not.

If you pressed a wrong key, for example, if you spelled red "r-e-g," you don't have to go back to the first screen to start over. Just press "Back Space" and retype the correct letter, "d."

At the bottom of the screen you are given two commands: "Start Over" and "Help." You don't need to use either at this time.

You have entered the title for which you are searching, but your computer hasn't gone to the next screen. How can you get to the next screen? (Press "Return.")

Do that.

Look at Worksheet 23a.

You are told that your search is for *Big Red*. You are also told that the title may be truncated. Truncated means shortened.

There are seven listings. Notice that number 3 has a < in front of it. (Computer trainers refer to this as a "less than sign" although that is not its meaning here.) On the computer, that line will light up.

Is number 3 the title we want? (yes)

We are told to enter the line number for more detail. Enter 3 on your keyboard. Then press a return key to get to the next screen.

Let's look at the commands listed at the bottom of Worksheet 23a. We could have pressed "S" and "O" to start over, if we desired.

The key labeled "B" to go back is rather complex. If you typed the subject "dog" into the computer, you'd find a list of subjects in which dogs would appear alphabetically: (1) Dogmatic theology, (2) Dogmatism . . . (6) Dogs . . . You'd press number 6 for dogs. There you'd find possibly 200 titles. Maybe when you got to title 86, you pressed the "B" to go back. You would not go back to title 1, you'd go back to the screen before that, back before this list started, back to the list of subjects: (1) Dogmatic theology, (2) Dogmatism . . . (6)Dogs . . . . So "Back" means back one screen before the multi-part screen you're on. If you're looking at a one-screen projection, then it'd be the screen before that.

By pressing the "P" key, you'll go back to the previous screen. If you press the return key, you'll go to the next screen. By pressing a "?" you'll get a screen of helpful ideas, if that key is programmed.

Look at Worksheet 23b.

We are reminded that we are searching for *Big Red*. You see a list of five authors. Number 3 is designated by a < and is lit up on the computer.

The author of *Big Red* is Jim Kjelgaard, who was born in 1910 and died in 1959.

Kjelgaard is pronounced Kel-guard.

Notice that the publication date of 1976 is for copy 1.

If a "c" appears in front of the date, it's a copyright date. Otherwise it's a publication date.

The "c" after the 1973 date (c1973, c) is probably a typo, a typing error.

On line 4, the brackets around 1966 mean this is an estimated date.

We are told that the five titles are the end of the list. We are asked to enter a title number for more detail.

On you keyboard, press 3. Then press "Return" to go to the next screen.

Look at Worksheet 24a.

The second line tells us that the call number we are looking for is located in the Children's Area, Juvenile Section, and is specifically J KJE: J for Juvenile and KJE for the first three letters of the author's name. The status of the book is that it's checked in. There is one other copy also.

Look at the author line. You see the author's name and dates: Jim Kjelgaard, 1910–1959.

Look at the title information line. *Big Red* was written by Jim Kjelgaard.

Look at the publishing information line, which is abbreviated Pubinfo. The book was published in New York by Bantam Books in 1976. It was copyrighted in 1973.

The collation line tells us that the book has 218 pages and is 20 centimeters in length. Collation refers to the technical description of a book: the number of pages, any illustrations, etc.

The subjects of the book are Dogs—Fiction and Outdoor life—Fiction. Notice that the computer doesn't put subjects in full capitalization like the card catalog does.

You are told that there's more on the next screen.

How do you get to the next screen? (Press "Return")

Do that.

For a minute, let's look back at the commands we could have used. The ones we haven't discussed yet are RW, C, and PH. If you'd like to see a list of related works, you can press RW. If you want to know the copy status of the book, press C.

By pressing PH you can request that a hold be placed on a book—that a book be held for you when it comes in. We will see how to do that a little later.

Look at Worksheet 24b.

The first lines are similar to those on the previous screen.

See the word "Continued." This is a continuation of the previous screen.

On the left you see the word "Notes." You are told that this is "A Bantam Skylark book."

The next line gives a summary: "The most famous action-filled adventure of them all. A boy and a dog battle for survival in the wilderness."

ISBN, on the next line, means International Standard Book Number.

OCLC once meant Ohio College Library Center. It now means Online Computer Library Center.

Dynix 112911 is the manufacturer's number.

You are told that this is the end of title information. However, you are also told that if you press the return key, you'll find the copy status.

Press "Return."

Before we go to the next screen, look at the commands listed. We've discussed all of them except for "First page." In this context or usage, "First page" doesn't mean the first page of the book, which you might expect. The word "page" means screen. If you are reading a list of 200 titles on numerous screens, to go back to the beginning of the list, press "F" for First page, meaning first screen. First page means first screen of a multi-part screen.

Look at Worksheet 25a.

This screen tells us about the copies of Jim Kjelgaard's book *Big Red.*

After the word "Holds," we see a zero. No one currently has placed a hold on the book—no one has asked for the book to be held for him or her.

Look at #1. In the Children's Area, Juvenile Section, under J KJE one copy of the book can be found. The status of the book is that it's checked out, but it's due February 19, 1995. That copy is part of the Cottonwood Public Library's collection.

Look at #2. In the Children's Area, Juvenile Section, under J KJE a copy 2 is located. The book is checked in. It's at the Cottonwood Public Library.

Look at #3. This copy is located in Fiction under KJE. It is checked in. It's located at Chino Valley High School.

Look at #4. *Big Red* is located in Children's Fiction under KJE. It's checked out, but it's due February 13, 1995. It belongs to Prescott Valley Public Library.

Look at the commands. The only one we aren't acquainted with is "O" for "Other Locations." The computer catalog will tell you where the book you're looking for can be found in other locations—locations in the network but which are farther away from you than those listed on the screen above.

You can borrow a book from a public library other than your own through interlibrary loan. In other words, if you place a request for a book that your library doesn't have, the library staff can borrow it from another library. After you pick the book up, finish, and return it, the library staff will return it to the library from which it was borrowed.

Let's find out how to place a hold—how to ask for the book to be held for us. Press PH for "Place Hold," meaning to place a hold. Then press "Return."

Look at Worksheet 25b.

Here we find that there are five copies of *Big Red* and there are no holds on the book. We can go to the shelf and get a copy. Let's pretend all copies are checked out and we want to have the book held for us.

Follow as I read: "You may place a hold on this title. When a copy becomes available, it will be held for you and you will be notified. To reserve this book, enter the barcode from your library card, then press <Return>."

After giving instructions, the screen commands you to "Type your library barcode."

The barcode is the long number on your library card.

Let's look back at the first screen. How can we get there? (Press "S" and "O" or "Start Over.")

Look at item #9, Your library record. If you would like to find out if you have any overdue books, or if you'd like to find out other information about your library record, you can press 9. Press it now on your keyboard. Then which key do you have to press to move to the next screen? ("Return")

Look at Worksheet 26a, which is on the back of the keyboard page. If you have pressed 9 and "Return," you will see this on the screen.

You are instructed to enter the barcode number from you library card. Let's pretend your number is 123456789. Turn over to your keyboard. Press those numbers.

What do you need to press to go on to the next screen? ("Return")

Press "Return."

Look at Worksheet 26b.

What are you told to do? ("Please enter a home telephone number.")

Turn back to the keyboard and enter your phone number. You won't need to enter the area code. Press "Return" to go to the next screen.

Look at Worksheet 26c.

You are told that for corrections or concerns, please see the library staff.

There are five choices on the menu.

1. Blocks
2. Items checked out
3. Holds
4. Patron's information
5. Quit

Item #1, Blocks, is not available to you. The library staff keeps records of unresolved problems there, such as overdues, lost books, etc.

You are told to select an option above or a command below.

If you want to know which items you have checked out, you'll press #2.

If you want to know if any items are being held for you, press #3, Holds.

If you'd like to review the information the library has about you, press #4, Patron's information. After you've pressed a number, press "Return" and you'll see the appropriate screen.

Worksheet 26d shows an example of information about a patron.

Read that to yourself.

   Pause.

If you're finished, press "Start Over" on your computer so that the catalog will be ready for the next patron.

Today we've gone step-by-step through a title search. When you have an opportunity to use an actual computer catalog, you'll have a basic understanding of how to proceed. You won't always do a title search. You can search under one of the other listings of the menu. You may find that the computer catalog that you have access to differs somewhat from the one we considered. However the general knowledge and confidence you've gained today will provide a basic approach to mastery of any computer catalog. Also the catalog you use will instruct you as to how to proceed. In the future, exciting new features will be added to the computer catalog, and you'll be ready to learn how to use each of them.

NOTE

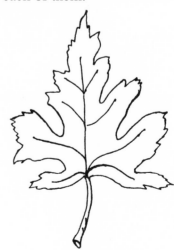

If your school library has one or more computer catalogs, you may want to teach an equal number of students at the computer(s). Thereafter, each one can teach one until everyone has learned to use the computers proficiently. If there are reasons why each of the students might not want to teach another, you could teach several competent students to use the computer and have them teach all the other students.

COMPUTER CATALOG KEYBOARD

F1	F2	F3	F4	F5	F6	F7	F8	F9	F10	F11	F12	Start Over	Srch Again	Print	Help

! 1	@ 2	# 3	$ 4	% 5	< 6	& 7	* 8	(9	) 0	_ -	+ =	Back Space △					7	8	9	-

| Q | W | E | R | T | Y | U | I | O | P | { [| }] | ~ ` | | 4 | 5 | 6 | , |

| A | S | D | F | G | H | J | K | L | : ; | " ' | | | 1 | 2 | 3 | Return |

| Shift | Z | X | C | V | B | N | M | < , | > . | ? / | Shift | | 0 | . |

| Caps Lock | | | | | | | | | : \ |

Excerpted from the Dynix Computer Catalog. Used by permission.

```
11 FEB 95            COTTONWOOD PUBLIC LIBRARY            10:38 am
                     Welcome to the Computer Catalog

              Please choose a number from the menu and press [RETURN]


      1. TITLE       —Alphabetical    (BROWSE)
      2. TITLE       —Any word(s) (KEYWORD)
      3. AUTHOR      —Alphabetical    (BROWSE)
      4. AUTHOR      —Any word(s) (KEYWORD)
      5. SUBJECT     —Alphabetical    (BROWSE)
      6. SUBJECT     —Any word(s) (KEYWORD)
      7. SERIES      —Alphabetical    (BROWSE)
      8. CONTENTS —(if available)
      9. Your library record
      10. Quit searching

 Enter your selection (1-10) and press <Return>:
 Commands: ?=Help, BB=Bulletin Board
```

Worksheet 22a

```
11 FEB 95            COTTONWOOD PUBLIC LIBRARY            10:39 am
                     TITLE—Alphabetical (BROWSE)

    Examples:

      GONE WITH THE WIND (Complete title)
      FROM HERE TO          (OK to shorten titles)

 Enter the title:
 Commands: SO: Start Over, ?=Help
```

Excerpted from the Dynix Computer Catalog. Used by permission.

Your Search: Big Red
TITLE (May be truncated)
  1. The big race/
  2. The big rain.
<3. Big Red/
  4. Big red barn
  5. Big Red confidential: inside Nebraska football/
  6. Big red drawing book.
  7. Big red fire engine/

Enter line number for more detail:
Commands: SO=Start Over, B=Back, P=Previous Screen, <Return>=Next Screen, ?=Help

Worksheet 23a

Your search: Big Red/

	AUTHOR/TITLE	DATE
1.	Kjelgaard, Jim, 1910–1959	
	Big Red/	c1973, c
2.	Kjelgaard, Jim, 1910–1959	
	Big Red/	1973, c19
<3.	Kjelgaard, Jim, 1910–1959	
	Big Red/	1976, cl
4.	Kjelgaard, Jim, 1910–1959	
	Big Red/	[1966]
5.	Haase, John	
	Big red/	c1980.

— —5 titles, End of List— —

Enter a title number for more detail:
Commands: SO=Start Over, B=Back, ?=Help

Excerpted from the Dynix Computer Catalog. Used by permission.

Worksheet 23b   **104**

```
┌─────────────────────────────────────────────────────────────────────────┐
│                                                                           │
│  11 FEB 95           COTTONWOOD PUBIC LIBRARY              10:42 am        │
│                                                                           │
│  Call Number   CHILDREN'S AREA—JUVENILE      Status: CHECKED IN           │
│                J KJE                         1 other copy                 │
│                                                                           │
│                                                                           │
│       AUTHOR                    Kjelgaard, Jim, 1910–1959.                │
│     TITLE INFO                  Big Red/ by Jim Kjelgaard.                │
│      PUBINFO                    New York: Bantam Books, 1976, c1973.      │
│     COLLATION                   218p.; 20cm.                              │
│    SUBJECT(S)                   1) Dogs—Fiction                           │
│                                 2) Outdoor life—Fiction                   │
│                                                                           │
│                                 ——More on Next Screen——                   │
│                                                                           │
│                                                                           │
│  Press <Return> to see next screen:                                       │
│  Commands: SO=Start Over, B=Back, RW=Related Works, C=Copy Status, PH=Place│
│  Hold, <Return>=Next Screen, ?=Help                                       │
│                                                                           │
│                                                                           │
└─────────────────────────────────────────────────────────────────────────┘
```

Worksheet 24a

```
┌─────────────────────────────────────────────────────────────────────────┐
│                                                                           │
│  11 FEB 95           COTTONWOOD PUBLIC LIBRARY            10:43 am         │
│                                                                           │
│  Call Number   CHILDREN'S AREA—JUVENILE      Status: CHECKED IN           │
│                J KJE                         1 other copy                 │
│                                                                           │
│                  Continued . . .                                          │
│       NOTES                     1)"A Bantam Skylark book"                 │
│      SUMMARY                    The most famous action-filled adventure of them all.│
│                                 A boy and a dog battle for survival in the wilderness.│
│       ISBN                      0553154346                                │
│      OCLC#                      yfI00000961                               │
│      DYNIX#                     112911                                    │
│                                                                           │
│                                 ——End of Title Info——                     │
│                                                                           │
│                                                                           │
│  Press <Return> to see Copy status:                                       │
│  Commands: SO=Start Over, B=Back, RW=Related Works, PH=Place Hold, F=First Page,│
│  ?=Help                                                                   │
│                                                                           │
│                                                                           │
└─────────────────────────────────────────────────────────────────────────┘
```

Excerpted from the Dynix Computer Catalog. Used by permission.

Worksheet 24b   **105**

```
┌──────────────────────────────────────────────────────────────────────┐
│ 11 FEB 95            COTTONWOOD PUBLIC LIBRARY              10:42 am    │
│                                                                        │
│ Author          Kjelgaard, Jim, 1910–1959.                             │
│ Title           Big Red /                                              │
│                                                              Holds: 0  │
│                                                                        │
│                                                                        │
│ CALL NUMBER                        STATUS          LIBRARY             │
│ 1.  CHILDREN'S AREA—JUVENILE       Due date        COTTONWOOD PUBLIC   │
│     J KJE                          19 FEB 95                           │
│ 2.  CHILDREN'S AREA—JUVENILE       CHECKED IN      COTTONWOOD PUBLIC   │
│     J KJE c.2                                                          │
│ 3.  FICTION                        CHECKED IN      CHINO VALLEY HIGH   │
│     FIC/KJE                                                            │
│ 4.  CHILDREN'S FICTION             13 FEB 95       PRESCOTT VALLEY     │
│     KJE                                                    PUBLIC      │
│                                                                        │
│                                                                        │
│ Choose a command:                                                      │
│ Commands: SO=Start Over, B=Back, O=Other Locations, PH=Place Hold, ?=Help │
│                                                                        │
└──────────────────────────────────────────────────────────────────────┘
```

Worksheet 25a

```
┌──────────────────────────────────────────────────────────────────────┐
│ 11 FEB 95            COTTONWOOD PUBLIC LIBRARY              10:43 am    │
│                          HOLDS/RECALLS                                 │
│                                                                        │
│                                      31929000454226                    │
│                                                                        │
│ Author          Kjelgaard, Jim, 1910–1959.            Copies:  5       │
│ Title           Big Red /                             Holds:  0        │
│                                                                        │
│ YOU MAY PLACE A HOLD OR RESERVE ON THIS TITLE. WHEN A COPY BECOMES     │
│ AVAILABLE, IT WILL BE HELD FOR YOU AND YOU WILL BE NOTIFIED.           │
│                                                                        │
│ TO RESERVE THIS BOOK, ENTER THE BARCODE FROM YOUR LIBRARY CARD,        │
│ THEN PRESS <RETURN>.                                                   │
│                                                                        │
│ Type your library barcode:                                            │
│                                                                        │
│                                                                        │
│                                                                        │
└──────────────────────────────────────────────────────────────────────┘
```

Excerpted from the Dynix Computer Catalog. Used by permission.

```
                    Review Patron Record

Enter the barcode from your card:
(or enter "Q" to quit)

Commands: SO=Start Over, ?=Help.
```

Worksheet 26a

```
                    Review Patron Record

Please enter your home telephone number.



Commands: SO=Start Over, B=Back, ?=Help.
```

Worksheet 26b

```
                    Review Patron Record

For corrections or concerns, please see library staff.

        1.      Blocks
        2.      Items checked out
        3.      Holds
        4.      Patron's information
        5.      Quit

Select an option above or a command below:
Commands: SO=Start Over, B= Back, ?=Help.
```

Worksheet 26c

```
                    Review Patron Record

Name                            Doe, John
Street                          123 Apache Trail
City, State, Zip                Cottonwood, Arizona 86326
Phone                           555-638-9240
Patron's Library:               Cottonwood Public Library
Card expiration date            11 JUL 96
```

Excerpted from the Dynix Computer Catalog. Used by permission.

Worksheet 26d   **107**

BIOGRAPHY AND AUTOBIOGRAPHY

OBJECTIVES

1. To discuss the meanings of biography, collective biography, and autobiography
2. To discuss how biography, collective biography, and autobiography are classified and shelved
3. To check mastery with a follow-up worksheet

MATERIALS

1. If available, a biography, a collective biography, and an autobiography. Suggestions: Biography—*Lincoln: A Photo-biography* by Russell Freedman. Collective biography—*Western Lawmen* by Frank Surge. Autobiography—*The Story of My Life* by Helen Keller. These particular titles aren't required; they are only ideas. There are very few autobiographies; finding one may be difficult.
2. A chalkboard, chalk, and eraser
3. Reproductions of the ditto follow-up, Worksheet 27
4. If you plan to have students read and report on a biography or autobiography, reproduce Worksheets 28a and 28b, back-to-back.
5. If you plan to have students report on an author/celebrity, reproduce Worksheet 29.

PREPARATION

Teacher. Find out which of these classifications is used to classify biography in your school library: 921, 920, 92, B.

NOTE

If you have time to prepare three book reviews, review a biography, a collective biography, and an autobiography, instead of introducing them.

Individual biography will be classified 921 and collective biography will be classified 920 in this lesson. If your school classifies biography either 92 or B, substitute your own classification.

LESSON

Hold up a biography. Read its title.

This is the true story of the life of _____. It was written by _____.

What do we call this type of book? (a biography)

What is this book's call number? (921, 92, or B, plus the first one, two, or three letters of the *biographee's* last name)

Individual biography—a biography about one person—is shelved under 921/92/B in our school library.

Libraries vary in the way they classify individual biography. Some classify it 921. Others classify it 92 or B. However, they all put one, two, or three letters from the biographee's last name under the classification.

>   Write this on the board: 599
>   Smi

Look at this call number. What does Smi stand for? (the first three letters of the *author's* last name)

The letters under a class number always represent the *author's* last name, except in the case of individual biography.

>   Write this on the board: 921
>   Lin

The number 921 is the class number for individual biography. The letters under 921 represent the last name of the person the book is about: the biographee.

Individual biography is the only classification in the library in which the letters under the classification *do not* represent the author's last name. They represent the *biographee's* last name.

It's very easy to locate an individual biography. For example, if you want a biography about George Washington, you don't have to refer to the card catalog; you can go to the shelves and look under 921 W.

Where would you look for a biography about Christopher Columbus? (921 C/921 Co/921 Col)

Thomas Edison? (921 E)

Clara Barton? (921 B)

Remember. Individual biography is the only section in the library in which the letters under the classification don't represent the author's last name. They represent the biographee's last name.

>   Hold up a collective biography. Read the title and the author's name.

This book contains a collection of biographies. It's called a collective biography.

>   Elaborate on the contents. Read the names of some of the biographees. Tell how many biographies are in the book.

Collective biography is classified 920.

>   Write on the board: 920

Who can tell me whose last name will be represented under the class number? (the author's)

The author of this collective biography is _____.

>   Write the first three letters of the author's last name under 920.

There are two ways to remember that the letters on a collective biography are those of the author. First, since there are many life stories in a collective biography, it wouldn't be fair to single out one biographee and use the letters of his or her last name. Second, remember that there is only one section in the library in which the letters under the class number are not the author's letters. That section is individual biography: 921.

What's the call number for these collective biographies?

Great Americans of the Twentieth Century by John Baker? (920 B/920 Ba/920 Bak)

Sports Heroes by Bill Smith? (920 S)

Presidents of the United States by Ann Brown? (920 B)

Some libraries classify all collective biographies 920. Other libraries classify collective biographies under other numbers of the 920s. For example, a book about artists might be classified 927.

>   Hold up an autobiography. Read the title.

This is the life story of _____. She/he wrote the book herself/himself.

What do we call the true story of a person's life written by herself or himself? (an autobiography)

Auto means self. An *auto*mobile is self-moving. An autobiography is a self-biography.

Autobiographies have the same class number as biographies.

>   Write this on the board: 921.

Autobiographies are individual biographies.

Will the letters under 921 represent the biographee or the author? (the biographee, who is also the author)

>   Write the first three letters of the biographee's last name under 921.

What would the call number be for Booker T. Washington's autobiography *Up from Slavery*? (921 W)

Benjamin Franklin's autobiography? (921 F)

Will Rogers's autobiography? (921 R)

I'm going to distribute a paper for you to do. Study the definitions at the top and then complete the paper.

Distribute reproductions of Worksheet 27.

FOLLOW-UP

Select from these ideas.

1. Teach the lessons, in this manual, on *Junior Book of Authors, Twentieth-Century Authors, Something About the Author, Current Biography, Webster's New Biographical Dictionary, Who's Who in America*. These reference book lessons, plus this lesson on biography and autobiography, constitute a biography unit. Extend the unit with the ideas below.

   Have students write a report about a favorite author or about a famous person. Use the form on Worksheet 29.

2. Have your students write autobiographies. To make the autobiographies special, students should present them in book form. If possible, have students include a snapshot on the frontispiece, the title page, or the first page. Have an art project to create covers or provide colored construction paper for bindings.

   If a particularly interesting autobiography is submitted, ask the student author if you may read it to the class.

3. Have a Student of the Day celebration.

   At the beginning of the period, announce who the Student of the Day is. Feature the Student of the Day's name and, if possible, his or her photograph on the bulletin board. Photograph sources: School pictures and students' pictures brought from home. If you have a Polaroid camera, take a picture of each student or, at least, take a picture of those who can't supply a photograph themselves.

   Go through your roll book, student by student, until each girl and boy has been proclaimed Student of the Day. You may want to have the Student of the Day stand and give a brief autobiographical report. If the student has formulated some goals, they can be presented.

   The Student of the Day should do all of the special jobs, such as taking messages to the office, erasing the board, passing papers, etc. The student should also line up first at the end of the period.

The instructor should make a point to speak to the Student of the Day and compliment him or her about something. The compliment can be about handwriting, work, a personal quality, or even a good-looking garment.

4. Have your students write biographies about their classmates or their parents.

5. Have your students read a biography or autobiography. You may want to assign written and/or oral reports. For a report form, see Worksheets 28a and 28b. (There are very few autobiographies, so be sure to tell students they may read either a biography or an autobiography.)

Name _____ Date _____

BIOGRAPHY

A *biography* is the true story of a person's life, written by another person. It is classified 921. (Some libraries classify biography 92 or B.) The letters under the class number represent the biographee's last name.

A *collective biography* is a collection of biographies bound together. It is classified 920. The letters under the class number represent the author's last name.

An *autobiography* is a self-biography: the story of one's life, written by oneself. It is classified 921. (Some libraries classify autobiography 92 or B.) The letters under the class number represent the biographee, who is also the author.

Write the call numbers for the following biographies.

Example: *921* Bow *Carry on, Mr. Bowditch*, by Jean Latham

1. _____ *Jim Bridger*, by Shannon Garst

2. _____ *Heroes of the American Revolution*, by Burke Davis

3. _____ *Benjamin Franklin*, by Milton Meltzer

4. _____ *Famous Modern Explorers*, by Bernadine Bailey

5. _____ *Daniel Boone*, by Laurie Lawlor

6. _____ *Great Indian Chiefs*, by Albert Roland

7. _____ *Our Heroes' Heroes*, by I. G. Edmonds

8. _____ *Winston Churchill*, by Quentin Reynolds

9. _____ *Jesse James*, by John Ernst

10. _____ *Heroines of the Early West*, by Nancy Wilson Ross

11. _____ *America's Abraham Lincoln*, by May McNeer

12. _____ *Five Artists of the Old West*, by Clide Hollmann

13. _____ *Marcus and Narcissa Whitman*, by James Daugherty

14. _____ *Anne Frank*, by Vanora Leigh

15. _____ *Queen Elizabeth II*, by Dorothy Turner

BIOGRAPHY REPORT

1. Biographee _____

2. Title _____

   _____

3. Author _____

4. Identify the biographee in one sentence. (Example: Abraham Lincoln was the sixteenth president of the United States.)_____

   _____

5. List the biographee's date of birth (and death, if deceased.) _____

6. Describe the biographee's childhood. _____

   _____

   _____

   _____

7. What goals did the biographee have? _____

   _____

   _____

8. What obstacles did he or she have to overcome?_____

   _____

   _____

9. What were the biographee's accomplishments? _____

   _____

   _____

   _____

10. Summarize the biographee's life. _____

_____

_____

_____

_____

11. Compare life at the time the biographee lived with times today. _____

_____

_____

_____

12. Name any famous people who were mentioned in the book. _____

_____

_____

13. Is the book interesting? Tell why or why not. _____

_____

14. Was the whole person, good and bad, presented? _____

Explain. _____

_____

_____

15. Give an example of good writing from the book. _____

_____

_____

_____

_____

_____

Name _____ Date _____

AUTHOR/CELEBRITY REPORT

1. Name _____

2. Date of birth (and death, if deceased) _____

3. Place of birth _____

4. Parents _____

5. Brothers and sisters _____

_____

6. Education _____

_____

_____

7. Obstacles to success_____

_____

_____

8. Career _____

_____

_____

9. Major accomplishments _____

_____

_____

10. Family _____

11. Hobbies, recreations, interests_____

_____

12. Source(s) of your information _____

_____

TYPES OF LITERATURE

LESSON 1: Poetry, Biography, Autobiography, Fiction, Nonfiction, Historical Fiction, Science Fiction, Classics

OBJECTIVES

1. To introduce/review the following types of literature: poetry, biography, autobiography, fiction, nonfiction, historical fiction, science fiction
2. To introduce the classics

MATERIALS

If it is inconvenient to gather all of the books listed below, gather only those from which you plan to read. Refer to the other books by title.

Read excerpts from these books:

1. Several books of poetry. Select a poem or poems to read to the class. You may want to read a long poem, a short poem, a humorous poem, and a limerick or two. See "Renascence" and Resources at the end of this lesson. Also refer to poetry in the index.
2. A biography and/or autobiography
3. A classic. See the list at the end of this lesson.

Refer to these books, as you hold up examples:

1. A collective biography
2. Two or three fiction titles. Suggestions: *Old Yeller* by Fred Gipson, *Seventeenth Summer* by Maureen Daly, and *All-American* by John Tunis
3. Several nonfiction books: books on history, science, sports, and so forth
4. Several volumes of historical fiction. Suggestions: *The Bronze Bow* by Elizabeth George Speare, *Johnny Tremain* by Esther Forbes, and a Laura Ingalls Wilder book
5. Two or three science fiction books. Suggestions: *Twenty Thousand Leagues Under the Sea* by Jules Verne, a book by Robert Heinlein, and a book by Ray Bradbury

Optional. If desired, reproduce Worksheet 30, a list of classics, and distribute it to the students. The worksheet can also be used as a reference list for the instructor.

PREPARATION

Use bookmarks to designate the pages you plan to read. See Materials above.

NOTE

You may want to present this lesson in several sessions.
If you want to read passages from books other than those designated for reading aloud, such as historical fiction and science fiction, do so.

LESSON

Can you tell me what type of literature this is?

Read a poem to the students.

What type of literature did I read? (poetry)

Are your textbooks written in the form of poetry? (no)

What form are they written in? (prose)

The ordinary form of writing is called prose. Novels, your textbooks, and nearly everything you read is written in prose.

Poetry has characteristics that differentiate it from prose.

What are some of poetry's characteristics? (Poetry has a rhythmic arrangement of words, is sometimes rhymed, is in meter or in free verse, expresses emotions and ideas in a more imaginative and powerful way than ordinary speech, is a concentrated form of expression.)

Present those characteristics that you are unable to elicit from the students.

Read several examples of poetry.

Hold up several books of poetry and read their titles.

Poetry is found in the nonfiction section of the library in the 800s, Literature. If you look in the card/automated catalog under the subject poetry, you'll be directed to the correct location.

Pick up a book of prose, a novel or an informational book, and read several lines.

Is this poetry? (no)

What is it? (prose)

Now let's go on to another form of literature. Listen and see if you can identify this type.

Hold up a biography. Read the title, and then read a passage.

What kind of book have I just read from? (a biography)

What is a biography? (the story of a person's life, written by another person)

What is an autobiography? (the story of one's life, written by oneself)

Hold up a copy of a collective biography. Read the title, and explain that the biographies of a number of people have been gathered together in one volume.

What do we call a book that has a number of biographies bound together? (a collective biography)

Now let's consider another form of literature.

Hold up two or three fiction books, and read their titles.

These stories aren't true. What do we call books that aren't true? (fiction)

Hold up several nonfiction books, and read their titles.

What kind of books are these? (nonfiction)

How are nonfiction and fiction books different? (Nonfiction books are true. Fiction books are not true.)

We say loosely that nonfiction is true; however, there are a few exceptions. Fairy tales aren't true, poems aren't necessarily true. In spite of the exceptions, nonfiction is referred to as true.

How is nonfiction arranged on the shelves? (by numbers)

Here's another form of literature: historical fiction.

Hold up several books of historical fiction, and read their titles.

In these books, the portrayal of the times is accurate, but the stories themselves are fiction: not true.

These books represent another type of literature.

Hold up several science fiction books and read their titles.

These books describe imaginary adventures in the world of the future, in outer space, and on other planets.

What do we call such books? (science fiction)

To find science fiction books, look in the card/automated catalog under the subject science fiction.

Fiction, historical fiction, and science fiction are shelved together in the fiction section of the library.

Who remembers how fiction is arranged? (by the authors' last names)

We've considered several types of literature. Now let's consider literature which is of the highest excellence. Let's consider the classics.

Classics are characterized by enduring qualities, such as a profound view of life; an expression of universal feelings, which can be understood by peoples of all times; and the highest excellence in writing. Classics have stood the test of time. Most classics were written before the twentieth century.

Classics are the most difficult and subtle pieces of literature. Appreciation and understanding of classics may not come without a measure of maturity.

The Bible, which was written thousands of years ago, is a classic. Shakespeare's works are classics.

> Hold up a few classics, if available. If not, give the names of a few. See the list that accompanies this lesson.

> Read a choice passage from a classic.

I'm going to describe some literature. See if you can tell me the name of each type:

Literature that has a rhythmic arrangement of words. Sometimes it's rhymed. (poetry)

Literature of the highest excellence. (classics)

The story of a person's life, written by another person. (biography)

Literature that describes imaginary adventures in the world of the future, in outer space, and on other planets. (science fiction)

The story of one's life, written by oneself. (autobiography)

Books that are made up, not true. (fiction)

True books. (nonfiction)

Books that accurately portray the life and times of a certain period, but their stories are made up. (historical fiction)

SUGGESTIONS

The list of classics that accompanies this lesson can be used for the instructor's reference, for familiarizing students with titles of classics, or for a recommended reading list.

> For a list of contemporary classics, see Worksheets 6a and 6b at the end of the lesson titled Fiction.

Teacher. A thorough study of each literary form would be ideal. For example, after presenting the material in this lesson about poetry, the teacher could stop and present a poetry unit. The unit could include some or all of these activities:

1. The reading of poems by the teacher
2. The silent or oral reading of poems by students
3. The writing of poems
4. The introduction of humorous poems, including limericks
5. The writing of limericks
6. The oral presentation of limericks by students

At the conclusion of the poetry unit, you may want to have a unit on biography and/or autobiography. Assign the reading of representative books. Require written or oral reports.

If you want to do a unit on fiction, nonfiction, historical fiction, or science fiction, stop after each form has been presented and have students read a book representative of the type being studied. You may want to require written or oral reports.

Review the material about classics. Have students read and report on any one of the titles listed on Worksheet 30. You may want to read an entire classic to your students, over a period of time.

Librarian. If time permits, and if the presentation of an in-depth study appeals to you, you may want to introduce only one type of literature at a session. Your presentation might consist of reading examples of a specific form and having students analyze the characteristics. Representative books should be introduced and left on a table for the students to examine or check out.

CLASSICS

Classics: literature of the highest excellence. Classics are characterized by enduring qualities, such as a profound view of life; an expression of universal feelings, which can be understood by people of all times; and the highest excellence in writing. Classics have stood the test of time. Most were written before the twentieth century.

Author	*Title*
Alcott, Louisa May	*Little Women* (1868–1869)
Barrie, J. M.	*Peter Pan* (1904)
Brontë, Charlotte	*Jane Eyre* (1847)
Brontë, Emily	*Wuthering Heights* (1847)
Burnett, Frances Hodgson	*The Secret Garden* (1911)
Cervantes, Miguel de	*The Adventures of Don Quixote de la Mancha* (1605 first part, 1615 second part)
Cooper, James Fenimore	*The Last of the Mohicans* (1826)
Crane, Stephen	*The Red Badge of Courage* (1895)
Defoe, Daniel	*Robinson Crusoe* (1719)
Dickens, Charles	*A Christmas Carol* (1843)
	David Copperfield (1849–1850)
	Great Expectations (1860–1861)
	Oliver Twist (1837–1839)
	A Tale of Two Cities (1859)
Doyle, Arthur Conan	*Sherlock Holmes: The Complete Novels and Stories*
Dumas, Alexandre	*The Count of Monte Cristo* (1844)
	The Three Musketeers (1844)
Hale, E. E.	*The Man Without a Country* (1863)
Henry, O.	*The Gift of the Magi* (1906)
Irving, Washington	*The Legend of Sleepy Hollow* (1819)
Kipling, Rudyard	*Captains Courageous* (1897)
	Kim (1901)
London, Jack	*The Call of the Wild* (1903)
	The Sea-Wolf (1904)
	White Fang (1906)
Poe, Edgar Allan	*The Complete Tales and Poems of Edgar Allan Poe*
Stevenson, Robert Lewis	*The Strange Case of Dr. Jekyll and Mr. Hyde* (1886)
	Kidnapped (1886)
	Treasure Island (1883)
Swift, Jonathan	*Gulliver's Travels* (1726)
Twain, Mark	*The Adventures of Huckleberry Finn* (1884)
	The Adventures of Tom Sawyer (1876)
	A Connecticut Yankee in King Arthur's Court (1889)
	The Prince and the Pauper (1882)
	The Tragedy of Pudd'nhead Wilson (1894)
	Tom Sawyer Abroad (1894)
	Tom Sawyer, Detective (1896)
Verne, Jules	*Around the World in Eighty Days* (1873)
	A Journey to the Centre of the Earth (1864)
	Twenty Thousand Leagues Under the Sea (1870)
Wyss, Johann	*The Swiss Family Robinson* (1812, 1813)

(The date listed is that of the first manuscript or of publication. Some books are published in parts, consequently two dates may be given.)

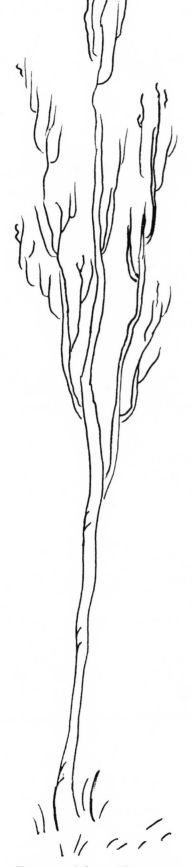

RENASCENCE

Edna St. Vincent Millay

All I could see from where I stood
Was three long mountains and a wood;
I turned and looked another way,
And saw three islands in a bay.
So with my eyes I traced the line
Of the horizon, thin and fine,
Straight around till I was come
Back to where I'd started from;
And all I saw from where I stood
Was three long mountains and a wood.

Over these things I could not see:
These were the things that bounded me.
And I could touch them with my hand,
Almost, I thought, from where I stand!
And all at once things seemed so small
My breath came short, and scarce at all.

But, sure, the sky is big, I said:
Miles and miles above my head.
So here upon my back I'll lie
And look my fill into the sky.
And so I looked, and after all,
The sky was not so very tall.
The sky, I said, must somewhere stop . . .
And—sure enough!—I see the top!
The sky, I thought, is not so grand;
I 'most could touch it with my hand!
And reaching up my hand to try,
I screamed, to feel it touch the sky.

I screamed, and—lo! Infinity
Came down and settled over me;
Forced back my scream into my chest;
Bent back my arm upon my breast;
And, pressing of the Undefined
The definition on my mind,
Held up before my eyes a glass
Through which my shrinking sight did pass
Until it seemed I must behold
Immensity made manifold;
Whispered to me a word whose sound
Deafened the air for worlds around,
And brought unmuffled to my ears
The gossiping of friendly spheres,
The creaking of the tented sky,
The ticking of Eternity.

Excerpted from "Renascence"
From *Collected Poems*, Harper & Row. Copyright 1912, 1940, Edna St. Vincent Millay

RESOURCES

POEMS

Here are some poems you may want to consider. They can be found in the books designated. *The Columbia Granger's Index to Poetry* (previously titled *Granger's Index to Poetry*) lists other sources. You may want to photocopy the poems for quick use in the future.

"Renascence," by Edna St. Vincent Millay
   (See the previous page in this book for an abridgement.)
"The Highwayman," by Alfred Noyes BeLS, FaPON
"Daniel Boone," by Arthur Guiterman FaPON
"Paul Revere's Ride," by Henry Wadsworth Longfellow BeLS, FaPON
"The Charge of the Light Brigade," by Alfred Tennyson BeLS, FaPON
"Casey at the Bat," by Ernest Lawrence Thayer BeLS, FaPON
"The Lady of Shalott," by Alfred Tennyson BeLS
"Barbara Fritchie," by John Greenleaf Whittier BeLS, FaPON
"Robinson Crusoe's Story," by Charles Edward Carryl BeLS

   Before reading the poem, explain that Robinson Crusoe, of the book by the same name, was castaway on an island where he and his native companion Friday tried to create a civilized life for themselves.

"The Barefoot Boy," by John Greenleaf Whittier FaPON (abridged)
"The Village Blacksmith," by Henry Wadsworth Longfellow FaPON

BeLS—*Best Loved Story Poems*

FaPON—*Favorite Poems Old and New*

LESSON 2: Fables, Fairy Tales, Folk Tales, Myths, Epics, Fantasy

OBJECTIVES

1. To introduce/review the following types of literature: fables, fairy tales, folk tales, myths, epics, fantasy
2. To test mastery of literary terms

MATERIALS

If it is inconvenient to gather all of the books listed below, gather only those from which you plan to read. Refer to the other books by title.

Read excerpts from these books:

1. A collection of Aesop's fables. Read one or more of these: "The Hare and the Tortoise," "The Lion and the Mouse," "The Town Mouse and the Country Mouse," "The Crow and the Pitcher," "Wolf! Wolf!" For a modern fable, present *Animal Farm* by George Orwell.
2. A book of myths. Read a brief account about Medusa, Pegasus, or Pandora.

Refer to these books:

1. Several fairy-tale books. Suggestions: *Grimm's Fairy Tales, Cinderella, The Sleeping Beauty.*
2. Several folk-tale books. Books about Paul Bunyan, Pecos Bill, Johnny Appleseed, and others.
3. Several epics. Suggestions: Books about Robin Hood and about King Arthur and the Knights of the Round Table. Also Homer's *Iliad* and *Odyssey*.
4. Some fantasies. Suggestions: *Alice's Adventures in Wonderland* by Lewis Carroll, *The Hobbit* by J. R. R. Tolkien, *Mr. Popper's Penguins* by Richard and Florence Atwater.

Reproduce these worksheets:

1. Types of Literature Study List, Worksheet 31
2. The test on types of literature, which covers lessons one and two, Worksheet 32

PREPARATION

Use bookmarks to designate the pages you plan to read from. See Materials above.

LESSON

Can you tell me what type of literature this is?

Read a fable.

What type of literature was that? (a fable)

Was the story short? (yes)

Were the characters animals? (yes)

What was the moral of the story?

You're probably familiar with a number of fables. How many of you have heard of the story of "The Hare and the Tortoise"?

You may want to read the fable.

Let's see if it measures up to the characteristics of fables.

Is it a short story? (yes)

Are the characters animals? (yes)

Is there a moral to the story? (yes)

What is the moral? (Slow and steady wins the race.)

Who remembers the fable about the boy who was always calling "wolf"?

If no one remembers, you may want to read it.

Was the story short? (yes)

Were the characters animals? (yes)

What was the moral of the story? (If you lie, you won't be believed when you tell the truth.)

Now let's consider another type of literature: fairy tales. Fairy tales are stories about imaginary beings who have magical powers, such as fairies, elves, pixies.

Hold up a few fairy-tale books, and read their titles.

Often the terms fairy tales and folk tales are used interchangeably. However, the terms refer to two different types of literature.

Is *Cinderella* a fairy tale? (yes)

The fairy godmother, who had magical powers, makes this a fairy tale.

Is *Rumpelstiltskin* a fairy tale? (yes)

What about *Sleeping Beauty*? (yes)

Fairy tales are found in the 398s.

Now let's consider folk tales. Folk tales are about ordinary people's legends, customs, superstitions, and beliefs. Stories about Paul Bunyan, Johnny Appleseed, and Pecos Bill are folk tales.

   Hold up a few folk tales, and read their titles.

Folk tales are found in the library in the 398s, too.

Listen to this piece of literature, and see if you can tell me what type it is.

   Read a myth.

What type of literature was that? (a myth)

Who can explain what a myth is? (It's a story that answers a question about the world for which the people of long ago had no explanation.)

What question was answered by the myth I read?

Another form of literature is the epic, which is a long poem about legendary heroes and their heroic deeds. Although epics are written in verse, some epics have been adapted to prose for young people.

   Hold up some epics, if available.

Now let's look at fantasy. Fantasy either concerns things that can't really happen or it's about people or creatures who don't exist.

You are all familiar with at least three well-known fantasies: *Mary Poppins, The Beauty and the Beast,* and *The Wizard of Oz.*

Here are some other fantasies.

   Hold up several fantasies, and read their titles.

I'm going to describe several types of literature. See if you can tell me the name of each kind.

Short stories in which the characters are usually animals. The action of the story leads to consequences which illustrate a moral. (fables)

Stories that answer questions about the world for which the people of long ago had no explanation. (myths)

Long poems about legendary heroes and their heroic deeds. (epics)

Stories about imaginary beings who have magical powers, such as fairies, elves, pixies. (fairy tales)

Stories about things that can't really happen or about people or creatures that don't exist. (fantasy)

Stories about ordinary people and their legends, customs, superstitions, and beliefs. (folk tales)

Distribute reproductions of the Types of Literature Study List, Worksheet 31.

Tell students to study the worksheet, including the spelling of the literary terms.

Some time thereafter, use Worksheet 32 to test the students.

TYPES OF LITERATURE STUDY LIST

FROM LESSON ONE

Autobiography—the story of one's life, written by oneself

Biography—the story of a person's life, written by another person

Classics—literature of the highest excellence. Classics are characterized by enduring qualities, such as a profound view of life; an expression of universal feelings, which can be understood by peoples of all times; and the highest excellence in writing. Classics have stood the test of time. Most were written before the twentieth century.

Fiction—books that are made up, not true

Historical fiction—fiction books that accurately portray the life and times of a certain period

Nonfiction—true books

Poetry—a rhythmic arrangement of words, sometimes rhymed, in meter or free verse, which expresses emotions and ideas in a more imaginative and powerful way than ordinary speech. A concentrated form of expression.

Prose—ordinary writing, without rhyme

Science fiction—books that describe adventures in the world of the future, in outer space, and on other planets

FROM LESSON TWO

Epics—long poems about legendary heroes and their heroic deeds. Some epics have been adapted to prose for young people.

Fables—short stories in which the characters are usually animals. The action of the story leads to consequences which illustrate a moral.

Fairy tales—stories about imaginary beings who have magical powers, such as fairies, elves, pixies

Fantasy—stories about things that can't really happen or about people or creatures that don't exist.

Folk tales—stories about ordinary people and their legends, customs, superstitions, and beliefs

Myths—stories that answer questions about the world for which the people of long ago had no explanation

Name _____ Date _____

LITERATURE TEST

Write the name of each type of literature described below.

1. Literature of the highest excellence_____

2. Fiction books that accurately portray the life and times of a certain period _____

3. Books that are made up, not true_____

4. The story of one's life, written by oneself _____

5. Books that are true _____

6. Highly concentrated literature that has a rhythmic arrangement of words_____

7. The story of a person's life, written by another person _____

8. Books that describe imaginary adventures in the world of the future, in outer space, and on other planets _____

9. Literature about things that can't really happen or about people or creatures that don't exist _____

10. Short stories in which the characters are usually animals. The action of the story leads to consequences which illustrate a moral. _____

11. Long poems about legendary heroes and their heroic deeds _____

12. Stories about fairies, elves, pixies _____

13. Stories that answer questions about the world for which the people of long ago had no explanation _____

14. Stories about ordinary people and their legends, customs, superstitions, and beliefs

_____

15. Ordinary writing, without rhyme _____

THE LIBRARY OF CONGRESS

OBJECTIVES

1. To acquaint students with the Library of Congress
2. To introduce the Library of Congress Classification

MATERIALS

1. If available, a picture of the Library of Congress
2. Books about the Library of Congress, if available

LESSON

What is the name of the world's largest library? (the Library of Congress)

Where is it located? (Washington, D.C.)

   If you have a picture of the Library of Congress, show it to the students.

The Library of Congress was established in 1800 for the use of Congress.

Although the library's first responsibility is to provide research and reference assistance to the United States Congress, over the years it has extended its services until it now serves the general public.

Floor space of the Library of Congress covers almost 65 acres. Books and other materials are shelved on some 532 miles of shelves.

All Library stacks are closed. That means you can't go to the shelves yourself. You have to request a book, and it will be brought to you.

The Library of Congress is a research library and books are used only on the premises. Anyone over high-school age may use the collections. Children may go on Library tours.

The Library's collection includes more than 100 million items. Among those are 16 million books, 2.2 million recordings, 14 million photographs, and 4.2 million maps. The collection includes materials in more than 470 languages.

The Library has a staff of more than 5,000 and serves some two million readers and visitors annually.

Books for entertainment are not included.

The Library of Congress has more than 500,000 books and other materials in its Rare Book and Special Collections Division. It has more than 5,600 books which were printed before 1501.

The Library of Congress provides cataloging information to other libraries. It also provides books in Braille and recorded books for the blind and handicapped.

The Library of Congress administers the copyright law.

Who remembers what a copyright is? (protection of an author's work; the exclusive right to a literary work)

The current copyright law, effective since January 1, 1978, protects an author's writing the minute it is written on paper. Protection lasts for the author's life plus 50 years. It is no longer necessary for an author to register work for it to be copyrighted. However, the formal copyrighting of a work is an advantage in the case of a lawsuit.

To copyright a piece of writing, one fills out the proper form and sends it with $20 and one copy of the unpublished work, or two copies of a published work, to the Register of Copyrights, Library of Congress, Washington, D.C.

You are familiar with the Dewey Decimal Classification by which most school and public libraries classify and shelve their nonfiction books. The Library of Congress and many large research and university libraries use the Library of Congress Classification, which provides more precision and more room for expansion than the Dewey Decimal Classification.

The Library of Congress Classification classifies books with capital letters and numbers. Here's an example:

Write this on the board: Science

Botany

Trees of North America

QK 481

The Library of Congress is not only a depository of books, it's also a museum of art. It contains beautiful sculptures, murals, paintings, and so forth.

The Librarian of Congress is appointed by the President of the United States and must be approved by the Senate.

Let's see how much you remember of what I've said.

What is the name of the world's largest library? (the Library of Congress)

Where is it located? (Washington, D.C.)

When was it established? (1800)

Who was it established to serve originally? (Congress)

Can the general public use the Library of Congress? (Anyone over high-school age may use the Library. Children may go on tours.)

How does the Librarian of Congress get his or her job? (The Librarian is appointed by the President of the United States and is approved by the Senate.)

What does the Library of Congress offer besides access to its large collection of books and other materials? (cataloging information, copyright protection, books for the blind and handicapped)

Does the Library of Congress classify books according to the Dewey Decimal Classification? (no)

Which classification system does it use? (The Library of Congress Classification)

Hold up any books you have about the Library of Congress, and show pictures from each of them. Announce that the books will be left on a table for the students to examine or check out.

REFERENCE

LIBRARY OF CONGRESS CLASSIFICATION

A	General Works	M	Music
B	Philosophy and Religion	N	Fine Arts
C	History & Auxiliary Sciences	P	Language & Literature
D	History & Topography excluding America	Q	Science
E-F	America	R	Medicine
G	Geography & Anthropology	S	Agriculture
H	Social Sciences	T	Technology
J	Political Science	U	Military Science
K	Law	V	Naval Science
L	Education	Z	Bibliography and Library Science

Note that I, O, W, X, and Y are omitted.

There are 21 main classes in the Library of Congress Classification.

MAGAZINES

NOTE

If you don't have a school library, adapt the lesson to your situation.

OBJECTIVES

1. To introduce your school library's magazines
2. To acquaint students with magazine format and coverage
3. To have each student examine and evaluate a magazine
4. To lay a foundation for a lesson on the *Readers' Guide to Periodical Literature*

MATERIALS

1. If possible, one *news* magazine for each student. Alternative: A magazine of any kind for each student. (Library back issues can be used.)
2. Several copies of a weekly news magazine
3. One copy of each magazine title in your school library, grouped according to kind: general interest, teen, science, news, sports, women's, and so forth
4. If available, one bound magazine volume
5. Magazines to illustrate varying qualities of magazine print, paper, and illustrations
6. Back-to-back reproductions of the two-page magazine evaluation form, Worksheets 33a and 33b
7. *Librarian.* If you plan to have a magazine survey, reproductions of Worksheet 34. List the library's magazines on the left before reproducing copies.

PREPARATIONS

1. Select a news magazine to present to students. Designate the location of the following with bookmarks:

> notice of frequency of publication
> table of contents
> name of the editor
> subscription information

letters to the editor
editorials

2. *Teacher.* Find out whether the magazine back issues in your school library are bound or unbound. Ask where they are stored.

LESSON

Our school library has many kinds of magazines.

If this lesson is presented in the library, point out the magazine shelves.

We have teen magazines, such as _____.

Hold up a copy of each teen magazine your library has, and state its name.

We have magazines of general interest, such as _____.

Hold up any general interest magazines, such as *Reader's Digest, National Geographic,* and so forth.

We have these science magazines: _____.

Hold up your science magazines, and name them.

We have news magazines.

Hold up your news magazines, and name them.

We have sports magazines.

Hold up your sports magazines, and give their names. Continue with any other types, such as women's magazines, hobby magazines, and so forth.

How many of you read magazines?

Who would like to tell us which magazines you read?

Call on students who raise their hands.

Which magazines do you have at home?

Call on students.

Besides borrowing a magazine from a library, there are two other ways to obtain a magazine. What are they? (buy one off a rack or subscribe)

What does subscribe mean? (to agree to pay for a magazine which will be mailed to you for a certain period of time, usually one, two, or three years)

Libraries usually have a few of the most recent issues of their magazines on the shelves.

Back issues are sometimes boxed and shelved in the main library or boxed and shelved in a storage room.

Our school library's back issues are stored in _____.

Some libraries have their back issues bound in volumes.

    Hold up a few copies of a weekly news magazine.

The library sends a number of individual issues to a bindery and has them bound together in a hardcover volume so they can be shelved easily.

    Hold up a bound volume of magazines, if available.

The dates of the magazines are printed on the volume's spine.

A weekly magazine like *Newsweek* will have four volumes a year: January–March, April–June, July–September, and October–December.

A number is put on each bound volume to make it easier to shelve and easier to locate.

Our library has/doesn't have its back issues bound.

Let's examine a copy of _____ (a news magazine).

    Hold the magazine up.

Magazines are issued at various periods of time: weekly, monthly, quarterly, and so forth. There are two ways to find out how often a magazine is issued. You can check the date on the magazine's cover. If the date consists of a month and a year, the magazine is issued monthly. Example: October 1989.

If the date is October 6, 1989, the magazine is a weekly. The other weekly issues will be October 13, 20, and 27.

If a magazine is a quarterly, it may designate its issues like this: Spring 1990, Summer 1990, Fall 1990, Winter 1990.

The date on the cover of this magazine is _____.

In the front of a magazine, you'll find a notice of the frequency of publication.

    Show your magazine's notice of frequency, and read it.

The table of contents tells you what subjects are covered in a particular issue. The page number for each article is listed.

    Show the table of contents.

The table of contents classifies a magazine's contents. It states where you can find information about _____. (Read the subject headings from the magazine you are using. Example: Cover Story, Nation, World, Business, Science, Music, Art, Books, Editorial.)

Show the table of contents again.

The names of the editor, publisher, and others involved with producing the magazine are listed near the front of the issue.

Hold the magazine up, and show the page to the students.

Also show where the subscription cost and address are listed.

Letters to the editor are often featured in magazines.

Show an example. Read one or more letters.

Most magazines have editorials.

Who knows what an editorial is? (an article which states the opinions of the editor or publisher)

Show an example. Read a few lines.

Each of you will be given a magazine to evaluate. Here are some of the questions you should ask yourself.

Are the articles well written? Are they comprehensive: do they cover everything they should?

Is the length of the articles too long, too short, or just right?

Do the illustrations add to the text? Is the quality good? Are the illustrations drawings or photographs? Are they in color or are they black and white? Are there enough illustrations to inform and to create a pleasing effect?

If you have some examples of illustrations of varying quality, show and discuss them.

Is the print easy to read?

Is the paper the magazine is printed on of good quality?

Show varying examples of print and paper, and compare them.

What is the overall effect of the text, the illustrations, the print, and the paper?

I'm going to distribute a copy of a magazine and a two-sided worksheet to each of you. Examine the magazine, and answer the questions on the worksheet. If you need help, raise your hand.

Distribute a magazine and a reproduction of Worksheets 33a and 33b to each student.

FOLLOW-UP

1. Teach the *Readers' Guide* lesson next.
2. *Librarian.* If you'd like to have a magazine survey, use the form on Worksheet 34. List the library's magazines on the left before reproducing copies.

MAGAZINE EVALUATION

1. Which magazine are you evaluating? _____

   _____

2. What kind of magazine is it? (news, teen, science, general interest, sports, women's, hobby, etc.)

   _____

3. What is the frequency of publication? (Is the magazine a weekly, monthly, or quarterly?) _____

4. List the table of content's subject headings. _____

   _____

   _____

   _____

5. Who is the editor? _____

6. What is the subscription cost for one year? _____

7. To which address should subscriptions be sent? _____

   _____

   _____

   _____

8. Does the magazine include letters to the editor? _____

   If so, on which page(s) are they found? _____

9. Is there an editorial? _____ If so, on which page does it appear? _____

10. Evaluate an article. Consider the writing, length, and comprehensiveness. _____

_____

_____

_____

_____

_____

_____

11. Evaluate the illustrations. Discuss the kind, quality, and quantity. _____

_____

_____

_____

_____

12. Evaluate the print. Consider the size and ease of reading. _____

_____

_____

_____

13. Evaluate the paper on which the magazine is printed. _____

_____

14. Evaluate the magazine as a whole. _____

_____

_____

15. What could be improved? _____

_____

_____

MAGAZINE SURVEY

1. Which magazine is your favorite? _____

2. Do you read any magazines regularly? _____ If so, which ones? _____

   _____

Library Magazines	Library Magazines I've Read This Year	Reorder These	Add These

READERS' GUIDE TO PERIODICAL LITERATURE

Readers' Guide to Periodical Literature. New York: H. W. Wilson, 1905–.

A cumulative author subject index to 240 popular magazines. Includes a list of citations to book reviews.

Abridged Readers' Guide to Periodical Literature. New York: H. W. Wilson, 1936–.

Indexes 82 of the most popular general-interest magazines covered by *Readers' Guide*. Designed especially for smaller libraries.

OBJECTIVES

1. To introduce *Readers' Guide to Periodical Literature* and *Abridged Readers' Guide to Periodical Literature*.
2. To provide practice in the use of *Readers' Guide*.
3. To check mastery with a worksheet follow-up.

MATERIALS

1. If available, some monthly, cumulative, and hardbound issues of *Abridged Readers' Guide* or *Readers' Guide*.
2. If you are not going to reproduce the *Readers' Guide* abbreviations page, Worksheet 35, you will need a chalkboard, chalk, and eraser.
3. Reproductions of the following:
   a. Optional. *The Readers' Guide* abbreviations page, Worksheet 35. (Several abbreviations may be put on the chalkboard, instead of reproducing the page. If you would like reproductions, duplicate the page on the back of either Worksheet 38 or Worksheet 39.)
   b. Back-to-back reproductions of sample subject and author entries, Worksheet 36, and sample review entries, Worksheet 37. (These can be saved and used again.)
   c. Reproductions of the follow-up reference page, Worksheet 38.
   d. Reproductions of the follow-up page, Worksheet 39. This should not be put back-to-back with the follow-up reference page, Worksheet 38.

PREPARATIONS

1. If you are not going to reproduce the abbreviations page, Worksheet 35, put the following on the chalkboard:

> D   December
> por portrait
> ed edited, edition, editor
> Jl   July
> w   weekly

2. *Teacher.* Find out if your school library has *Readers' Guide to Periodical Literature* or *Abridged Readers' Guide to Periodical Literature.*

LESSON

Are you looking for some current information about a particular subject, perhaps for a science report? If so, you'll want to locate some magazine articles about your subject. Books aren't current since it takes two to three years to write books and to get them published.

Maybe your subject is acid rain.

What is acid rain? (rain, snow, or other precipitation that has been polluted by acids)

How can you locate some magazine articles about the subject? Will you go to the library and look through stacks of various magazines, or is there an easier way?

   Call on students who raise their hands.

When you go to the library to find a book on a specific subject, you don't look at all of the books on the shelves. You go to an index to the book collection: the card or automated catalog.

There's an index to magazines. It's called the *Readers' Guide to Periodical Literature.*

The term periodical literature refers to literature that is published at regular intervals of more than one day, such as a magazine. You might translate the title *Readers' Guide to Periodical Literature* to *Readers' Guide to Magazines.*

Readers' Guide to Periodical Literature indexes 240 magazines. It's found in most public and college libraries. Since school libraries don't usually have 240 magazines, they don't need an exhaustive index like *Readers' Guide to Periodical Literature.* Instead, schools usually have the shortened *Readers' Guide:* the *Abridged Readers' Guide to Periodical Literature,* which indexes 82 magazines.

   If you have some copies of *Abridged Readers' Guide* or of *Readers' Guide,* hold them up.

In a year, *Readers' Guide* is published twice a month in March, October, and December and once a month in January, February, April, May, June, July, August, September, and

November. The February, May, August, and November issues are quarterly cumulations. A hardbound cumulation is published yearly.

> If available, hold up some monthlies and explain how they are combined and superseded by a cumulative issue. Then explain how cumulative issues are combined and superseded by an annual hardbound volume.

Our school has the *Abridged Readers' Guide to Periodical Literature*/the *Readers' Guide to Periodical Literature*.

Readers' Guide, which is a shortened title, is used loosely to refer to either the abridged or the unabridged edition.

Readers' Guide is a reference work. It can't be checked out of the library.

I'm going to distribute some worksheets.

> Distribute back-to-back reproductions of Worksheets 36 and 37. If the *Readers' Guide* abbreviations page, Worksheet 35, has been reproduced, distribute it, too.

Readers' Guide and the abridged edition are author/subject indexes. That means to locate information, you need to look under either an author or a subject.

> Tell the students that a key to the abbreviations used in *Readers' Guide* appears in the front of every issue.

> Ask the students to look at the abbreviations on the board/on Worksheet 35.

What does the abbreviation "D" stand for? (December)

What does "por" mean? (portrait)

What does "ed" stand for? (edited, edition, editor)

Jl? (July)

What does "w" mean? (weekly)

Information about how to use the *Readers' Guide* is in the front of each issue.

Look at Worksheet 36.

There's a sample subject entry at the top of the page. Let's read it.

What's the subject of the entry? (ATHLETES)

What's the title of the article? (''Careers on ice and snow'')

Notice that *Readers' Guide* capitalizes only first words and proper names in titles.

When a title isn't very clear, *Readers' Guide* clarifies it in brackets. Clarifies means makes it clearer. The clarification tells us that the article is about athletes making a career of going to the Olympics.

Who is the author? (T. Callahan)

What does "il" mean? (illustration, -s)

What is the name of the magazine in which the article appears? (*U.S. News and World Report*)

What is the volume number? (volume 116)

Magazines are often sent to a bindery and bound into hardback volumes. The volumes are given numbers for ease of shelving.

On which page is the article found? (page 64)

What is the date of the magazine? (February 28, 1994)

Look at the box at the bottom of the page on the left side. It contains a subject entry.

Find the subject heading ATHLETES.

The first thing we notice is a "see also" reference. "See also" means you've found some articles on the subject, but for more you can see the additional headings which are listed. In this case, you can also see Baseball players, Basketball players, Boxers, Discrimination in sports, Football players, and Hockey players.

Then there's another "see also" reference. If you need more information, you can also look under the names of athletes.

How many articles are listed for athletes? (six)

The first line of each entry is farther to the left than the following lines. You can count the lines that extend farthest to the left to determine the number of entries.

Notice that the articles are arranged alphabetically.

Look at the third entry.

What is the title of the article? ("Guts and glory")

Who wrote it? (R. Weinberg)

What is the article about? (athletes overcoming difficulties)

In which magazine can you find this article? (*Sport*)

The magazine *Sport,* that you are referred to, is the one published in New York.

In which volume will you find the article? (volume 85)

On which pages is the article? (pages 23–24, plus there's more to which you'll be referred in the magazine)

What is the date of the magazine? (February 1994)

Find an article about the most influential people in professional sports.

What is the title of the article? (''Sport top 40'')

In which magazine can you find it? (*Sport*)

In which volume does it appear? (volume 85)

On which pages is the article? (pages 16–20+)

What is the date of the magazine? (January 1994)

Look at the subhead Awards. A "see" reference tells you to see Sports—Awards for information on that subject.

Indexers use "see" references to lead you from a subject heading they aren't using to one they are using.

Look at the subhead Health and Hygiene. You know that Health and Hygiene is a heading that's being used because you aren't told to see a different heading. It just happens that there aren't any articles on the subject indexed in this issue of *Readers' Guide*. You can see also the heading Drugs and Athletes.

Look at the box on the right, which contains a name entry.

Kathie Lee Gifford is the author of the *first* article.

What is the title of that article? (''A time to change'')

Who wants to read the title clarification? (excerpt from "I can't believe I said that")

In which magazine does the article appear? (*Ladies' Home Journal*)

What is the volume number? (volume 110)

On which pages will you find the article? (pages 186–189)

What is the date of the magazine? (September 1993)

Notice the word "about."

The next article is *about* Kathie Lee Gifford. She didn't write the article.

Who wants to read the entry and identify each part as you read? (Title: "Frank talk with Kathie Lee;" title clarification: cover story; author: J. Conant; illustrations; portrait; magazine: *Ladies' Home Journal*; volume 110; pages 124–5 plus more; date of magazine: September 1993.)

Turn the paper over.

What is a review? For example, what is a review of a TV program? (an evaluation: a critical discussion)

If you would like to know what the critics think about a certain TV program, you can read their reviews.

Under the heading TELEVISION PROGRAM REVIEWS, you see three general articles. Follow while I read their titles: "The best television of 1993," "Top twenty report card," and "Winter preview."

Next you see the subhead Single Works.

Notice that the reviews are listed in alphabetical order.

Find "The Cisco Kid."

Who wants to read the information about the review? (Magazine: New York; volume 27; pages 60–1; date of the magazine: February 7, 1994; author of the review: J. Leonard)

Find a review of "Wide world of sports."

Who wrote the review? (J. Baker)

In which magazine does it appear? (*TV Guide*)

What does "il" mean? (illustration, -s)

In which issue of *TV Guide* was the review published? (the January 8–14, 1994 issue)

On which page does the review appear? (page 30)

What is the volume number? (volume 42)

Look at THEATER REVIEWS.

The first review, "The best theater of 1993," covers a number of plays. Next you see the subhead Single Works. Under that you are instructed to "See name of author for full entry."

What would you look under if you wanted to find a review of "Family secrets"? (Glaser, Sherry)

In the same column, find the heading OTHER REVIEWS. There are eleven other types of reviews listed there.

Under which heading would you look if you wanted to find a movie review? (MOTION PICTURE REVIEWS)

Under which heading would you look for a review of a videotape? (VIDEODISC AND VIDEOTAPE REVIEWS)

Look below to BOOK REVIEWS.

Basically book reviews are arranged by the authors' last names. If a book is a compilation of many authors' works, it is arranged alphabetically by title.

Notice that the first two books listed are arranged by author. The third book, a compilation of many authors' works, is arranged alphabetically by title.

What is the title of the first book that's listed? (*Picturing nature*)

Who is the author of the book? (A. S. Blum)

When was the book published? (1993)

Which magazine has a review of the book? (*Science*)

Which volume is it in? (volume 262)

On which pages is it found? (pages 1752–1754)

Evidently *Science* numbers its pages consecutively from the first to the last issue of the year. We know it wouldn't have 1,700 pages in an issue.

What's the date of the magazine? (December 10, 1993)

Who reviewed the book? (W. Stanton)

What is the title of the second book? (*The cost of talent*)

What's different about the third entry? (It's not entered by author. It's a title entry.)

References to book reviews are found at the end of *Readers' Guide*.

> If you have a copy of *Readers' Guide,* open it to the book reviews, and hold the book up so the students can see it.

Look at the last entry in the second column: Creative Literature. References to fiction, poems, and short stories are included. You can see the instructions in the front of *Readers' Guide* regarding indexing.

When looking in *Readers' Guide,* you should refer to the most recent monthly or semimonthly issue, if you want the latest information. If you don't find what you need, examine a quarterly issue. If you still haven't found what you need, refer to an annual volume: a hardbound issue. Start with the latest issues, and go backward in time thereafter.

> Collect the papers.

I'm going to distribute a sample page from *Readers' Guide* and a worksheet for you to do.

> Distribute Worksheets 38 and 39.

NOTE

There are three complete *Readers' Guide* presentations you may want to use:

1. The lesson presented in this book
2. The 16-page *Readers' Guide* booklet *How to Use the Readers' Guide to Periodical Literature*. (This booklet is free in quantities up to 50 copies; additional copies are available at two cents each.) Order a class set plus a few extra copies, or order more. Write to:

> Customer Services Department
> The H. W. Wilson Company
> 950 University Avenue
> Bronx, N.Y. 10452

3. *How to Use the Readers' Guide Video* (length: 20 minutes). This video replaces the *How to Use the Readers' Guide Filmstrip,* which is no longer available. (Cost: With a subscription to *Readers' Guide to Periodical Literature* or *Abridged Readers' Guide to Periodical Literature:* $49 U.S. and Canada, $59 foreign. Without a subscription: $69 U.S. and Canada, $79 foreign. Order from the H. W. Wilson address listed under item 2.

Here are some ways to use the presentations.

1. Use only the lesson with which you feel most comfortable: the lesson presented in this book, the booklet *How to Use the Readers' Guide to Periodical Literature,* or the *Readers' Guide Video.*
2. Use one lesson as an introduction. The next year, use another lesson for a review. If you feel a lesson a year is needed, use a different lesson the third year.
3. Use the lesson most appropriate for each individual class.

ABBREVIATIONS

+	continued on later pages of same issue	Ltd	Limited
		m	monthly
Ag	August	Mr	March
ann	annual	My	May
Ap	April		
Assn	Association	N	November
Aut	Autumn	no	number
Ave	Avenue		
		O	October
bi-m	bimonthly		
bi-w	biweekly	p	page
bibl	bibliography	por	portrait
bibl f	bibliographical footnotes	pt	part
bldg	building		
		q	quarterly
Co	Company		
cont	continued	rev	revised
Corp	Corporation		
		S	September
D	December	semi-m	semimonthly
Dept	Department	Spr	Spring
		Sr	Senior
ed	edited, edition, editor	St	Street
		Summ	Summer
F	February	supp	supplement
f	footnotes		
		tr	translated, translation, translator
il	illustration, -s		
Inc	Incorporated		
introd	introduction, introductory	v	volume
Ja	January	w	weekly
Je	June	Wint	Winter
Jl	July		
Jr	Junior	yr	year
jt auth	joint author		

By permission. *Readers' Guide to Periodical Literature*. The H. W. Wilson Company.

READERS' GUIDE
TO PERIODICAL LITERATURE

SUBJECT ENTRY

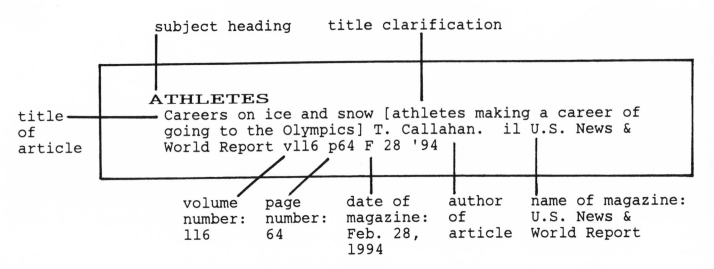

subject heading   title clarification

ATHLETES

title of article → Careers on ice and snow [athletes making a career of going to the Olympics] T. Callahan. il U.S. News & World Report v116 p64 F 28 '94

volume number: 116

page number: 64

date of magazine: Feb. 28, 1994

author of article

name of magazine: U.S. News & World Report

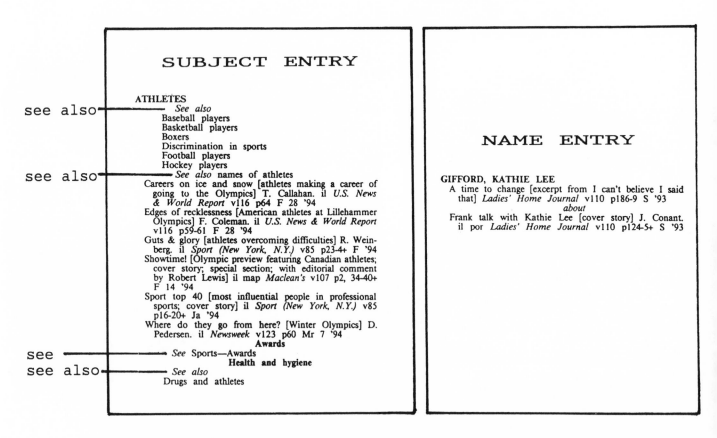

SUBJECT ENTRY

ATHLETES

see also →
See also
Baseball players
Basketball players
Boxers
Discrimination in sports
Football players
Hockey players

see also → *See also* names of athletes
Careers on ice and snow [athletes making a career of going to the Olympics] T. Callahan. il *U.S. News & World Report* v116 p64 F 28 '94
Edges of recklessness [American athletes at Lillehammer Olympics] F. Coleman. il *U.S. News & World Report* v116 p59-61 F 28 '94
Guts & glory [athletes overcoming difficulties] R. Weinberg. il *Sport (New York, N.Y.)* v85 p23-4+ F '94
Showtime! [Olympic preview featuring Canadian athletes; cover story; special section; with editorial comment by Robert Lewis] il map *Maclean's* v107 p2, 34-40+ F 14 '94
Sport top 40 [most influential people in professional sports; cover story] il *Sport (New York, N.Y.)* v85 p16-20+ Ja '94
Where do they go from here? [Winter Olympics] D. Pedersen. il *Newsweek* v123 p60 Mr 7 '94

Awards

see → *See* Sports—Awards

Health and hygiene

see also → *See also*
Drugs and athletes

NAME ENTRY

GIFFORD, KATHIE LEE
A time to change [excerpt from I can't believe I said that] *Ladies' Home Journal* v110 p186-9 S '93
about
Frank talk with Kathie Lee [cover story] J. Conant. il por *Ladies' Home Journal* v110 p124-5+ S '93

Excerpts from the *Readers' Guide to Periodical Literature*. Printed by permission of The H. W. Wilson Company.

TELEVISION PROGRAM REVIEWS

TELEVISION PROGRAM REVIEWS
The best television of 1993. il *Time* v143 p71 Ja 3 '94
Top twenty report card. il *TV Guide* v42 p18-24+ Ja 22-28 '94
Winter preview [cover story] il *TV Guide* v42 p8-14+ Ja 22-28 '94

Single works
American detective
   Harper's il v287 p50-7 N '93. D. Seagal
Armistead Maupin's Tales of the city
   The New Yorker il v69 p74-5 Ja 10 '94. J. Wolcott
   TV Guide il v42 p26-8 Ja 8-14 '94. A. Maupin
Beavis and Butt-head
   Commonweal v121 p28+ Ja 14 '94. F. D. McConnell
Birdland
   TV Guide il v42 p6 Ja 8-14 '94. J. Jarvis
The Buddha of suburbia
   The New Yorker il v69 p75 Ja 10 '94. J. Wolcott
Chantilly lace
   Glamour il v91 p95 Ag '93. J. Kirchner
The Cisco Kid
   New York v27 p60-1 F 7 '94. J. Leonard
The critic
   New York il v27 p60 Ja 31 '94. J. Leonard
   Newsweek il v123 p62 Ja 24 '94. H. F. Waters
Dieppe
   Maclean's il v107 p62 Ja 3 '94. J. L. Granatstein
Frasier
   TV Guide il v42 p36-7 Ja 29-F 4 '94. J. Rhodes
Fresh Prince of Bel-Air
   Jet il v85 p64 Ja 10 '94
The frightening frammis
   Premiere il v6 p40-1 Ag '93. C. K. Cordero
The good life
   TV Guide il v42 p10 Ja 29-F 4 '94. J. Jarvis
Harts of the West
   TV Guide il v42 p28-31 Ja 1-7 '94. J. Rhodes
Homicide: life on the street
   New York il v27 p52 Ja 10 '94. J. Leonard
I spy returns
   New York il v27 p60 F 7 '94. J. Leonard
Jane's house
   New York il v27 p54 Ja 3 '94. J. Leonard
The Jerry Springer show
   People Weekly il v41 p73+ Ja 24 '94. M. S. Goodman
The Jon Stewart show
   New York il v27 p36-9 Ja 10 '94. C. S. Smith
Late night with Conan O'Brien
   New York il v27 p16 Ja 24 '94. K. O'Hara
Late night with David Letterman
   The New York Times Magazine il p28-34 Ja 30 '94. B. Carter
Malcolm X: make it plain
   Newsweek il v123 p65 Ja 31 '94. E. Cose
Mighty Morphin Power Rangers
   TV Guide il v42 p20-1 Ja 1-7 '94. P. Patsuris
The mommies
   TV Guide il v42 p7 Ja 1-7 '94. J. Jarvis
NYPD blue
   New York il v27 p34-9 F 7 '94. C. S. Smith
Phenom
   TV Guide il v42 p9 Ja 15-21 '94. J. Jarvis
Pierre Elliott Trudeau: memoirs
   Maclean's il v107 p54 Ja 10 '94. E. K. Fulton
Saturday night live
   New York il v27 p16 Ja 24 '94. K. O'Hara
The state
   Newsweek il v123 p55 Ja 31 '94. H. F. Waters
TekWar
   TV Guide il v42 p16-17 Ja 15-21 '94. C. E. Cohen
To play the king
   New York il v27 p58 Ja 17 '94. J. Leonard
   The New Yorker il v69 p82-3 Ja 17 '94. J. Wolcott
   Time il v143 p62 Ja 24 '94. R. Zoglin
The tonight show
   The New York Times Magazine il p28-34 Ja 30 '94. B. Carter
Unnatural pursuits
   New York il v27 p54 Ja 24 '94. J. Leonard
Viper
   TV Guide il v42 p7 Ja 22-28 '94. J. Jarvis
Wide world of sports
   TV Guide il v42 p30 Ja 8-14 '94. J. Baker
The X-files
   TV Guide il v42 p20-1 Ja 15-21 '94. D. Infusino

THEATER REVIEWS

THEATER REVIEWS
The best theater of 1993. il *Time* v143 p83 Ja 3 '94
   Single works
   See name of author for full entry
All in the timing. Ives, David
Angels in America: Perestroika. Kushner, Tony
Arcadia. Stoppard, Tom
The ash fire. Kostick, Gavin
Booth. Pendleton, Austin
East Texas hot links. Lee, Eugene
Edith Stein. Giron, Arthur
Family secrets. Glaser, Sherry
The gift of the Gorgon. Shaffer, Peter
The government inspector. Gogol', Nikolai Vasil'evich, 1809-1852
The illusion. Corneille, Pierre, 1606-1684
An imaginary life. Parnell, Peter
It's a great big shame! Leigh, Mike, 1943-
The Kentucky cycle. Schenkkan, Robert
Moonlight. Pinter, Harold, 1930-
No man's land. Pinter, Harold, 1930-
Ricky Jay & his 52 assistants. Jay, Ricky
Timon of Athens. Shakespeare, William, 1564-1616
Wildest dreams. Ayckbourn, Alan, 1939-
Wonderful Tennessee. Friel, Brian

OTHER REVIEWS

BALLET REVIEWS
COMPACT DISC REVIEWS
DANCE REVIEWS
MOTION PICTURE REVIEWS
MUSICALS, REVUES, ETC.
OPERA AND OPERETTA REVIEWS
PHONOGRAPH RECORD REVIEWS
PRODUCT REVIEWS
RADIO PROGRAM REVIEWS
TAPE RECORDING REVIEWS
VIDEODISC AND VIDEOTAPE REVIEWS

BOOK REVIEWS

BLUM, A. S. Picturing nature. 1993
   Science v262 p1752-4 D 10 '93. W. Stanton
BOK, D. C. The cost of talent. 1993
   The New Leader v76 p17-18 D 13 '93. E. T. Chase
   The New York Review of Books v41 p20-4 Mr 3 '94. A. Hacker
THE BOOK OF VIRTUES. 1993
   Time v143 p78 Mr 7 '94. L. Morrow

CREATIVE LITERATURE

Fiction, Poems and Short Stories
(See the instructions in the front
of READERS' GUIDE REGARDING INDEXING.)

Excerpts from the *Readers' Guide to Periodical Literature*. Printed by permission of The H. W. Wilson Company.

READERS' GUIDE TO PERIODICAL LITERATURE

EARTH—Crust—*cont.*
Was continental crust born in a geologic moment? [research by Samuel Bowring] R. A. Kerr. *Science* v262 p992-3 N 12 '93
Internal structure
Earth's heart beats with a magnetic rhythm [research by Jean-Pierre Valet and Laure Meynadier] R. Monastersky. il *Science News* v144 p327 N 20 '93
Mantle
See Earth—Internal structure
Observations from space
See also
Artificial satellites—Earth sciences use
Earth—Photographs and photography
Photographs and photography
A new view of earth [Galileo images] D. Stover. il *Popular Science* v243 p34 N '93
Surface
See Earth—Crust
EARTH, EFFECT OF MAN ON *See* Man—Influence on nature
EARTH REMOTE-SENSING SATELLITES *See* ERS (Earth remote-sensing satellites)
EARTH SCIENCES
See also
Artificial satellites—Earth sciences use
Geology
Radar in earth sciences
EARTH TREMORS *See* Earthquakes
EARTHQUAKE PREDICTION
The next big one . . . [network of underground faults crisscross southern California] J. M. Nash. il map *Time* v143 p45-6 Ja 31 '94
Rumblings coast to coast [risk of an earthquake in the Midwest] W. F. Allman. il map *U.S. News & World Report* v116 p41 Ja 31 '94
The ultimate nightmare [predictions of an earthquake along the Newport-Inglewood fault zone in California] S. Brownlee. il map *U.S. News & World Report* v116 p38-9 Ja 31 '94
EARTHQUAKES
Prediction
See Earthquake prediction
California
See also
Los Angeles earthquake, 1994
Disassembling California [plate tectonics] il *The New Yorker* v69 p4+ Ja 31 '94
The next big one . . . [network of underground faults crisscross southern California] J. M. Nash. il map *Time* v143 p45-6 Ja 31 '94
The ultimate nightmare [predictions of an earthquake along the Newport-Inglewood fault zone in California] S. Brownlee. il map *U.S. News & World Report* v116 p38-9 Ja 31 '94
Middle Western States
Rumblings coast to coast [risk of an earthquake in the Midwest] W. F. Allman. il map *U.S. News & World Report* v116 p41 Ja 31 '94
EARTHQUAKES AND BRIDGES
Quakeproofing the freeways [repairing damaged overpasses as a result of the Los Angeles earthquake] W. J. Cook. il *U.S. News & World Report* v116 p40 Ja 31 '94
EARTHWORK
See also
Dams
EAST AFRICA
See also
Somalia
Indigenous peoples
See also
Masai (African people)
EAST ASIA
See also
Pacific region
Securities—East Asia
Economic relations
The coming Pacific century? T. Inoguchi. bibl f *Current History* v93 p25-30 Ja '94
Politics and government
The coming Pacific century? T. Inoguchi. bibl f *Current History* v93 p25-30 Ja '94
EAST HARLEM SCHOOL (N.Y.)
School-based management. C. Atamian. il pors *New York* v27 p14 Ja 10 '94
EAST TEXAS HOT LINKS [drama] *See* Lee, Eugene
EASTERN EUROPE
See also
Investments, American—Eastern Europe
Investments, Foreign—Eastern Europe

Poland
Relief work—Eastern Europe
Securities—Eastern Europe
Yugoslavia
Defenses
The case for a bigger NATO. M. Kramer. il map *Time* v143 p36-7 Ja 10 '94
Clinton in Europe. *National Review* v46 p14 Ja 24 '94
Compromise, appeasement and sugarcoating [Clinton administration] C. W. Weinberger. il *Forbes* v153 p35 Ja 17 '94
Debating NATO's future. R. Knight. il *U.S. News & World Report* v116 p46-7 Ja 17 '94
NATO looks eastward, with trepidation. P. Mann. il *Aviation Week & Space Technology* v140 p20-2 Ja 17 '94
Putting Russia first [Partnership for Peace plan] J. Joffe. il *U.S. News & World Report* v116 p52 Ja 17 '94
Whither NATO? (No, really). il *The New Yorker* v69 p6-7 Ja 17 '94
Foreign relations
Russia (Republic)
Debating NATO's future. R. Knight. il *U.S. News & World Report* v116 p46-7 Ja 17 '94
Putting Russia first [Partnership for Peace plan] J. Joffe. il *U.S. News & World Report* v116 p52 Ja 17 '94
Whither NATO? (No, really). il *The New Yorker* v69 p6-7 Ja 17 '94
EASTERN OREGON CORRECTIONAL INSTITUTE (PENDLETON, OR.) *See* Prisons—Oregon
EASTERN ORTHODOX CHURCH *See* Orthodox Eastern Church
EASTWOOD, CLINT
about
Clint Eastwood: riding high. G. Gibson. il pors *Ladies' Home Journal* v110 p42+ Ag '93
Shot by shot. C. Bagley. il pors *Premiere* v6 p66-8 Ag '93
EATING
See also
Diet
The ins and outs of eating: do's and don'ts for dining out or eating in. H. Rubenstein. il *Interview* v23 p106 Ag '93
Etiquette
See Etiquette
Psychological aspects
See also
Food cravings
EATING DISORDERS
See also
Anorexia nervosa
Food cravings
Coping with a consuming obsession. T. Allis. il *People Weekly* v41 p56+ Ja 31 '94
EATON, CHARLES EDWARD, 1916-
The pond [poem] *Commonweal* v121 p16 Ja 28 '94
EBERLY, JOSEPH H., AND KULANDER, KENNETH C.
Atomic stabilization by super-intense lasers. bibl f il *Science* v262 p1229-33 N 19 '93
EC *See* European Community
ECKSTEIN, EVE
(jt. auth) *See* Firkins, June, and Eckstein, Eve
ECLIPSES, LUNAR *See* Lunar eclipses
ECLIPSES, SOLAR *See* Solar eclipses
ECM (ELECTRONIC COUNTERMEASURES ON JET AIRPLANES) *See* Airplanes, Jet—Radar equipment
ECOLOGICAL ART *See* Environment (Art)
ECOLOGICAL MOVEMENT *See* Environmental movement
ECOLOGICAL RESEARCH
See also
National Biological Survey (U.S.)
The information gap [lack of knowledge about the ecological makeup of the parks] B. Sharp and E. Appleton. il *National Parks* v67 p32-7 N/D '93
ECOLOGY
See also
Environment
Human ecology
Snow ecology
The world between our walls. S. Weidensaul. il *Country Journal* v21 p53-5 Ja/F '94
ECONOMETRICS
A forecaster who usually hits his targets [L. H. Meyer] H. Banks. il por *Forbes* v153 p35 Ja 3 '94
ECONOMIC ASSISTANCE
See also
Relief work

Reproduced from *Readers' Guide to Periodical Literature*, March 1994. The H. W. Wilson Company. Used by permission.

Worksheet 38   156

READERS' GUIDE
TO PERIODICAL LITERATURE

Find the answers to these questions on Worksheet 31.

1. What is the title of the *second* article about earthquakes?

   _____

   _____

2. What is the title clarification for that article?

   _____

   _____

   _____

3. To which "see also" reference does the subject heading Earthquakes direct you?

   _____

4. If you look under Earthquakes and then its subhead Prediction, you will learn that the subhead Prediction isn't being used. You are told to see which heading?

   _____

5. What is the title of the first article about Clint Eastwood?

   _____

6. In which magazine does it appear?

   _____

7. What is the volume number of the magazine? _____

8. What is the magazine's date? _____

9. On which pages will you find the article? _____

10. Who is the article's author? _____

NEWSPAPERS

OBJECTIVES

1. To formally introduce students to newspapers
2. To cite the source of freedom of the press: the First Amendment to the Constitution
3. To define, discuss, and examine a news story, a feature story, an editorial, and an editorial cartoon
4. To have students examine a newspaper in detail

MATERIALS

1. A newspaper for each student. (See Suggestions at the end of this lesson regarding a class set of newspapers.) If a class set of papers isn't affordable, newspapers varying in title and date can be used.
2. Back-to-back reproductions of the news story on Worksheet 40 and the feature story on Worksheet 41
3. Back-to-back reproductions of the editorial on Worksheet 42 and the editorial cartoon on Worksheet 43
4. If making the homework assignment, reproductions of Worksheet 44. Cut in half.

LESSON

Did you know that there are 1,570 *daily* newspapers in the United States?

Pause to emphasize the fact.

There are also thousands of *weekly* newspapers and hundreds of *semiweekly* newspapers. Semiweekly means twice a week.

By what right are newspapers permitted to present and comment on the news? (the right of freedom of the press, which is derived from the First Amendment to the Constitution)

The First Amendment to the Constitution says: "Congress shall make no law respecting an establishment of religion, or prohibiting the free exercise thereof; or abridging the freedom of speech, or of the press; or the right of the people peaceably to assemble, and to petition the government for a redress of grievances."

We're going to study several parts of a newspaper. Afterwards I'll pass a newspaper out to each of you, and you'll have the opportunity to find the parts we've discussed.

First, let's consider a news story. Listen to this definition and see if you hear a very important word: a word that distinguishes a news story from an editorial. Here's the definition. A news story is an objective account of a significant event or occurrence.

Which word distinguishes a news story from an editorial? (objective)

What does objective mean? (without bias or prejudice)

News stories are supposed to be objective. Only the facts are to be presented in news stories, not the personal feelings of the writers.

What is an antonym of objective: a word that is the opposite of objective? (subjective)

What does subjective mean? (determined by a person's feelings; a personal viewpoint about a subject)

An editorial is subjective. It expresses the newspaper's view on a subject. Editorials are usually presented on one or two pages designated Editorials, Opinion, or Debate.

I'm going to distribute some newspaper excerpts.

> Distribute back-to-back reproductions of the news story on Worksheet 40 and the feature story on Worksheet 41.

Look at Worksheet 40.

What is a headline? (the words in large type at the top of a story)

Who wants to read the headline of this news story? ("Young prisoner's dad urges Singapore to cane him instead")

Which news service released this article? (The Associated Press)

Which news service contributed to the article? (Cox News Service)

How do you know? (A note at the end of the story states that fact.)

Where was George Fay interviewed? (Dayton, Ohio)

Read the first paragraph to yourself.

> Wait until the students finish.

Newspaper stories start with the who, what, where, when, why, and how of a story. The reader can read the first paragraph and get the main facts. If the reader wants all of the details, the entire story can be read. Otherwise, the reader can go on to other stories. This inverted pyramid style of putting the who, what, where, when, and how first allows the editor to shorten stories easily. If the editor needs to shorten a story, he or she can just cut from the end.

Finish the story. See if it's objective. See if the reporter kept his personal views out. The reporter may quote other people's views, but his own should not be stated. The quoting of other people's views should not be slanted to make the reader come to a particular conclusion.

   Wait until the students finish.

Is the story objective? (yes)

Turn the paper over.

This is a feature: a human-interest story.

The headline reads: "Being Miss America is not an easy job." Is that hard news, urgent news? (no)

It's included in the newspaper because it's of human interest. It adds another dimension to the newspaper.

   If desired, give the students time to read part or all of the story.

Look at Worksheet 42.

This is an editorial, a column written to express the newspaper's view on a subject. Editorials don't appear on news pages; they appear separately on editorial pages. Subjective stories, stories expressing personal feelings about a subject, should be separated from news stories.

Editorial pages are usually designated Editorials, Opinion, or Debate. If editorials aren't designated, there are two ways you can identify them besides identifying them from content. First, the index states on which pages editorials can be found. Second, editorials usually begin on the page where the masthead appears.

The masthead is that part of a newspaper that states the name of the publishers, owners, and editors and gives the location of the newspaper's offices.

Editorials give personal comments. They may discuss, praise, or criticize. Sometimes they encourage action that they feel will benefit the community.

Who wants to read the headline? ("Let's crack down on abuse of steroids")

Read the editorial and see if you can find any of the characteristics I've just mentioned.

   Give the students time to read the entire editorial.

Who has found some editorial characteristics? (personal comment, discussion, criticism, and encouragement for action)

Any others?

This particular editorial is not all opinion. A number of facts have been stated to support the editor's viewpoint.

Some editorials are controversial. Others aren't. What does controversial mean? (subject to clash of opposing opinion)

Sometimes editorials are highly controversial. If an editorial urges readers to support gun control, that would be controversial. All of those opposed to gun control would be of a different opinion.

Editorials state personal opinion. They should be found on editorial pages, separate from news stories.

Turn your paper over.

This is an editorial cartoon.

Some editorial cartoons include a few words of comment, others don't. In this example, the editorial cartoonist has sent his message through an illustration.

What is the cartoon saying? (Taking steroids is like taking a bomb into your body.)

With one illustration the cartoonist has said what an editor might need several hundred words to say.

Some newspapers publish reviews. Reviews are analyses of books, plays, movies, restaurants, musical performances, and so forth.

I'm going to give a newspaper to each of you.

> If the newspapers are not all alike, tell the students this fact.

> During the following newspaper examination, move about the room and check the students or have the students hold up the appropriate pages so you can check from the front of the room.

If you are using *Usa Today,* see "Suggestions, Teaching with *USA Today*" at the end of this lesson.

Look at page one.

Find the newspaper's name at the top of the page. Point to it.

That's a logo. It's sometimes called a flag or nameplate.

Point to the index.

Read it to yourself.

Wait.

Use the index to find the editorial pages.

Check students.

If the newspaper that is being studied indexes obituaries, television information, and the weather forecast, have students tell you on which pages each can be found.

If obituaries are indexed, explain that they are death notices.

Turn to the sports section.

Is there an index to sports?

Point to it.

Find the classified ads.

Hold up an example, if necessary.

Classified ads are small ads usually placed by individuals to sell a product or service. You will also find listings of job openings in the classified ads.

Retail stores and manufacturers often buy large ads which are frequently illustrated. Such ads appear throughout newspapers. They're called display ads.

Show an example.

Find a display ad and point to it.

Let's review. What do we call a cartoon that illustrates a newspaper's opinions? (an editorial cartoon)

What is an analysis of a book, movie, restaurant, and so forth called? (a review)

Which of these two, an editorial or a news story, should not give the writer's personal opinion? (a news story)

What do we call a column that isn't urgent news, but is of general interest? (a feature story; a human interest story)

Give the students time to read the reproductions and the newspapers.

FOLLOW-UP

For a homework assignment, see Worksheet 44.

SUGGESTIONS

Utilizing a Class Set of Newspapers Economically

1. Use the same newspapers with more than one class.
2. Share the newspapers with teachers of current events or with teachers of other classes.

Subscribing to USA Today's *Daily Teaching System*

If your school can afford to purchase a class set of *USA Today,* you may want to enroll in the *USA Today* Daily Teaching System.

Under this program, you may select any day or days of the week for delivery of *USA Today* for as many weeks as you choose. There is a 10-copy minimum.

Teaching guides, to be used in combination with *USA Today,* are available for the following programs:

Business Today
Careers: A Lifetime Journey
Earth Today: Your Place in the Environment
Economics Today
English: Critical Thinking and Writing
Geographic Connections
How to Teach Math with *USA Today*
Journalism: A *USA Today* Perspective
Power Teaching with *USA Today*
Today's Issues
USA Decision: The Power of Each Voice
USA Freedom: Voices That Shaped Our Nation
Visions of Exploration

For information on the *USA Today's* Daily Teaching System, contact your local *USA Today* office or call 1-800-USA-0001.

Teaching with USA Today

Teach the lesson in this manual first. Then go through *USA Today* page by page.

On page one of *USA Today,* discuss the blocks of copy on either side of the logo at the top of the front page. (These blocks of copy are called ears.) Discuss how one can get a quick summary of the news by reading the Newsline column. Discuss the index and any other items of interest.

Have the students examine how the paper is divided into four sections: A, B, C, and D. On the first page of all four sections, there's a summary of the news covered in the particular section. Call attention to each summary: newsline, moneyline, sportsline, and lifeline.

Go through the paper, pointing out and discussing graphs and any other items of interest. Call attention to news from every state in Section A. Discuss the extensive weather coverage.

Continue through the other sections, specifically mentioning various items that are covered.

Give the students time to read the paper on their own.

Young prisoner's dad urges Singapore to cane him instead

The Associated Press

DAYTON, Ohio — Wracked by guilt for advising his son to plead guilty to vandalism, George Fay is willing to do the ultimate for the young man now facing six strokes of a rattan cane in Singapore: trade places with him.

"If you're going to penalize somebody, then penalize me, and I'll take his place," George Fay said this week. Today is the deadline to appeal for a presidential pardon from President Ong Teng Cheong.

Fay's 18-year-old son, Michael, was arrested in October and accused of 53 acts of vandalism, including spray-painting cars.

In March, he pleaded guilty to reduced counts and was sentenced to six strokes of a split-bamboo cane, four months in prison and a $2,230 fine.

Michael said police coerced the confession from him by slapping and punching him, but authorities have denied his coercion charges and the allegations have been dismissed by the courts here.

President Clinton, who has appealed for leniency, suggested for the first time that the confession may not have been voluntary.

"It's not entirely clear that his confession wasn't coerced from him,"

George Fay /
Blames himself for advising his son to plead guilty to reduced charges, not realizing that the sentence would include caning.

Clinton said Tuesday in Washington.

George blames himself for advising his son to plead guilty to the reduced charges, not realizing that the judge was going to order his son caned.

But George also believes the caning would be wrong even if his son had taken part in the vandalism.

"But you know what? He didn't. And he's going to get it anyway," George said. "He's going to come out of this thing, and there's going to be a hell of a lot of hatred."

George and Randy Chan, Michael's mother, divorced in 1984, when Michael was 9. They got joint custody of Michael, but he chose to live with his father.

In 1992, George agreed to allow his son to attend school in Singapore, where Chan and her husband were living. George said he warned Michael about the strict rules there.

Now, all he can do is hope his son has "enough inner strength that he'll come out of this OK."

Meanwhile, in Singapore, Michael's mother emerged Tuesday from a tearful visit with him, saying there was "not very much" hope that the government would spare him from the beating.

Caning in Singapore consists of six strokes on the bare buttocks with a water-soaked rattan rod wielded by a martial-arts expert. The lashes can tear the flesh, bloody the buttocks and leave scars.

"I still hold out some hope, but not very much," Chan told reporters after a 40-minute meeting with her son at Singapore's Queensland Remand Prison. It was her first meeting with Michael since she returned Monday night from the United States, where she made media appearances and collected what she claims are "thousands" of signatures on a petition seeking clemency for her son.

"He told me that I should stay strong and that he's ready," she said, struggling to speak through tears, "and to thank everybody for everything they're trying to do."

Contributing to this article was *Cox News Service.*

By permission. The Associated Press, April 20, 1994.

Worksheet 40

FEATURE STORY

● THE FRESNO BEE   Thursday, February 23, 1989   E3

Being Miss America is not an easy job

By BRUCE BENIDT
Scripps Howard News Service

ST. PAUL, Minn. — Gretchen Carlson is always eager to speak or play her violin instead of just standing there looking pretty when she makes appearances as Miss America.

"It shows that I'm not a bimbo, that I do have intelligence and that I do represent what every woman wants to be in this society, which is a career woman, and be respected for her intelligence," she said.

When she was crowned five months ago, the Anoka, Minn., woman said her selection showed that the pageant is interested in women with brains and talent, not just stunning looks.

The Stanford University junior has continued that theme in her travels since then: "I don't want to say that I have changed the image of the pageant; I think I've contributed to it."

Carlson is crisscrossing the nation at a breathless pace, promoting the pageant that gave her national fame as well as promoting products from pantyhose to hair coloring and doing good deeds.

The work is physically and emotionally exhausting, she said, but it has rewarded her with increased confidence. "I could handle anything right now, and I never thought I would be saying that.

"A lot of times people think that the pageant is a glamorous job, and it's exactly the opposite. I would never think of it as a glamorous job. It's the hardest job I've ever had in my whole life, and I've been a person who's been busy my whole life, so that's saying a lot."

It will make going back to Stanford look easy, she said. She has one year left, then hopes to use her scholarship money at Harvard Law School. But the Miss Minnesota and Miss America competitions have taken two years out of her academic life.

The pace is so fast that she says she has no time to be a student, no time to be sick, and "I don't have time to be Gretchen when I'm Miss America," she told a group of children at Children's Hospital here.

An accomplished violinist, Carlson impressed the audience and judges in Atlantic City last year with her virtuosity, poise and intelligence.

She said that Miss America, which she is careful to call a scholarship pageant rather

CARLSON

than a beauty pageant, has always valued talent and brains, but that it will take time to dispel the myth that it's just about beauty. "I always say if I can change one person's mind a day, then I've been successful in my mission."

One of the things that has surprised her, she said, has been "how on-guard you have to be all the time. You always have to be on, and that's difficult at times.

"Miss America is always friendly and warm and receptive and approachable, and I'm only human. It's hard to be that way all the time. Sure we're upset, we're frustrated, and I've had to learn to deal with those emotions in my private time."

The job demands great patience, and "You have to be flexible. Those are all surprising things coming from a person who's used to being very independent and having absolutely no patience and no flexibility," she said. "It's testing me."

The children in the hospital were happy to see Miss America. "It kind of makes us feel a little happy," said Chia Vang, 14.

Carlson autographed pictures for them while hospital staff people took snapshots of her with each child.

Said Marcus Jackson, 15: "I like to meet somebody like Gretchen. Not everybody gets to meet her."

When Carlson went over to Marcus, he looked at her hands and said, "Miss America with no fingernails?!"

"I know, isn't that refreshing?" Carlson said, laughing and displaying her close-trimmed nails. "I'm probably the first Miss America ever to not have any fingernails, and I'm kind of proud of it."

Printed by permission. "Being Miss America is not an easy job," by Bruce Benidt. *Star Tribune,* Minneapolis-St. Paul.

Worksheet 41   **166**

Let's crack down on abuse of steroids

All athletes, from junior high through the pros, have heard how steroids can make them faster, stronger. Even non-athletes think they'll give them sexy, sinewy bodies.

But steroids can destroy livers, change sexual characteristics, cause heart disease. They also can mess up minds.

▶ Tommie Chaikin, a star defensive lineman at the University of South Carolina, nearly committed suicide after a series of violent episodes. He had a .357-caliber Magnum pressed under his chin when his father knocked on his door and saved his life. Chaikin blames his troubles on steroids.

▶ Rocky Rauch, a nationally known body builder from Allentown, Pa., has cancer. He blames it on steroids.

▶ Benji Ramirez, a 200-pound high school tackle in Ashtabula, Ohio, keeled over and died of a heart attack. The county coroner attributed his death in part to steroids.

But those stories don't mean much to athletes driven to win at any cost. They don't think it can happen to them.

They saw Ben Johnson lose his Olympic medal for using steroids. But they learned the wrong lesson. They think: "Steroids made him fast. They can do the same for me."

Even some coaches and doctors become friendly pharmacists, handing out steroids — or looking the other way. They pretend that what athletes do is no one else's business. You can read those views across this page.

The results are insane — and not just for athletes. About 10% of high school kids have tried steroids, too.

Steroid abuse is the other side of anorexia. Teenage boys want to match the muscled men in magazines. Girls want the long, lean look. They think a pill or an injection will make them attractive.

But steroids can make them sick or turn them into walking bombs, with hair-trigger tempers. None of us should have to worry that the driver in the car behind us, or the person drinking at the bar beside us, may be on the verge of a steroid rage.

Unfortunately, education alone won't stop steroid abuse. Nationwide surveys show that not even absolute proof of physical harm would be enough to stop the abuse.

Users' only real fear: loss of an athletic scholarship.

That's why every sport, from junior high to the pros, should guard against the use of steroids. Athletes who don't want to abuse their bodies with dangerous drugs should not have to compete against those who will take any risk to win.

It's time to crack down on steroids:

▶ Sports officials must conduct vigorous, effective and fair testing programs and punish offenders.

▶ Police and federal drug authorities must crack down on illegal sellers — often the same people selling cocaine and crack.

▶ Medical associations must stop doctors who prescribe steroids for other than treating diseases and injuries.

Families, schools and churches should join the fight, too. They can teach young people to respect themselves, not some huckster's vision of the perfect body.

Sure, steroids helped Tommie Chaikin bench press 500 pounds. They also drove him to the brink.

Steroids can make you strong and beautiful. But if your body is polluted, the beauty is only skin deep.

EDITORIAL CARTOON

By David Seavey, USA TODAY

NEWSPAPER ASSIGNMENT

Clip an example of each of the following from a newspaper:

News story
Human interest story
Editorial
Editorial cartoon
Review
Classified ad
Display ad

Label and paste each example on an 8½″ by 11″ sheet of paper. More than one item can be pasted on a page, if desired. Clip or staple the pages together.

Don't forget to put your name on the assignment.

Worksheet 44

NEWSPAPER ASSIGNMENT

Clip an example of each of the following from a newspaper:

News story
Human interest story
Editorial
Editorial cartoon
Review
Classified ad
Display ad

Label and paste each example on an 8½″ by 11″ sheet of paper. More than one item can be pasted on a page, if desired. Clip or staple the pages together.

Don't forget to put your name on the assignment.

Worksheet 44

THE VERTICAL FILE

NOTE

This is a very short lesson. If you don't have vertical file folders that you can distribute to each of your students, combine this lesson with another lesson or with some book reviews.

OBJECTIVES

1. To introduce vertical files and their indexing and arrangement
2. To present your school's vertical file

MATERIALS

If you have a vertical file in your school library, gather the following:

1. Several high-interest folders for demonstration
2. A vertical file folder for each of your students
3. Reproductions of Worksheet 45

PREPARATIONS

Teacher. Familiarize yourself with your school library's vertical file(s). Find out the answers to these questions:

1. How many vertical files does your school library have?
2. Where are they located?
3. What kind are they? General? Career? Other?
4. What kinds of materials are contained? Pamphlets? Newspaper clippings? Pictures?
5. Are the files indexed?
6. Are the subjects arranged alphabetically? If not, how are they arranged?
7. Can the materials be checked out?

LESSON

Many libraries have vertical files. A vertical file is a file cabinet or box which contains materials such as pamphlets, newspaper clippings, or pictures.

A library may have more than one vertical file. For example, it may have a career file and a general file.

The file may have an index, or it may not.

The folders in the file may be arranged alphabetically, or they may be arranged by some other method.

Some libraries allow vertical file materials to be checked out, others don't.

Our school library has/doesn't have a vertical file.

> *If your school doesn't have a vertical file,* tell your students to look for one at the public library. End your lesson here.

> *If your school has a vertical file,* tell your students:

1. Where the file is located
2. What kind of file it is (general? career? other?)
3. What kinds of materials are contained in the file (newspaper clippings? magazine clippings? pictures? pamphlets?)

Hold up several high-interest folders. Show your students what they contain.

4. Whether the file is indexed or not
5. How the file is arranged (alphabetically? other method?)
6. Whether the materials can be checked out or not

I'm going to distribute a folder from the vertical file to each of you. Look over all the materials in your folder and then complete the worksheet that I'm going to pass out to you.

Distribute a folder and a reproduction of Worksheet 38 to each student.

Later, grade or write a comment on each student's paper.

Name _____ Date _____

THE VERTICAL FILE

1. The folder I have is titled _____

2. It contains the following kinds of materials: _____

   _____

   _____

3. Write a paragraph or two about the subjects contained in your folder. Be sure to use
   your own words. _____

   _____

   _____

   _____

   _____

   _____

   _____

   _____

   _____

   _____

   _____

   _____

   _____

Worksheet 45

PART 2

REFERENCE BOOK LESSONS

BIOGRAPHY

Current Biography

Current Biography. New York: H. W. Wilson, 1940–. Profiles of people in the news. Published every month except December. Each issue contains 14–15 profiles. A portrait accompanies each biography. A cumulative index is part of each issue listing all those profiled in the current volume year. Updates. Obituaries.

Current Biography Yearbook, New York: H. W. Wilson, 1940–.

In December, the 11 monthly issues of *Current Biography* are cumulated in one alphabet in a hardcover volume. A cumulative index to all previous yearbooks of the decade is included. Also featured is a classification of the subjects of articles by their professions.

Current Biography Cumulated Index 1940–1990. New York: H. W. Wilson, 1991. 133 p.

Indexes all of the articles in *Current Biography* from 1940–1990.

OBJECTIVES

1. To introduce *Current Biography,* its yearbook, and index
2. To present a sample page from *Current Biography*
3. To familiarize students with *Current Biography's* coverage

MATERIALS

1. If available, *Current Biography* (1–11 copies), *Current Biography Yearbook,* and *Current Biography Cumulated Index 1940–1990.* (The preferred issue of *Current Biography* is the one for November 1987, in which Michael J. Fox is profiled; however, any

issue will suffice. If the latest issue of *Cumulated Index* isn't available, an older index can be used.)
2. Reproductions of a sample page from *Current Biography,* Worksheet 46
3. Reproductions of the follow-up paper, Worksheet 47
4. If assigning a *Current Biography* report, reproduce the form on Worksheet 48.

PREPARATIONS

1. If you plan to have a whole class use *Current Biography* at the same time, find out if there are enough copies available.
2. If the November 1987 *Current Biography* is available, designate Michael J. Fox's biography, page 17, with a bookmark.
3. If you have a *Yearbook,* use a bookmark to designate the Classification by Profession pages.

LESSON

If you are interested in finding information about a person in the news, for example, Michael J. Fox, you may want to refer to *Current Biography.*

  If available, hold up a copy of *Current Biography* (a monthly paperback).

Who remembers what the word "biography" means? (the story of a person's life, written by another person)

What does current mean? (now in progress)

Current Biography contains life histories of people who are currently in the news. It features artists, politicians, business people, journalists, actors, authors, sports figures, scientists, and others.

It is published every month except December. Each issue contains 14–15 profiles.

What does the word "profile" mean? (a short biography)

  Hold up a copy of *Current Biography,* if available, and show one of the portraits to the class. A portrait of Michael J. Fox is preferred, but any portrait will do. If a book is unavailable, hold up the portrait of Michael J. Fox, which you reproduced on Worksheet 46.

A portrait accompanies each biography.

Sometimes if a person featured in an earlier issue continues to make news, his original biography is rewritten and updated.

Obituaries are included.

What is an obituary? (a notice of someone's death)

Do you remember that I said *Current Biography* is issued every month except December? In December, the 11 monthly issues are cumulated in one alphabet in a hardcover volume. This hardcover book is titled *Current Biography Yearbook.*

> If you have 11 issues of *Current Biography,* hold them up, and reiterate that in December the 11 monthly issues are put into one alphabet in a hardcover volume called a yearbook. Then hold up a copy of *Current Biography Yearbook,* if available.

> Alternative: If you have only a *Current Biography Yearbook,* hold it up.

In a way, the 11 individual paperback issues aren't needed any more, are they? Their biographies have been combined and put in alphabetical order in a hardbound volume. Of course, the paperbacks can still be used.

A yearbook is a book that is published annually.

What does "annually" mean? (yearly)

Yearbooks usually give information about the preceding year.

Current Biography was first published in 1940. That means if a library has all of the yearbooks, it has _____ volumes. (Subtract 1940 from the current year and add one to get the correct answer.)

Current Biography Yearbook has a classification of subjects by profession. If you want to know which sports personalities are featured in a particular *Yearbook,* look in the back of the volume under sports. If you're interested in finding out which television personalities are in a *Yearbook,* look in the classification pages under television.

> If you have a *Yearbook,* show the classification pages to the students. Read a few listings.

In *Current Biography Yearbook,* you'll find a cumulative index to all of the previous yearbooks of the decade.

What's a decade? (10 years)

If you want to locate a biography about Michael J. Fox, start by looking in *Current Biography Cumulated Index 1940–1990,* which indexes 51 yearbooks.

> If available, hold up a copy of *Current Biography Cumulated Index 1940–1990.*

If you don't find Michael listed in the 1940–1990 cumulated index, look in the index of the latest *Yearbook.*

Current Biography, the *Yearbook,* and the *Index* are found in most public libraries and colleges. They are also found in many junior and senior high schools.

Our library has/doesn't have copies.

If your library has *Current Biography,* point to its location, if you are in the library.

I'm going to distribute a sample page from *Current Biography.*

Distribute copies of Worksheet 46.

The article about Michael J. Fox starts about three inches from the top of the page.

Is Michael entered under his first or last name? (last)

Under Michael's portrait, you see the date June 9, 1961. What do you think that date represents? (Michael's birth date)

After "Actor," you see the word "Address" followed by the letter "b." What is "b" an abbreviation for? (business)

What does "c/o" represent? (in care of)

At the time this article was published, Michael's business address was "c/o NBC-TV, 3000 W. Alameda Ave., Burbank, Calif. 91523." If you were writing a letter to Michael, you'd put his name first, of course. Since the article about Michael was written in 1987 and since his series is no longer on TV, this address is no longer current. You can refer to *Who's Who in America* for Michael's current address.

I have been distinguishing between *Current Biography* and *Current Biography Yearbook* by using their precise titles when referring to them. However, in general use, they are both loosely referred to as *Current Biography.*

I'm going to distribute a worksheet for you to do. Read the questions on the worksheet first so you'll know what you're looking for. Then read Michael's biography and answer the questions.

Distribute Worksheet 47.

After the students have completed their papers, collect the worksheets.

Have a quick review by asking the following question.

What information can you find in *Current Biography?* (the subject's full name; birth date; field or profession; subject's views and attitudes; observations of journalists, colleagues, and associates; photograph; reference to additional sources of information)

How would you go about finding a biography of a particular celebrity? (Look in *Current Biography Cumulated Index 1940–1990.* If you were unsuccessful, you'd look in the index of the latest *Yearbook.*)

FOLLOW-UP

If your library has *Current Biography,* you may want to do one of the following:

1. Assign a *Current Biography* report. Tell students to locate information about one of the

three people they listed as an answer for item #10 on Worksheet 47. Provide reproductions of Worksheet 48 for the report. Let students go individually to the library to do research.

2. When the class is in the library as a group, pass out a copy of *Current Biography* or *Current Biography Yearbook* to each student. Have the students select a profile and report about it. Use the form on Worksheet 48. Check to make sure the library has enough books for your class.

NOTE

You may want to discuss the meanings of the following words when discussing Michael J. Fox's biography:

quondam—former
elan (ā′län′)—impetuosity, enthusiasm

Like Mickey Mouse and the other characters who decorate the $300 million worth of Disney products, including watches and T-shirts, that he markets worldwide, Eisner himself has become a highly visible symbol of the company. As host of the *Disney Sunday Movie* he appears briefly on each week's program, sometimes joking with actors costumed as Mickey, Goofy, and other cartoon characters. Although he concedes that he "can't act," he appears relaxed, good-humored, and personable.

Six-foot-three inches tall and slender, with thinning dark curly hair, Eisner is decidedly informal in his manner. His expensive suits are often rumpled and his ties askew. He best expressed his childlike enthusiasm when he was chosen as Disney's chairman and said that he felt like he had been set free in a toy store: "I don't know which toy to take home because they're all fabulous and they

all work and I'm so excited I can't sleep at night." Fiercely devoted to his family, Eisner has been married to the former Jane Breckenridge for some twenty years. He recalls that the happiest moment of his life was when his first child was born, and he regularly spends Saturday mornings watching his sons, Michael, Eric, and Anders play basketball, football, and soccer. He has often put helping them with their schoolwork or taking them to Boy Scout meetings ahead of business matters. Eisner also finds time to serve on the boards of Denison University, the California Institute of the Arts, the American Film Institute, and the Performing Arts Council of the Los Angeles Music Center.

References: Bsns W p62+ Mr 9 '87 por; N Y Newsday mag p1+ Ap 19 '87 por; N Y Times Mag p13+ D 29 '85 por; New York p25+ Jl 30 '84 pors; Vanity Fair 46:76+ Jl '83 por; Who's Who in America, 1986–87

Fox, Michael J.

June 9, 1961– Actor. Address: b. c/o NBC-TV, 3000 W. Alameda Ave., Burbank, Calif. 91523

Endowed with the same energy and drive that his characters display on the screen, Michael J. Fox has achieved the distinction of starring simultaneously in the top-grossing film of 1985, *Back to the Future*, and in the second most popular situation comedy of the mid-1980s, *Family Ties*, for which he received an Emmy. Demonstrating "an incredible comic sensibility," "agile timing," and "infallible charm," in the words of various admir-

ing critics, he continues to attract large audiences, even in mediocre films. Once aiming no higher than supporting roles, the quondam short and chubby youth has been transformed into a teeny-bopper's sex symbol.

Noting Fox's "large, expressive face and . . . wise guy's élan," Paul Attanasio of the *Washington Post* (July 3, 1985) praised his ability to "modulate" his "big TV-style delivery" in film roles "while making use of the shortcuts that TV teaches, that way of conveying a character in a few broad strokes." According to Lloyd Sachs of the Chicago *Sun-Times*, (February 8, 1987), Michael J. Fox, Tom Cruise, and Matthew Broderick are prototypes of the "more clean-cut, value-oriented young leading man" that has reemerged in the 1980s in the wake of the ascendancy of the "brat pack." The director Paul Schrader believes that Fox is shooting for "a career in the direction of . . . Jimmy Stewart, primarily light comedy but turning to heavier fare if the situation is just right." The initial "J" in Fox's show business name is a gesture he made in honor of Michael J. Pollard, a character actor whom he much admires.

Michael Andrew Fox was born on June 9, 1961 in Edmonton, Alberta, Canada, the fourth of five children of Bill Fox, a retired veteran of the Canadian army who later served fifteen years with the Edmonton police, and Phyllis Fox, a payroll clerk whom her famous son describes as a "5-foot-2, round and sexy Irish lady." "My parents are their best friends in the world," Fox told Mark Morrison of *Rolling Stone* (March 12, 1987), in describing their relationship ("always together—an unmovable force") as a crucial aspect of his happy childhood. His humor is homegrown too, as he observed in the *Rolling Stone* interview. "The oldest form of theater is the [family] dinner table. It's got five or six people, new show every night, . . . same players. Good ensemble; the people have worked together a lot."

November 1987 CURRENT BIOGRAPHY   17

CURRENT BIOGRAPHY

1. When was Michael J. Fox born?

   _____

2. What is his business address?

   _____

   _____

   _____

3. Name two qualities that Michael and the characters he plays on the screen have in common. _____

   _____

4. For his work in which TV show did Michael receive an Emmy? _____

   _____

5. What have some of his critics said about him? _____

   _____

   _____

6. What is Michael J. Fox's middle name?_____

7. Where was Michael born? _____

8. Name Michael's father and mother. _____

   _____

9. What is the name of the 1985 top-grossing film in which Michael starred? _____

   _____

10. Name three people in the news about whom you would like to know more. _____

    _____

Name _____ Date _____

CURRENT BIOGRAPHY REPORT

1. Biographee _____

2. Birth date_____

3. Field or profession _____

4. For what is the biographee best known? _____

   _____

5. Address _____

   _____

6. Does the article give some of the biographee's views? If so, give an example. ____

   _____

   _____

   _____

7. Does the article include observations of journalists, colleagues, or associates? If so,

   give an example. _____

   _____

   _____

   _____

8. Is there a photograph of the biographee? _____

9. Additional sources of information are listed at the end of the article. Name one.____

   _____

10. What was one of the most interesting things you learned about the biographee?____

   _____

   _____

   _____

Webster's New Biographical Dictionary

Webster's New Biographical Dictionary. Springfield, Mass.: Merriam-Webster, 1988. 1,152 p.
Concise biographies of more than 30,000 noteworthy deceased persons from all parts of the world, all eras, and all occupations. No longer includes living persons. Pronunciation of names included.

OBJECTIVES

1. To introduce *Webster's New Biographical Dictionary*
2. To give students practice in locating, reading, and interpreting biographical entries.

MATERIALS

1. If available, a copy of *Webster's New Biographical Dictionary*
2. Reproductions of a sample page from *Webster's New Biographical Dictionary,* Worksheet 49
3. Reproductions of the follow-up assignment, Worksheet 50

PREPARATION

If your school library has *Webster's New Biographical Dictionary,* check the copyright date. Books copyrighted prior to 1983 contained biographies of living persons as well as deceased ones.

LESSON

If you are interested in finding a concise biography of a famous deceased person, for example, Helen Keller, you can refer to *Webster's New Biographical Dictionary.*

Hold up a copy of *Webster's New Biographical Dictionary,* if available.

What is the meaning of the word concise? (short)

What does the word deceased mean? (dead)

Webster's New Biographical Dictionary contains concise biographies of more than 30,000 important, celebrated, or notorious deceased persons from the last five thousand years. All parts of the world and all occupations are included.

Webster's New Biographical Dictionary is a standard reference book, which is found in most public, college, junior high school, and senior high school libraries.

Prior to 1983, *Webster's New Biographical Dictionary* contained biographies of both living and deceased people. Thereafter, the book has contained biographies of deceased people only.

Our library has/doesn't have *Webster's New Biographical Dictionary.*

If your school library has the book, tell the students whether the book was copyrighted prior to 1983 and contains both living and deceased people or if it was copyrighted after 1983 and contains deceased people only.

I'm going to distribute a sample page from the book.

Distribute reproductions of Worksheet 49.

To be able to include more than 30,000 people in one book, the publisher had to keep the biographies brief, and he had to have the book printed in small type.

At the top of the page there are two names in boldface type. What do we call those words? (guide words)

What is their purpose? (They are alphabetical guides that tell you whether the name you are looking for will be found on a particular page.)

The first guide word represents the first name on the page, and the second guide word represents the last name on the page. By looking at the two, you can determine whether the name for which you are looking will be found on that page.

Find the entry for Helen Keller.

Who would like to read it?

Call on a student.

What is Helen Keller's full name? (Helen Adams Keller)

When was she born? (1880)

When did she die? (1968)

What does the letter "b" on the first line of this entry mean? (born)

What does mute mean? (unable to speak)

On line three of this entry you see the abbreviation q.v. What does the abbreviation mean?

How can we find out? (Check the pages that list abbreviations.)

If you refer to the pages that list abbreviations, you'll find that q.v. is from the Latin quod vide (pronounced quod vidē). It means "which see." The abbreviation q.v. comes after the name Anne Sullivan Macy. It means see Anne Sullivan Macy in this book.

Let's look at another biography. Look at the first name on the page.

Who would like to read it?

   Call on a student.

Originally Harry Kellar spelled his last name K-e-l-l-e-r. As you can see, *Webster's New Biographical Dictionary* includes name changes.

Notice that pronunciation of names is given. Look at entries one and two for examples.

Find the entry for Emmett Lee Kelly.

Who wants to read it?

   Call on someone.

Find the entry for Alvin Kelly.

Who wants to read it?

   Call on someone.

Find the entry for Grace Kelly.

Who wants to read it?

   Call on someone.

Follow me as I read the nationality and occupation of the biographees listed on this page. Look at the first entry.

American magician.

Follow me as I read the others.

Swiss archeologist, Swiss writer, American author and lecturer. . . .

   If desired, continue reading the identifications.

From what I read, what did you learn about the coverage of *Webster's New Biographical Dictionary?* (People of all nations and all occupations are included.)

Let's review.

How is the book arranged? (alphabetically)

Would you look in this book if you wanted to find a biography of our current president? (No. The book contains biographies of deceased people only.)

Are the biographies short or long? (short)

> If you have presented lessons on other biographical books, name one of the other books, and ask students to compare it to *Webster's New Biographical Dictionary.* You may want to ask for comparisons of the following:
>
> > number of volumes
> > arrangement
> > people included (living/deceased)
> > length of the articles
> > portraits
> > readability
> > number of biographies included

I'm going to distribute a worksheet for you to do. Refer to the sample page from *Webster's New Biographical Dictionary* for the information you will need to complete the paper.

> Distribute reproductions of Worksheet 50.

Look at item number 10 on Worksheet 50.

Who wants to read the item? (For what did he gain notoriety?)

What does the "l" after notoriety mean? (It refers you to the footnote below.)

Who wants to read the footnote? (notoriety: the quality of being widely, but unfavorably, known)

You may begin work.

> After the students have completed their worksheets, collect them. You may also want to collect the sample page from *Webster's New Biographical Dictionary.*

Kel·lar \\'kel-ər\\, Harry. *Surname orig.* Keller. 1849–1922. American magician, b. Erie, Pa. First great magician native to U.S. Opened his first full evening show (1884); reigned supreme (1896–1908); called "dean of magic".

Kel·ler \\'kel-ər\\, Ferdinand. 1800–1881. Swiss archaeologist. A founder of Zürich Antiquarian Society (1832); pioneer in European prehistoric archaeology. Discovered lake dwellings of Obermeilen on Lake Zürich (1854); organized researches on Swiss lake dwellings.

Keller, Gottfried. 1819–1890. Swiss writer. Most representative national author of the German-speaking Swiss. Author of collections of verse, novels *Der grüne Heinrich* (autobiographical, 1854–55, rev. 1879–80) and *Martin Salander* (1886), and short stories of Swiss provincial life, some collected in *Die Leute von Seldwyla* (1856–74) and *Sieben Legenden* (1872).

Keller, Helen Adams. 1880–1968. American author and lecturer, b. Tuscumbia, Ala. Left blind, deaf, and mute by illness at age of 19 months. Educated (1887–1936) by Anne Sullivan Macy (*q.v.*). Lecturer in U.S. and abroad on behalf of the blind. Author of *The Story of My Life* (1902), *The World I Live In* (1908), *Out of the Dark* (1913), *My Religion* (1927), *Helen Keller's Journal* (1938), *The Open Door* (1957), etc.

Kel·ler·mann \\'kel-ər-,män\\, Bernard. 1879–1951. German novelist. Author of *Yester und Li* (1904), *Ingeborg* (1906), *Der Tor* (1909), *Das Meer* (1910), *Der Tunnel* (1913), *Der Krieg im Westen* (1915), *Krieg in Argonnerwald* (1916), *Der Neunte November* (1920), *Die Brüder Schellenberg* (1925), *Das blaue Band* (1938); also of works on his travels in Japan and the East.

Kel·ler·mann \\kä-ler-mán\\, François-Christophe. Duc de Val·my \\də-val-mē\\. 1735–1820. French soldier. Entered army (1752); fought with distinction in Seven Years' War (1756–63); promoted field marshal (1788), lieutenant general (1792). Commanded army of the Moselle (1792) and cooperated with Dumouriez in defeating the Prussians at Valmy (Sept. 20, 1792). Commanded army of the Alps (1792–93, 1795–97); recaptured Savoy (1793); appointed senator (1804); created marshal of France (1804), duc de Valmy (1808), and a peer (1814). His son ¶François-Étienne (1770–1835) was one of Napoléon's generals; brigadier general (1797); led decisive charge at Marengo (1800) and was promoted general of division; prominent at Austerlitz and Waterloo.

Kel·ley \\'kel-ē\\, Florence. 1859–1932. American reformer, b. Philadelphia. Resident at Hull-House, Chicago (1891–99); helped create and first holder of post of Illinois state factory inspector (1895–97); general secretary, National Consumers' League, New York City (1899–1932); founded National Child Labor Committee (1902); helped found National Association for the Advancement of Colored People (1909). Author of *Some Ethical Gains through Legislation* (1905), *Modern Industry* (1913).

Kelley, Oliver Hudson. 1826–1913. American agricultural organizer, b. Boston. An organizer (1868) and secretary (1868–78) of National Grange of the Patrons of Husbandry; zealous in promoting its growth; wrote *Origin and Progress of the Patrons of Husbandry* (1875).

Kell·gren \\'kel-grän\\, Johan Henrik. 1751–1795. Swedish poet. Cofounder and critic (1778), then owner and editor (from 1788) of the journal *Stockholmsposten*; championed rationalism. Librarian (1780), private secretary (from 1785), and literary adviser to Gustav III. Author of satirical, lyrical, and patriotic verse, esp. *Mina löjen* (1778) and *Den Nya Skapelsen eller Ibillningens värld* (1789); also wrote verse dramas and collaborated with Gustav on opera *Gustaf Wasa* (1786).

Kel·logg \\'kel-,ôg, -,äg\\, Frank Billings. 1856–1937. American lawyer, politician, and diplomat, b. Potsdam, N.Y. Practiced law in Minnesota; special counsel for government in successful antitrust suits against Standard Oil (1906) and Union Pacific Railroad (1907). U.S. senator (1917–23); U.S. ambassador to Great Britain (1923–25); U.S. secretary of state (1925–29). With Aristide Briand negotiated Kellogg-Briand Pact to outlaw war as an instrument of national policy (1928). Awarded Nobel peace prize for 1929. Judge, Permanent Court of International Justice (1930–35).

Kellogg, John Harvey. 1852–1943. American physician, b. Tyrone, Mich. Superintendent, Battle Creek (Mich.) Sanitarium (from 1876); founder and president (1923–26), Battle Creek College; founder (1931) and medical director, Miami-Battle Creek Sanitarium, Miami Springs, Florida. Aided by his brother Will, developed dry breakfast cereals for use in his sanitarium; wrote numerous medical books. His brother ¶Will Keith (1860–1951), b. Battle Creek, Mich., took position at Battle Creek Sanitarium (1880) and helped John in his nutritional experiments. Founder (1906), president (1906–29), board chairman (1929–46), W.K. Kellogg Co., which became a leading manufacturer of cornflakes and other prepared breakfast foods; established major philanthropic institution, W.K. Kellogg Foundation (1930).

Kel·ly \\'kel-ē\\, Alvin Anthony. *Known as* Shipwreck Kelly. 1893–1952. American stunt man. Famous during 1920s for spending long periods of time on high perches; sat atop a flagpole at Atlantic City for 1177 hours (1930).

Kelly, Colin P. 1915–1941. American army officer, b. Madison, Fla. Pilot of bomber that destroyed Japanese battleship *Haruna* (Dec. 9, 1941) following attack on Pearl Harbor; when his airplane was damaged by enemy fire, ordered crew to bail out; died in crash.

Kelly, Emmett Lee. 1898–1979. American clown, b. Sedan, Kans. Created (1923) role of "Weary Willie," a mournful tramp dressed in tattered business suit with a growth of beard and a bulbous nose; appeared in this role with English and American circuses, esp. Ringling Bros. and Barnum & Bailey Circus (1942–57), in films as *The Greatest Show on Earth* (1952).

Kelly, George. 1887–1974. American actor and playwright, b. Philadelphia. Author of *The Torchbearers* (1922), *The Show-Off* (1924), *Craig's Wife* (1925, Pulitzer prize), *Maggie the Magnificent* (1929), *Philip Goes Forth* (1931), *Reflected Glory* (1936), *The Fatal Weakness* (1946).

Kelly, George. *Known as* Machine Gun Kelly. *Orig.* George Kelly Barnes \\'bärnz\\, Jr. 1895–1954. American gangster, b. Memphis, Tenn. Gained notoriety (by 1933) for series of robberies and slayings in Midwest; kidnapped Oklahoma millionaire Charles F. Urschel (July 1933); arrested (Sept. 1933), convicted, and spent rest of life in prison.

Kelly, Grace. Princess Grace of Monaco. 1929–1982. American actress, b. Philadelphia. Known as a leading lady of patrician beauty and cool reserve. Niece of playwright George Kelly. Made film debut in *Fourteen Hours* (1951). Other films included *High Noon* (1952), *The Country Girl* (1954, Academy Award), *Dial M for Murder* (1954), *Rear Window* (1954), and *To Catch a Thief* (1955). m. (1956) Prince Rainier of Monaco and retired from films.

Kelly, Howard Atwood. 1858–1943. American physician, b. Camden, N.J. Professor of gynecology, Johns Hopkins, and chief gynecologist, Johns Hopkins Hospital (1899–1919). Devised operations to correct retroposition of the uterus; among first to use radium in cancer treatment; invented a rectal and vesical speculum. Author of *Operative Gynecology* (1898, 1906), *Cyclopedia of American Medical Biography* (1912), etc.

Kelly, Hugh. 1739–1777. Irish playwright. Author of comedies *False Delicacy* (1768), *A Word to the Wise* (1770), *The School for Wives* (1773), *The Romance of an Hour* (1774), *The Man of Reason* (1776); also of *Thespis* (1766–67, literary criticism) and *Memoirs of a Magdalen* (1767, novel).

Kelly, Ned, *in full* Edward. 1855–1880. Australian outlaw. Last and most famous bushranger (Australian rural outlaw); led gang in series of daring robberies on Victoria–New South Wales borderland (1878–80); captured and hanged; became symbol of protest against arbitrary authority and rich landowners.

Kelly, Walter Crawford, *known as* Walt. 1913–1973. American cartoonist and illustrator, b. Philadelphia. Worked as animator for Walt Disney Productions, Hollywood (1935–41); commercial artist in New York City (1941 ff.). Created (1948) comic strip "Pogo," eventually syndicated in over 450 newspapers; also illustrated children's books and published collections of "Pogo" strips.

Kelly, William. 1811–1888. American inventor, b. Pittsburgh. Invented (c.1850) converter (later known as Bessemer converter, from Sir Henry Bessemer's similar process) for the making of steel, utilizing an air blast on molten iron to obtain greater heat for the process; patent issued (1857).

Kel·sey \\'kel-sē\\, Henry. d. 1729. English explorer. Entered service of Hudson's Bay Company (1687); on expedition to Manitoba, Canada, to find new sources of fur (1690–92); possibly first European to explore central Canada.

Kelvin, Baron. See William THOMSON.

Ke·mal \\ke-'mäl\\, Namık, *in full* Mehmed Namık. 1840–1888. Turkish writer, journalist, and patriot. Became disciple of İbrahim Şinasi; edited (1865–67) Şinasi's newspaper *Tasvir-i Efkâr* after Şinasi fled to Paris; member of secret revolutionary society Young Ottomans; fled to London (1867), publishing newspaper *Hürriyet* there (1868) and continuing revolutionary novels in Paris and Vienna. Returned to Turkey (1871), becoming editor of newspaper *İbret*; enthusiastic reception of performance of his patriotic play *Vatan yahnut Silistre* (1872) caused his imprisonment (1873–76); governor of Sakız (1888). His ideas of *vatan* (fatherland) and *hürriyet* (freedom) helped establish a Turkish national consciousness and greatly influenced the Young Turk and other Turkish nationalist movements. Championed rejection of classical Ottoman literary forms and adoption of European models. Works included verse, plays *Zavallı çocuk* (1873) and *Akif Bey* (1874), historical novels *İntibah* (1874) and *Cezmi* (1887/88), political essays as *Rüya* (1907), historical works, and translations of Hugo, Rousseau, Montesquieu, and others.

Kemal Atatürk. See ATATÜRK.

Ke·mal·pa·şa·zâ·de \\kä-,mäl-pä-,shä-zä-'de\\. *Known also as* Ibn Kemal \\,ib-ən-kä-'mäl\\ *and* Ibn Kemal Pa·şa \\-pä-'shä\\. *In full* Şemseddin Ahmet ibn Süleyman ibn Kemal Paşa. c.1468–1534. Turkish scholar, poet, and historian. Taught at religious colleges; commissioned by Sultan Bayezid II to write *Tevarih-i Al-i Osman*, a chronicle covering Ottoman history of 1481–1526. Military judge of Anatolia (1516–17); appointed Shaykh al-Islām by Sultan

\\ə\\ abut	\\ᵊ\\ kitten, *Fr.* table	\\ər\\ further	\\a\\ ash	\\ā\\ ace	\\ä\\ cot, cart
\\aù\\ out	\\ch\\ chin	\\e\\ bet	\\ē\\ easy	\\g\\ go	\\i\\ hit	\\ī\\ ice	\\j\\ job	\\ŋ\\ sing
\\ō\\ go	\\ò\\ law	\\òi\\ boy	\\th\\ both	\\th\\ the	\\ü\\ loot	\\ù\\ foot	\\y\\ yet
\\zh\\ vision	\\à, b̲, g̲, k̲, ⁿ, œ, œ̄, ᵫ, ȳ\\ *see* Guide to Pronunciation

---

By permission. From *Webster's New Biographical Dictionary* © 1988 by Merriam-Webster, Inc., publisher of the Merriam-Webster ® Dictionaries.

WEBSTER'S NEW BIOGRAPHICAL DICTIONARY

On Worksheet 49, find the entry for George Kelly, actor and playwright. Refer to that entry to answer these questions.

1. When was George Kelly born? _____

2. When did he die? _____

3. What was his nationality? _____

4. Where was he born? _____

5. For which play did he receive a Pulitzer prize? _____

On Worksheet 49, find the entry for George Kelly, known as Machine Gun Kelly. Refer to that entry to answer these questions.

6. What was George Kelly's original name? _____

7. When was he born? _____

8. When did he die? _____

9. Where was he born? _____

10. For what did he gain notoriety[1]? _____

_____

_____

[1]notoriety—the quality of being widely, but unfavorably, known

Who's Who in America

Who's Who in America. New Providence, N.J.: Marquis
Who's Who, 1899–. 3 vols. Annual.
Standard directory of contemporary American biography
containing life and career information about noteworthy
individuals.

The 49th edition (1995) contains approximately 90,000
biographies. Prominent individuals from other countries,
particularly Canada and Mexico, are also included.

OBJECTIVES

1. To introduce *Who's Who in America*
2. To have the class read and interpret the sample profile on the Key to Information page
3. To provide a written follow-up that requires students to locate specific information
   from a second sample profile.

MATERIALS

1. Back-to-back reproductions of the Key to Information page, Worksheet 51, and the
   Shirley Temple Black profile, Worksheet 52
2. Reproductions of the follow-up paper, Worksheet 53

PREPARATION

Teacher. Find out if your school library has *Who's Who in America.*

LESSON

If you'd like to find some information about a well-known American, for example, Shirley
Temple, you can look in *Who's Who in America.*

Who's Who in America is a large three-volume reference book, which contains concise biographies of well-known Americans. Although the book focuses on Americans, prominent individuals from other countries, particularly Canada and Mexico, are included.

Who's Who in America contains biographies of living people only. That's easy to remember if you think of the first word of the title, Who's, as Who *Is—Who Is Who in America.* You wouldn't say "who is" if a person wasn't living, would you?

The biographical information in *Who's Who in America* was supplied by the biographees, which insures that the information is accurate and current.

What is a biographee? (a person a biography is about)

Prior to 1994, *Who's Who in America* was a biennial.

What does the word biennial mean? (happening every two years)

The 1994 *Who's Who in America* had two major differences from previous editions. For the first time in its history, *Who's Who in America* was issued as an annual.

What does the word annual mean? (happening every year)

The second difference was that a third volume was added. The first two volumes were an A–Z directory of biographies. The third volume was a *Geographic/Professional Index.*

The Geographic Index listed cities and the biographees living in each. The Professional Index listed professions and the biographees who were engaged in them.

Who's Who in America is found in most college and public libraries. Some junior and senior high schools have copies, too.

Our school library has/doesn't have *Who's Who in America.*

The book titled simply *Who's Who* is international, principally British. People often get confused and don't realize that. If you're looking for the biography of a living American, look in *Who's Who in America.*

The biographies of famous Americans who are no longer living are published in *Who Was Who in America.*

The publisher of *Who's Who in America* is publishing a total of 17 Who's Who books. Other publishers are also publishing some Who's Who titles.

The 1995 *Who's Who in America* contains approximately 90,000 biographies. To be able to include that many biographies in one work, the publisher did three things. He compiled information and recorded it in the briefest way, which means he recorded it without putting it into sentences. He used small print, and he divided the biographies into two volumes.

I'm going to distribute back-to-back reproductions of two pages from *Who's Who in America.*

Distribute back-to-back reproductions of Worksheets 51 and 52.

Look at Worksheet 51.

This is a sample biography that has been enlarged for study. The key on the right helps the reader understand what information has been included in the profile.

Who would like to read the biographee's name? It's designated number 1. (Oscar Julius Gibson)

If the student you call on doesn't read the first name first, say, "Good. That's the way the name is entered in the book. Now read the first name first."

Call on someone after each of the following biographical references.

Number 2, occupation. (physician, medical educator)

Number 3, vital statistics. (born Syracuse, N.Y., on Aug. 31, 1937)

Number 4, parents. (son of Paul Oliver and Elizabeth H. [Thrun] Gibson)

If the student didn't translate the "G" into Gibson, ask what the "G" stands for.

What is the word in parentheses? (the mother's maiden name: the mother's name before marriage)

What does the letter "s" stand for? (son)

If the subject had been a woman, a "d" for daughter would have been used.

Number 5, marriage. (married Judith S. Gonzalez on April 28, 1968)

Number 6, children. (Richard Gary, Matthew Cary, Samuel Perry)

Number 7, education. (BA: Bachelor of Arts degree, magna cum laude: with high honors, University of Pennsylvania, 1960; MD: Doctor of Medicine degree, Harvard University, 1964)

Number 8, professional certifications. (diplomate American Board of Internal Medicine, American Board of Preventive Medicine.)

Explain that diplomate (dip′ lə-māt′) means the subject (Gibson) is certified as a specialist in a particular branch of medicine.

Definitions for words found in the following paragraph:

intern—a doctor who is serving in a hospital just after his graduation from medical school
resident—a doctor who is living or staying in a hospital while working there
clinical associate—a doctor who has secondary status in a clinic
chief resident—head of trainees
NIH—National Institutes of Health
v.p.—vice president

Number 9, career. (Intern Barnes Hospital, St. Louis, 1964–1965, resident 1965–1966; clinical associate National Heart Institute, NIH, Bethesda, Maryland, 1966–1968; chief resident medicine University of Oklahoma Hospitals, 1968–1969; assistant professor of community health Oklahoma Medical Center, 1969–1970, associate professor, 1970–1974, professor and chairman of the department, 1974–1980; dean of the University of Oklahoma College of Medicine, 1978–1982; v.p. of medical staff affairs Baptist Medical Center, Oklahoma City, 1982–1986, executive vice president 1986–1988, chairman 1988–)

Number 10, career-related. (member of governing board of the Ambulatory Health Care Consortium, Inc., 1979–1980; member of Oklahoma Board of Medicolegal Examiners, 1985–)

After the last date, 1985, there is a line. What does that line mean? (Dr. Gibson is still a member of the Oklahoma Board of Medicolegal Examiners. He became a member in 1985. If he were no longer a member there would be a date after the line telling when he discontinued membership.)

Number 11, writings and creative works. (contributes articles to professional journals)

Number 12, civic and political activities. (board of directors, vice president Oklahoma Arthritis Foundation, 1982–; trustee North Central Mental Health Center, 1985–)

What is a trustee? (A trustee is a person to whom another's property, or management of another's property, is entrusted. In this case, Dr. Gibson is entrusted with North Central Mental Health Center.)

Number 13, military. (served with the U.S. Army 1955–1956)

Number 14, awards and fellowships. (recipient R. T. Chadwick award NIH, 1968; American Heart Association grantee, 1985–1986, 1988)

What does recipient mean? (one who receives)

What does grantee mean? (a person who receives a grant, a sum of money)

Definitions of words found in the following paragraph:

fellow—has had specialty training
AAAS—American Association for Advancement of Science
AMA—American Medical Association
Sigma Xi—a fraternity
fraternity—a group of people with the same work, belief, or interests, such as a medical fraternity

Number 15, professional and association memberships, clubs and lodges. (fellow of the Association of Teachers of Preventive Medicine; member of the American Federation of Clinical Research. Association of Medical Colleges, AAAS, AMA, Masons, Shriners, Sigma Xi)

What is a lodge? (an association or fraternal organization in which the members are joined for mutual benefit or for a common goal)

Number 16, political affiliation. (Republican)

Number 17, religion. (Roman Catholic)

Number 18, avocations. (swimming, weight lifting, travel)

What is an avocation? (something one does for fun)

Number 19, home address. (6060 N. Ridge Ave., Oklahoma City, OK 73126)

Number 20, office address. (Baptist Medical Center, 1986 Cuba Highway, Oklahoma City, OK 73120)

The key at the right is a summary of what is covered in each biography.

Call on someone to read the key.

Turn your paper over.

We were considering finding information about Shirley Temple. In *Who's Who in America,* Miss Temple is listed under her married name, Black. Some women biographees are listed under their married names, others are not.

Miss Temple's biography has been enlarged for your ease of reading.

Read either the first six lines or the entire entry with the students.

I'm going to distribute a worksheet for you to do. For the answers, refer to Shirley Temple's biography on Worksheet 52.

Distribute the follow-up paper, Worksheet 53.

For a change, you may want to have the students correct their own papers. If so, call on one student at a time to read a question and answer. Collect the papers.

Key to Information

[1] **GIBSON, OSCAR JULIUS,** [2] physician, medical educator; [3] b. Syracuse, N.Y., Aug. 31, 1937; [4] s. Paul Oliver and Elizabeth H. (Thrun) G.; [5] m. Judith S. Gonzalez, Apr. 28, 1968; [6] children: Richard Gary, Matthew Cary, Samuel Perry. [7] BA magna cum laude, U. Pa., 1960; MD, Harvard U., 1964. [8] Diplomate Am. Bd. Internal Medicine, Am. Bd. Preventive Medicine. [9] Intern Barnes Hosp., St. Louis, 1964-65, resident, 1965-66; clin. assoc. Nat. Heart Inst., NIH, Bethesda, Md., 1966-68; chief resident medicine U. Okla. Hosps., 1968-69; asst. prof. community health Okla. Med. Ctr., 1969-70, assoc. prof., 1970-74, prof., chmn. dept., 1974-80; dean U. Okla. Coll. Medicine, 1978-82; v.p. med. staff affairs Bapt. Med. Ctr., Oklahoma City, 1982-86, exec. v.p., 1986-88, chmn., 1988—; [10] mem. governing bd. Ambulatory Health Care Consortium, Inc., 1979-80; mem. Okla. Bd. Medicolegal Examiners, 1985—. [11] Contrb. articles to profl. jours. [12] Bd. dirs., v.p. Okla. Arthritis Found., 1982—; trustee North Central Mental Health Ctr., 1985—. [13] Served with U.S. Army, 1955-56. [14] Recipient R.T. Chadwick award NIH, 1968; Am. Heart Assn. grantee, 1985-86, 88. [15] Fellow Assn. Tchrs. Preventive Medicine; mem. Am. Fedn. Clin. Research, Assn. Med. Colls., AAAS, AMA, Masons, Shriners, Sigma Xi. [16] Republican. [17] Roman Catholic. [18] Avocations: swimming, weight lifting, travel. [19] Home: 6060 N Ridge Ave Oklahoma City OK 73126 [20] Office: Bapt Med Ctr 1986 Cuba Hwy Oklahoma City OK 73120

KEY

[1] Name
[2] Occupation
[3] Vital statistics
[4] Parents
[5] Marriage
[6] Children
[7] Education
[8] Professional certifications
[9] Career
[10] Career related
[11] Writings and creative works
[12] Civic and political activities
[13] Military
[14] Awards and fellowships
[15] Professional and association memberships, clubs and lodges
[16] Political affiliation
[17] Religion
[18] Avocations
[19] Home address
[20] Office address

BLACK, SHIRLEY TEMPLE (MRS. CHARLES A. BLACK), ambassador, former actress; b. Santa Monica, Calif., Apr. 23, 1928; d. George Francis and Gertrude Temple; m. John Agar, Jr., Sept. 19, 1945 (div. 1949); 1 dau., Linda Susan; m. Charles A. Black, Dec. 16, 1950; children: Charles Alden, Lori Alden. Ed. under pvt. tutelage; grad., Westlake Sch. Girls, 1945. Rep. to 24th Gen. Assembly UN, N.Y.C., 1969-70; amb. to Ghana Accra, 1974-76; chief of protocol White House, Washington, 1976-77; amb. to Czechoslovakia Prague, 1989-92; mem. U.S. Delegation on African Refugee Problems, Geneva, 1981; mem. public adv. com. UN Conf. on Law of the Sea; dep. chmn. U.S. del. UN Conf. on Human Environment, Stockholm, 1970-72; spl. asst. to chmn. Pres.'s Council on Environ. Quality, 1972-74; del. treaty on environment USSR-USA Joint Commn., Moscow, 1972; mem. U.S. Commn. for UNESCO, 1973— . Began film career at age 3 1/2; first full-length film was Stand Up and Cheer; other films included Little Miss Marker, Baby Take a Bow, Bright Eyes, Our Little Girl, The Little Colonel, Curly Top, The Littlest Rebel, Captain January, Poor Little Rich Girl, Dimples, Stowaway, Wee Willie Winkie, Heidi, Rebecca of Sunnybrook Farm, Little Miss Broadway, Just Around the Corner, The Little Princess, Susannah of the Mounties, The Blue Bird, Kathleen, Miss Annie Rooney, Since You Went Away, Kiss and Tell, 1945, That Hagen Girl, War Party, The Bachelor and the Bobby-Soxer, Honeymoon, 1947; narrator, actress: TV series Shirley Temple Storybook, NBC, 1958, Shirley Temple Show, NBC, 1960; author: Child Star: An Autobiography, 1988. Dir. Bank of Calif.; dir. Fireman's Fund Ins. Co., BANCAL Tri-State Corp., Del Monte Corp.; Mem. Calif. Adv. Hosp. Council, 1969, San Francisco Health Facilities Planning Assn., 1965-69; Republican candidate for U.S. Ho. of Reps. from Calif., 1967; bd. dirs. Nat. Wildlife Fedn., Nat. Multiple Sclerosis Soc., UN Assn. U.S.A.; bd. dirs. exec. com. Internat. Fedn. Multiple Sclerosis Socs. Appointed col. on staff of Gov. Ross of Idaho, 1935; commd. col. Hawaiian N.G.; hon. col. 108th Rgt. N.G. Ill.; dame Order Knights Malta, Paris, 1968; recipient Ceres medal FAO, Rome, 1975, numerous other state decorations. Mem. World Affairs Council No. Calif. (dir.), Council Fgn. Relations, Nat. Com. for U.S./China Relations. Club: Commonwealth of Calif. Office: Care Academy of Motion Picture Arts & Sciences 8949 Wilshire Blvd Beverly Hills CA 90211

Name _____ Date _____

WHO'S WHO IN AMERICA

Biographee: Shirley Temple Black

1. Where was Shirley Temple born? _____

2. Who were her parents? _____

3. Name Miss Temple's three children? _____

4. From which school did Miss Temple graduate? _____

5. To which country was Miss Temple an ambassador from 1989–1992? _____

6. How old was she when she began her film career? _____

7. What was the name of her first full-length film? _____

_____

8. With which political party is she affiliated? _____

9. To which club does she belong? _____

_____

10. What is her address? _____

ENCYCLOPEDIAS

LESSON 1: Guide Words; Subject Location

OBJECTIVES

1. To review the following information about encyclopedias: definition, arrangement, guide words, subject location
2. To test mastery with a worksheet

MATERIALS

1. If available, a volume from *The World Book Encyclopedia*. If not available, use a dictionary to show the location of guide words.
2. A chalkboard, chalk, and eraser
3. Back-to-back reproductions of the oral practice items on Worksheet 54 and the follow-up paper, Worksheet 55

PREPARATIONS

Write the following on the chalkboard.

Word-by-word Arrangement	*Letter-by-letter Arrangement*
AIR FORCE	AIRCRAFT
AIR POLLUTION	AIR FORCE
AIRCRAFT	AIRPLANE, MILITARY
AIRPLANE, MILITARY	AIR POLLUTION
AIRSHIP	AIRSHIP

On another area of the chalkboard, write: S–Sn

So–Sz

LESSON

Who can tell us what an encyclopedia is? (1. a book, or a set of books, which contains articles on subjects from all branches of knowledge; or 2. a book, or a set of books, which contains information on one field of knowledge)

Some encyclopedias, for example, *The World Book Encyclopedia, Encyclopaedia Brittanica,* and *Compton's Encyclopedia,* contain articles on subjects from all branches or knowledge. Other encyclopedias contain articles on only one subject. *New Encyclopedia of Science* is an example of a set of encyclopedias limited to one subject.

Encyclopedias are usually arranged alphabetically. They may be arranged alphabetically word by word or letter by letter.

The World Book Encyclopedia arranges its entries word by word. Let's look at the chalkboard at some examples.

    Point to AIR FORCE and AIR POLLUTION in the word-by-word list.

AIR FORCE comes alphabetically before AIR POLLUTION.

    Point to AIR POLLUTION and AIRCRAFT in the same column.

Remember, we are alphabetizing word by word.

    Point to AIR in AIR POLLUTION.

AIR in the subject AIR POLLUTION comes before AIRCRAFT.

    Point to AIRCRAFT; AIRPLANE, MILITARY; and AIRSHIP.

These three all start with the word AIR.

    Point to the fourth letter of each.

C, P, S. These subjects are in alphabetical order.

Some encyclopedias arrange subjects letter by letter.

    Point to the list of words that illustrates this method of alphabetizing.

Are these words in the same order as the words in the letter-by-letter column? (no)

    Point to AIR FORCE.

With letter-by-letter alphabetizing, the space after AIR is disregarded. AIR FORCE is alphabetized as if it were joined.

Why is it important to consider the way entries are alphabetized? (If a person is thinking in terms of one of the methods of alphabetizing and doesn't find what he or she wants, the person may conclude that the subject isn't covered and stop looking. It could be that the book is alphabetized another way and the person just hasn't looked far enough.

Open an encyclopedia and point to the guide words. If you don't have an encyclopedia, explain that the guide words are located at the top of the pages similar to the guide words in a dictionary, and use a dictionary to illustrate.

What's the purpose of encyclopedia guide words? (By looking at the guide words, which represent the first and last words on the page, or pages, you can determine whether your subject will be found between them. If the subject you're looking for isn't on the page, you can use the guide words to tell you whether to turn towards the front or towards the back of the volume.)

I'm going to distribute some worksheets that will help us review encyclopedias.

Distribute back-to-back reproductions of Worksheets 54 and 55.

Look at Worksheet 54.

The examples we'll consider are from *The World Book Encyclopedia,* which alphabetizes word by word.

In the first example, you see two guide words. They are RAIN and RAINBOW. Does RAIN DANCE come between those two guide words in a word-by-word arrangement? (yes)

Explain why.

Look at number two.

Will GREAT BRITAIN be found between the guide words GRAY FOX and GREAT BEAR LAKE? (no)

Should you turn back or forward in the volume to look for GREAT BRITAIN? (forward)

Look at number three.

Will you find the subject WILLIAM TELL between TELEVISION and TELSTAR? (yes)

Did you look under William Tell's last name? (yes)

Look at number four.

Will the subject TIGER be found between TIJUANA and TIMBUKTU? (no)

Should you turn towards the front or towards the back of the book to find the subject TIGER? (towards the front)

Look at number five.

Does LOCOMOTIVE come between LOCK and LOCOMOTION? (no)

Should you look towards the front or the back of the volume to find LOCOMOTIVE? (the back)

Find the heading "Locating Subjects."

Five rules are listed. Follow while I read them to you.

Read the rules.

I'm going to give you a couple of minutes to read the rules to yourself and to study them.

Give the students time to read and study the rules.

Look at the practice items at the bottom of the page. There are eight subjects listed.

If an encyclopedia set has one volume for each letter of the alphabet, in which volume will you find GEORGE BERNARD SHAW? (S)

DINOSAUR NATIONAL MONUMENT? (D)

ST. PAUL? (S)

What if there were two S volumes: S–Sn and So–Sz?

Point to S–Sn and So–Sz on the board.

In which volume would you look? (S–Sn)

You spelled ST. out: S-A-I-N-T, didn't' you? (yes)

In which volume would you find *UNCLE TOM'S CABIN?* (U)

What does the underlining mean? (*UNCLE TOM'S CABIN* is a title.)

QUEEN BEATRIX? (B)

LIBERTY BELL (L)

TEAM HANDBALL? (T)

ABRAHAM LINCOLN? (L)

Once more, for locating encyclopedia subjects, remember these rules: (1) Look people up under their last names. (2) Most other subjects should be looked up under their first words. (3) Spell abbreviations out. (4) Books are located by the first words of their titles. (5) Don't look up royal persons by their titles.

Turn your papers over to Worksheet 55. Complete the papers.

After the students finish, have them grade their own papers. Discuss the rules when reading the answers.

ENCYCLOPEDIAS

GUIDE WORDS

Guide Words	*Subjects*
1. RAIN/RAINBOW	RAIN DANCE
2. GRAY FOX/GREAT BEAR LAKE	GREAT BRITAIN
3. TELEVISION/TELSTAR	WILLIAM TELL
4. TIJUANA/TIMBUKTU	TIGER
5. LOCK/LOCOMOTION	LOCOMOTIVE

LOCATING SUBJECTS

Rules

1. People. Look under their last names.
   Example: GEORGE WASHINGTON. Look under WASHINGTON.
2. Most other subjects. Look under the first word.
   Example: LAVA BEDS NATIONAL MONUMENT. Look under LAVA.
3. Abbreviations. Spell abbreviations out.
   Example: ST. LOUIS. Look under S-A-I-N-T Louis.
4. Book titles. Look under the first word.
   Example: *DAVID COPPERFIELD*. Look under DAVID.
5. Royalty. Look under the first name. Don't look under a title. Example: QUEEN ELIZABETH. Look under ELIZABETH.

Practice Items

1. GEORGE BERNARD SHAW
2. DINOSAUR NATIONAL MONUMENT
3. ST. PAUL
4. *UNCLE TOM'S CABIN*
5. QUEEN BEATRIX
6. LIBERTY BELL
7. TEAM HANDBALL
8. ABRAHAM LINCOLN

Name _____ Date _____

ENCYCLOPEDIAS
GUIDE WORDS AND SUBJECT LOCATION

Circle the subjects that can be found between the guide words.

Guide Words	*Subjects*
Example: SNAKE CHARMING/SNEAD, SAM	(SNAPPER)
1. MOHAIR/MOLAR	MOHAWK TRAIL
2. MILLER, LEWIS/MILNE, A. A.	MILLION
3. MASADA/MASK	JOHN MASEFIELD
4. MILITARY SCIENCE/MILK	MILITIA
5. MEDICINE HAT/MEDITERRANEAN SEA	MEDICINE

Circle the letter under which you'd look for each subject.

Example: (A)IR FORCE

1. NORTH POLE	11. QUEEN VICTORIA
2. KING GEORGE VI	12. BOSTON TEA PARTY
3. SAINT BERNARD	13. PRINCE CHARLES
4. JOHN QUINCY ADAMS	14. TRACK AND FIELD
5. BOY SCOUTS	15. STATUE OF LIBERTY
6. PRESIDENT CLINTON	16. LIGHTNING ROD
7. ST. PATRICK'S DAY	17. SCOTLAND YARD
8. TROPICAL RAIN FOREST	18. RALPH WALDO EMERSON
9. *TOM SAWYER*	19. RED CROSS
10. BLACK SEA	20. HONG KONG

LESSON 2: Cross-References; Key Words

OBJECTIVES

1. To review the use of cross-references.
2. To provide practice in picking out key words.

MATERIALS

Back-to-back reproductions of an oral exercise on cross-references and key words, worksheet 56, and a follow-up on key words, worksheet 57

LESSON

Distribute back-to-back reproductions of worksheets 56 and 57.

Sometimes when you look a subject up in an encyclopedia, you find a reference to a different heading.

Look at the cross-reference examples on worksheet 56.

If you look in *The World Book Encyclopedia* under the subject "snowstorm," you'll find a crossreference directing you to the word blizzard instead. There's nothing wrong with the word snowstorm. The encyclopedia's staff just happened to select the word blizzard. The staff has anticipated that some people will look under "snowstorm," so they've entered "snowstorm" and a cross-reference to direct people to the heading "blizzard."

If you look in the *The World Book Encyclopedia* under "wild canary," you'll find a cross-reference telling you to see "goldfinch."

If you look under "First Amendment" in an encyclopedia, you'll probably see this cross-reference: See "Constitution of the United States (Amendment 1)." You've been directed to where the information you're seeking can be found.

A "see" reference refers you from a heading that isn't being used to one that is.

A "see also" reference refers you to additional material about a subject. Also means in addition.

If you look goldfish up in *The World Book Encyclopedia,* you'll find an article on the subject. At the end there's a "see also" reference, which says, "See also Carp."

At the end of the article TEPEE, there are three "see also" cross references. You're referred to "Indian, American," where you'll find pictures of tepees. You're also referred to an article titled "Tent" and another titled "Wigwam."

The article "WILDCAT" has two references to additional material. One is to "Bobcat," the other is to "Serval."

When you need information, you have to look in the right place to find it. Determining specifically what your subject is will enable you to find your information quickly.

Look at number one under Key Words.

Who wants to read it?

Which key words name the subject? (Washington, D.C.)

Let's say we're using an encyclopedia set that has a volume for each letter of the alphabet. Which letter will you look under? (W)

Who'd like to read item two and tell us the key word or words and the volume in which you'd look? (fox, Volume F)

Item 3? (Liberty Island, Volume L)

Item 4? (Korea, Volume K)

Item 5? (lead, Volume L)

Item 6? (whale, Volume W)

Item 7? (Robert Frost, Volume F)

Item 8? (Kilimanjaro, Volume K)

Item 9? (Joan of Arc, Volume J)

Item 10? (Flag Day, Volume F)

Turn the worksheet over.

Explain whether the students are to circle the key words only or whether they are also to answer the questions. Access to encyclopedias will be one of the determining factors. You may want to assign this worksheet for homework or for extra credit.

ENCYCLOPEDIAS:
CROSS REFERENCES; KEY WORDS

CROSS-REFERENCE EXAMPLES

"See" References

1. SNOWSTORM. See Blizzard.
2. WILD CANARY. See Goldfinch.
3. FIRST AMENDMENT. See Constitution of the United States (Amendment 1).

"See Also" References

1. GOLDFISH. See also Carp.
2. TEPEE. See also Indian, American (pictures); Tent; Wigwam.
3. WILDCAT. See also Bobcat; Serval.

KEY WORDS

1. What is the population of Washington, D.C.?
2. To which family does the fox belong?
3. For what is Liberty Island in Upper New York Bay known?
4. What is the capital of the east Asian country Korea?
5. For what is lead, one of the world's oldest known metals, used?
6. To which group of animals does the whale belong?
7. When was the popular American poet Robert Frost born?
8. How many peaks does the extinct volcano Kilimanjaro have?
9. For what is the French national heroine Joan of Arc known?
10. When is Flag Day celebrated?

ENCYCLOPEDIAS: KEY WORDS

In the questions below, circle the key words, and then find answers to the questions in an encyclopedia.

1. Who won the Nobel Prize for literature in 1985? _____

2. What was O. Henry's real name? _____

3. In which city is the Alamo located? _____

4. Where were the Olympic Games held in the summer of 1980? _____

5. From which language did the word robot come? _____

6. What was the Titanic's destination when it struck an iceberg and sank? _____

7. On which dates did Charles Augustus Lindbergh make the first solo nonstop flight

   across the Atlantic Ocean? _____

8. About how many miles does the Mojave Desert cover? _____

   _____

9. In which city is Scotland Yard located? _____

10. In which part of the world did martial arts originate? _____

LESSON 3: Articles; Study Aids

OBJECTIVES

1. To consider the following elements of several *World Book Encyclopedia* articles: birth and death dates, introductory paragraphs, headings, subheadings, authors' credits, cross references, bibliographies, pronunciation
2. To examine the various study aids at the end of *The World Book Encyclopedia* article "Careers"

MATERIALS

Back-to-back reproductions of a page of encyclopedia articles, Worksheet 58; and a page of study aids, Worksheet 59.

LESSON

Today we're going to review encyclopedia articles and study aids.

I'm going to distribute back-to-back reproductions of two pages from *The World Book Encyclopedia*.

   Distribute Worksheets 58 and 59.

Look at Worksheet 58.

At the top, after the page number, you see the guide word, Carrousel.

What is the purpose of guide words? (To tell you the first and last entries on a page, or on facing pages, so you can determine whether the subject you're looking for will be found between them. They also guide you as to whether you should turn forwards or backwards in the book if you have turned to the wrong place.)

The guide word Carrousel represents the first entry of two facing pages. The guide word on the facing page represents the last entry for the two pages.

How many articles are on page 250? (four)

Who'd like to read the titles of the four articles? ("Johnny Carson," "Kit Carson," "Rachel Carson," and "Carson City")

Look at the Johnny Carson article.

What does the date 1925 represent? (the year Johnny Carson was born)

Why is there a blank space inside the parentheses? (Johnny Carson is still living. The space was left for a death date.)

Who'd like to read the paragraph?

   Call on someone.

What does that first paragraph do? (It identifies Johnny Carson and gives some of his characteristics.)

At the end of the article you see the name Joe Robinowitz. Who is Joe Robinowitz? (the author of the Johnny Carson article)

Look at the next article, "Kit Carson."

When was Kit Carson born? (1809)

When did he die? (1868)

Who'd like to read the first paragraph of the entry?

   Call on someone.

That paragraph identifies Kit Carson and tells some of his characteristics.

Who'd like to read the article's three subheads? ("Early life," "Rise to prominence," "Military career")

What is the purpose of the subheads? (to help you find the information you're looking for)

Who wrote the article about Kit Carson? (Howard R. Lamar)

Where can we find more information about Kit Carson? (in the article about John C. Frémont and in the article about Stephen W. Kearny)

At the end of the article you see the subhead "Additional resources." What information is given there? (information about two books on Kit Carson)

What are the titles of the books? (*Kit Carson* and *Kit Carson: A Pattern for Heroes*)

How do you know those are titles? (They're printed in italics.)

What's a bibliography? (a list of sources of information about a particular subject)

Could the word bibliography have been used as a subhead instead of the words "Additional resources"? (yes)

Who wants to read the first paragraph of the next article?

Call on someone.

Rachel Carson is identified in that paragraph. If we want more information, we can read the remaining three paragraphs.

Who wrote the article? (Sheldon M. Novick)

Look at the last entry.

Who wants to read the paragraph about Carson City?

Call on someone.

Make sure that the abbreviation "pop." is read "population."

The article is continued on the next page.

The four articles on this page are short. Some articles are many pages long.

Turn your paper over.

At the end of long articles you often find some study aids to help you.

The study aids on this page are found at the end of the article on careers.

Who wants to read the guide word? (Careers)

Follow me as I read. "Related articles in *World Book* include: Career opportunities. The following articles contain information helpful to a general understanding of a career area. Many of the articles include a *Careers* section and give qualifications and sources of further information."

There's a long list of articles that would be helpful in career research, such as "Accounting," "Advertising," "Agriculture," and so forth.

Next there's a list of "Other related articles." Read that list to yourself.

An outline of the career article is next. It tells you what the article covers.

After the outline, there's a list of questions, which will help you determine whether you've absorbed the information in the career article. If not, you can look back at the article and reread the parts you haven't mastered.

Next is a list of additional resources. What's another name for such a list? (a bibliography)

That completes the study aids for the article on careers.

There are a couple of other entries on the page that we can consider in our review.

Look at the next entry: "Cargo."

Is there an article there? (no)

The encyclopedia staff felt that someone might look under that heading, so it's been entered. The reader is referred to some articles where he or she will find some information about cargo. Look at the entry while I explain it. The reader is told to see the article "Airplane." Then the reader is referred to the article "Airport." To find the specific information about cargo in the "Airport" article, one should look under two subheads: "Cargo handling" and "Airport terms." A picture is included.

The reader can also read the article on "Aviation." The last article the reader is referred to is titled "Ship." It refers the reader to the subhead "Classification of cargo ships" and the subhead "General cargo ships." Pictures are included.

Notice that a semicolon is used to separate articles and to separate subheads. If a comma were used, there might be confusion as to where some titles or subheads ended. A semicolon separates and acts as a double comma or a reduced period.

Look at the next entry: "Carib Indians." Notice that the pronunciation of Carib is given. The pronunciation is presented phonetically, which means by sound. The accent is on the first syllable. Instead of using an accent mark to tell you what to emphasize, the first syllable is capitalized.

As you can see, these encyclopedia articles provide pronunciation, subject information, subheadings, authors' names, cross references, bibliographies, and study aids. The material is presented in an easy-to-use format.

Encyclopedias are good, convenient sources of information.

ily, Apiaceae or Umbelliferae. They are *Daucus Carota,* variety *sativus.*   Albert Liptay

See also **Vitamin** (Vitamin A); **Wild carrot.**

Carrousel. See **Merry-go-round.**

Carson, Johnny (1925-   ), a popular American entertainer, became famous as host of "The Tonight Show" on television. He appeared as a guest host on "The Tonight Show" in 1958 and was the regular host from 1962 to 1992. Carson became noted for his quick sense of humor and natural performing style.

Carson was born in Corning, Iowa, and grew up in Norfolk, Neb. He began his career in Lincoln, Neb., as a radio announcer in the late 1940's. During the early 1950's, Carson worked as a writer and performer in radio and television in Los Angeles. In 1955, he starred in "The Johnny Carson Show," a weekly TV program. Then, for five years, Carson hosted a daytime game show called "Who Do You Trust?"   Joe Robinowitz

Carson, Kit (1809-1868), was a famous American frontiersman. He became known as a skillful and daring hunter, guide, and soldier. People described Carson as brave, gentle, honest, and wise.

Early life. Carson, whose real first name was Christopher, was born in Madison County, Kentucky. His family moved to Boon's Lick, Mo., near Arrow Rock, when he was 1 year old. At the age of 14 or 15, Kit was sent to work for a saddlemaker. He hated the job and ran away in 1826 to join a group of traders headed for Santa Fe, in what is now New Mexico. From 1829 to 1841, Carson worked in the fur trade. He trapped beavers in Arizona, California, Idaho, Wyoming, and the Rocky Mountains and took part in many fights with Indians.

Culver

Kit Carson

Rise to prominence. John C. Frémont, who became a famous government explorer, hired Carson in 1842 to guide his party along the Oregon Trail to South Pass in the Rockies in Wyoming. The expedition passed safely through land of hostile Sioux Indians. Frémont praised Carson in his official reports, which helped make Carson well known. In 1843 and 1844, Carson helped guide Frémont's second expedition, which included a survey of Great Salt Lake in Utah and part of the Oregon Trail. In 1845, Carson guided the explorer's third expedition from Colorado to California and north into Oregon.

The Mexican War broke out in 1846, and Frémont and his group returned to California. They joined the American settlers there in a revolt against the Mexicans who controlled the region. The Americans defeated the Mexicans, and Frémont sent Carson to Washington, D.C., with messages, including news of the victory. But at Socorro, N. Mex., General Stephen W. Kearny ordered Carson to guide him to California. Kearny's troops were attacked by Mexicans at San Pasqual, Calif., near Escondido. Carson and two others slipped through the enemy lines to seek help from American forces stationed in San Diego. They had to walk or crawl for about 30 miles (48 kilometers), but Kearny's troops were rescued.

Military career. After the Civil War began in 1861, Carson was made colonel of the New Mexico Volunteer Regiment. In 1862, he fought the Confederate forces in a battle at Valverde, N. Mex., near Socorro. Carson was later ordered to lead a campaign against the Apache Indians to force them to live on a reservation. In the fall of 1862, Carson gathered together about 400 Apaches and placed them on a reservation that was near Fort Sumner, N. Mex.

Carson then led a campaign against the Navajo Indians. By destroying their crops and animals, he forced about 8,000 Navajos to accept reservation life (see **Navajo Indians**).

In November 1864, Carson fought the Kiowas, Comanches, and other Plains Indians at Adobe Walls, an abandoned trading post in Texas. His force of about 400 men retreated after being attacked by 1,500 to 3,000 Indians. Carson was made a brigadier general in 1865 and took command of Fort Garland in Colorado the following year. Carson resigned from the Army in 1867 because of illness.   Howard R. Lamar

See also **Frémont, John C.; Kearny, Stephen W.**

Additional resources

Gleiter, Jan, and Thompson, Kathleen. *Kit Carson.* Raintree, 1987. For younger readers.
Guild, Thelma S., and Carter, H. L. *Kit Carson: A Pattern for Heroes.* Univ. of Nebraska Pr., 1984.

Carson, Rachel (1907-1964), was an American marine biologist and science writer. She wrote several books that reflect her lifelong interest in the life of the seas and the seashores.

In her writings, Carson stressed the interrelation of all living things and the dependence of human welfare on natural processes. *The Sea Around Us* (1951) describes the biology, chemistry, geography, and history of the sea. *Silent Spring* (1962) called public attention to the wasteful and destructive use of pesticides.

Carson warned that pesticides poison the food supply of animals and kill large numbers of birds and fish. She pointed out that pesticides could also contaminate human food supplies. Carson's arguments helped lead to restrictions on the use of pesticides in many parts of the world.

Rachel Louise Carson was born in Springdale, Pa. She graduated from the Pennsylvania College for Women in 1929 and received a master's degree from Johns Hopkins University in 1932. She worked for the United States Fish and Wildlife Service for most of her adult life.   Sheldon M. Novick

Erich Hartmann, Magnum

Rachel Carson

Carson City (pop. 40,443) is the capital of Nevada and a tourist center. It lies at the eastern base of the Sierra Nevada, near the Nevada-California border. For location, see **Nevada** (political map). Carson City ranks as one of the fastest-growing cities in Nevada. The population increased from 32,022 in 1980 to about 40,500 in 1990.

Related articles in *World Book* include:

Career opportunities

The following articles contain information helpful to a general understanding of a career area. Many of the articles include a *Careers* section and give qualifications and sources of further information.

Accounting	Forestry	Pharmacy
Advertising	Gardening	Photography
Agriculture	Geology	Physical education
Air conditioning	Government	Physical therapy
Air Force, U.S.	Hairdressing	Physics
Anthropology	Home economics	Plastics
Archaeology	Hospital	Police
Architecture	Hotel	Psychiatry
Army, U.S.	Industrial arts	Psychology
Astronomy	Industrial design	Public relations
Audiology	Industry	Publishing
Automobile	Insurance	Radio
Aviation	Interior decoration	Railroad
Ballet	Iron and steel	Real estate
Bank	Journalism	Recording indus-
Biology	Law	try
Bookkeeping	Library	Recreation
Botany	Marine Corps, U.S.	Religious educa-
Building trade	Mathematics	tion
Business	Mechanical drawing	Restaurant
Chemistry	Medicine	Retailing
Chiropractic	Merchant marine	Salesmanship
City planning	Metallurgy	Science
Clothing	Meteorology	Secretarial work
Coal	Mining	Social work
Coast Guard, U.S.	Modeling	Sociology
Commercial art	Motion picture	Speech therapy
Computer	Music	Surveying
Conservation	Navy, U.S.	Taxidermy
Crime laboratory	Nuclear energy	Teaching
Criminology	Nursing	Telephone
Dental hygiene	Occupational ther-	Television
Dentistry	apy	Theater
Disabled	Ocean	Toolmaking
Economics	Ophthalmology	Veterinary medi-
Electronics	Optometry	cine
Engineering	Osteopathic medi-	Vocational rehabil-
Entomology	cine	itation
Federal Bureau of	Personnel manage-	Writing
Investigation	ment	Zoology
Fire department	Petroleum	

Other related articles

Apprentice	Foreign Service	Universities and
Career education	Guidance	colleges
Civil service	Job Corps	Vocational educa-
Community college	Letter writing	tion
Correspondence	Peace Corps	Women's move-
school	Scholarship	ments (Impact of
Employment agency	Service industries	women's move-
Fellowship		ments)

Outline

I. Choosing and planning a career
 A. Learning about oneself   C. Exploring career fields
 B. Discovering the   D. Preparing for a career
    world of work
II. Getting a job
 A. Finding job   D. Completing
   opportunities   application forms
 B. Contacting employers   E. Being interviewed
 C. Writing a résumé
III. The world of work
 A. Agribusiness and natural resources
 B. Business and office
 C. Communications and media
 D. Construction

E. Environment
F. Fine arts and humani-
   ties
G. Health
H. Home economics
I. Hospitality
   and recreation

J. Manufacturing
K. Marine science
L. Marketing and distribution
M. Personal services
N. Public service
O. Transportation

Questions

Why is it important to learn about yourself before exploring career fields?
In what ways can a person learn about job openings?
What are some job characteristics to consider when you explore an occupation?
In what ways can the career you have affect your life?
What is a résumé? Why is it used?
How can high schools help students prepare for a career?
How can abilities influence a person's career choice?
What are the four main levels of career preparation?
What are some sources of information that can help you explore a career field?

Additional resources

Bolles, Richard N. *What Color Is Your Parachute? A Practical Manual for Job Hunters & Career Changers.* Rev. ed. Ten Speed, 1990.
The Encyclopedia of Careers and Vocational Guidance. Ed. by W. E. Hopke. 7th ed. 3 vols. J. G. Ferguson, 1987.
Figler, Howard. *The Complete Job-Search Handbook: All the Skills You Need to Get Any Job and Have a Good Time Doing It.* Holt, 1988.
Krannich, Ronald L. *Careering and Re-Careering for the 1990's: The Complete Guide to Planning Your Future.* Impact, 1989.
Phifer, Paul. *College Majors and Careers: A Resource Guide for Effective Life Planning.* Garrett Park, 1987.
Shanahan, William F. *College—Yes or No.* 2nd ed. Arco, 1983.
Shields, Charles J. *How to Help Your Teenager Find the Right Career.* College Board, 1988.
U.S. Department of Labor. *Occupational Outlook Handbook.* U.S. Government Printing Office. Published every two years.
Several publishers issue series of books covering a wide range of careers. Some examples are *Career Concise Guides* (Watts); *Career Choices* (Walker); and *Careers in Depth* (Rosen Pub.).

Cargo. See Airplane; Airport (Cargo handling; Airport terms; picture); **Aviation; Ship** (Classification of cargo ships; General cargo ships; pictures).

Carib Indians, *KAR ihb,* were a warlike group of South American tribes who lived mainly in the Amazon River Valley and the Guiana lowlands. These fierce Indians ate their war captives. Our word *cannibal* comes from the Spanish name for these Indians. About 1300, the Carib moved from northeastern South America to islands in the Caribbean Sea now known as the Windward Islands. They captured these islands from the Arawak Indians (see **Arawak Indians**).

The Carib were farmers and raised *cassava,* a root crop. They also fished, hunted, and gathered wild plants for food. They lived in small, independent villages. The people had no tribal chiefs or permanent village chiefs, but followed special leaders in time of war. The Carib, especially those who lived on the islands, were expert canoeists. They used large, planked dugouts. They hunted with traps, javelins, and clubs, and shot fish with poison arrows. The Carib are said to have valued personal independence so highly that they looked down on Spaniards who took orders from others.

Like other aggressive tribes, the Carib trained their sons for war from childhood. A boy had to prove his skill and endurance with weapons when he came of age. If he passed the tests, the tribe accepted him as a war-

LESSON 4: Indexes; Special Features

OBJECTIVES

1. To review the use of encyclopedia indexes
2. To give practice in the use of an index
3. To give an overview of some special features contained in *The World Book Encyclopedia*

MATERIALS

1. If available, *The World Book Encyclopedia* index volume
2. If available, Volume C–Ch of *The World Book Encyclopedia*
3. Reproductions of a sample index page, Worksheet 60

PREPARATION

If you have access to Volume C–Ch of *The World Book Encyclopedia,* use a bookmark to designate the article on California.

LESSON

If you want to find an article about Princess Diana in *The World Book Encyclopedia,* how will you go about it?

If someone says, "I'd look in Volume D of the encyclopedia," tell the student that's a good suggestion. Say that a person should always look directly under a subject first. Explain that, in this case, there isn't a direct listing.

If a student suggests looking under Diana's last name, explain that royal persons are listed under their first names.

If someone says, "Look in the encyclopedia index," agree.

If you can't find a subject by looking directly for it, refer to the index.

The World Book Encyclopedia hasn't included an article about Princess Diana. However, if you look in the index, you'll find that Diana has been referred to under two different subjects.

If you have a copy of *The World Book Encyclopedia* index, hold it up.

The last volume of *The World Book Encyclopedia* contains a research guide and an index.

I'm going to distribute a sample page from the index.

Distribute Worksheet 60.

Look at the guide word at the top of the page. That word represents the first entry on the page. Check to see if that is correct.

Wait.

The facing page, which we don't have before us, has a guide word that represents its last entry. The two facing pages are a unit. The guide word on the left page represents the *first* entry on that page. The guide word on the right page represents the *last* entry on that page.

What's the purpose of guide words? (to tell you the first and last words on a page, or on facing pages, so you can determine whether the subject you are seeking can be found between them. If you need to look on another page, you can refer to the guide words to tell you whether to go forward or turn back.)

There are five entries for the name Diana. Find them.

After each entry you'll see some information in brackets. That information identifies the subject.

Brackets look like this.

Draw some brackets on the board. If a board isn't available, draw brackets in the air with the index fingers of both hands.

Look at the first entry for the name Diana. Who would like to read the identifier in the brackets? (Roman mythology)

Since we aren't interested in the Diana of Roman mythology, we'll read further.

Look at the next entry.

Who wants to read the identifier? (book by Montemayor)

Since we're not looking for a book titled *La Diana* by Montemayor, we'll continue.

Who wants to read the identifier for the next entry? (wife of Prince Charles)

Is that the entry we want? (yes)

Since we've started reading the entries for the name Diana, let's finish them. We can come back to this one later.

Who'll read the identifier for *Diana in Love?* (book by Polo)

We're not interested in a book by Polo written in the 1500s about someone named Diana.

The last entry is *Diana of the Crossways,* which is a book by Meredith.

That isn't what we want, is it?

Go back to the entry for Diana, Princess of Wales.

We see two references. The first is a reference to an article about Prince Charles. We are told to look in Volume C, page 382, for a reference to Diana.

What is the relationship between Princess Diana and Prince Charles? (They are married.)

The second reference is to Elizabeth II.

What relation is Elizabeth II to Prince Charles and Princess Diana? (Elizabeth II is Prince Charles's mother and Princess Diana's mother-in-law.)

After the name Elizabeth II, you see the words "picture on ." A picture of Diana is included in the article Elizabeth II.

In which volume is the article? (E)

On what page? (241)

If you can't find a subject in an encyclopedia by looking directly for it, look in the index. The index may refer you to the location of some information under a different topic.

Find Diamond Head.

Who wants to find the identifier? (volcano, Hawaii)

Where will we find a picture of Diamond Head? (There's one in the article on Hawaii in Volume H, page 88. There's a picture in the article on Honolulu in Volume H, page 320.)

What is the purpose of the words "The City," which appear in parentheses after "Honolulu"? (They tell you which subhead to look under in the Honolulu article.)

Can you find an article about Diamond Head by looking directly for it in Volume D? (no)

   Give the students time to check the entry.

There are references to Diamond Head in the articles on Hawaii and Honolulu, but there isn't an article under Diamond Head.

Find the entry for the diamondback rattlesnake.

Can you find an article by looking directly under the subject diamondback rattlesnake? (no)

Where will you find an article that contains a reference to the diamondback rattlesnake? (in the article "Rattlesnake" in Volume R, page 149)

The next reference places the word "picture" before the volume number. It says, "Snake *picture on.*"

That reference has a picture only.

Look at the entry "Diamondback terrapin."

What's a terrapin? (a turtle)

How do you know? (The identifier says "turtle.")

Can you find the diamondback terrapin by looking directly in Volume D? (no)

Follow as I decode the references.

    Read slowly.

In the article "Terrapin" (pause), which is in Volume T, page 176 (pause), there's information about the diamondback terrapin. There's also a picture.

In the index volume of *The World Book Encyclopedia,* there's a section titled "Writing, Speaking, and Research Skills." The section tells how to write short reports, book reports, and term papers; how to prepare and deliver a speech; how to do research; how to take notes; and so forth.

Such information can be helpful.

    If you have Volume C–Ch of *The World Book Encyclopedia,* continue with the following, otherwise end the lesson here.

The World Book Encyclopedia presents information in a form that is easy to find and absorb.

    Hold up the article on California.

Here are some examples in the article on California.

    Hold the book open toward the students, and show and identify the information showcased in illustrations, maps, charts, and tables.

    As a confirmation, here's what you'll present in the 1994 edition: state flag, state seal, state bird, state flower, state tree, map, general information, state capitol, land and climate, timeline, people, population trend, economy, gross state products, government, and so forth.

    Encyclopedias vary. Some may have more depth, more pictures, and more coverage than others. Encyclopedias may vary in other ways, too. Some may have their indexes in separate volumes and others may not. Use different encyclopedias and compare them.

Dewberry [plant] D:176 *with picture*
  Boysenberry B:554
Dewclaw
  Cat *picture on* C:286
  Deer (Legs and hoofs) D:83 *with pictures*
  Dog (Body structure) D:264-265
Dewey, George [American admiral] D:176 *with portrait*
  Navy, United States (The Spanish-American War [1898]) N:88
  Spanish-American War (Manila Bay) So:753
Dewey, John [American philosopher] D:177
  James, William J:27
  Pragmatism P:729
  Progressive education (Progressive educators) P:813
Dewey, Melvil [American librarian] D:177
  Library (Libraries in the United States) L:261-262
Dewey, Nelson [American political leader]
  Wisconsin (table) W:367; (Statehood) W:368
Dewey, Thomas Edmund [American political leader] D:177 *with portrait*
  New York (table) N:313
  Public opinion poll (History) P:863
  Roosevelt, Franklin Delano (Election of 1944) R:461
  Truman, Harry S. (Vice President) T:468; (Election of 1948) T:470
Dewey Decimal Classification [library] D:177
  Dewey, Melvil D:177
  Library (Libraries in the United States) L:261-262
  A Guide to Research Skills **Research Guide:** 31, 40
De Witt Clinton [locomotive]
  Railroad (Developments in the United States) R:115
Dewlap [biology]
  Anole A:518 *with picture*
  Iguana I:50
DeWolfe, Florence Kling [wife of]
  Harding, Warren Gamaliel (Marriage) H:56; (Government scandals) H:58 *with picture*
Dexedrine [medication]
  Amphetamine A:439
  Drug abuse (table: Some commonly abused drugs) D:363
Dexter, Andrew [American settler]
  Montgomery (Government and history) M:766
Dexter, Samuel [American government official]
  Adams, John (table) A:38
  Jefferson, Thomas (table) J:83
  Treasury, Department of the (table) T:407
Dexter, Walter F. [American educator]
  Nixon, Richard Milhous (Education) N:429-430
Dexter Avenue Baptist Church
  Alabama (Places to visit) A:266
Dexter cattle
  Cattle (Other dairy cattle) C:311
Dexter side
  Heraldry (Expansion) H:194
Dextrin [chemical] D:178
Dextrose [sugar] D:178
  Glucose G:236
De Young Memorial Museum [San Francisco]
  California (Museums) C:41
  San Francisco (Libraries and museums) S:96
Dh
  Baseball (Players) B:125
Dhaka [Bangladesh] D:178
  Bangladesh *pictures on* B:079, B:082
Dhal [food]
  Chickpea C:446
Dhala [emirate]
  South Arabia, Federation of So:639
Dharma [religion] D:178
  Buddha (Later life) B:677
  Buddhism (The dharma) B:678
  Manu M:168
Dharma Chakra [symbol]
  India *picture on* I:111
Dharma Commentaries [religion]
  Dharma D:178
Dharma Sutras [religion]
  Dharma D:178
Dhaulagiri [mountain, Nepal]

Himalaya (Peaks) H:233
DHLPP [vaccine]
  Dog (Medical care) D:279
Dhofar [region]
  Oman (Land and climate) O:758
Dhoti [clothing]
  Bangladesh (Way of life) B:80-81
  India (Clothing) I:117
Dhow [boat]
  Ship (Sailing ships in the 1900's) S:411 *with picture*
Dia, Mamadou [Sengalese political leader]
  Senegal (History) S:299-300
Día de la Raza [custom]
  Columbus Day Ci:865
Diabetes [disease] D:178
  Banting, Sir Frederick Grant B:99
  Blindness (Diseases) B:417
  Glucose G:236
  Hypoglycemia H:479
  Insulin I:308
  Pancreas P:128
Diabetes insipidus [disease]
  Diabetes (Diabetes insipidus) D:179
Diabetes mellitus [disease]
  Diabetes (Diabetes mellitus) D:178
  Disease (Hormonal diseases) D:230
  Insulin I:308
Diabetic retinopathy [disorder]
  Blindness (Diseases) B:417
  Eye (Diseases of the retina) E:475
Diabolo [game]
  Top (History of tops) T:332
Diachronic linguistics
  Linguistics (Comparative and historical linguistics) L:336
Diaconate [religious office]
  Deacon D:55
Diacritical mark [language] D:180
Diaghilev, Sergei Pavlovich [Russian ballet director] D:180
  Ballet (Russian ballet) B:53-54
  Dancing (Dancing since 1900) D:30
  Stravinsky, Igor (Early works) So:922
Diagnosis [medicine]
  Blood (Diagnostic tests) B:425
  Disease (Diagnosing disease) D:232
  Internal medicine I:336
  Medicine (Diagnosis) M:364
  Oncology O:761
Diagnosis related group [insurance]
  Hospital (Recent developments) H:374
  Medicine (Government aid) M:371
Diagonal [chess]
  Chess (The board and the men) C:412 *with diagram*
Diagonal stride
  Skiing (Nordic skiing) S:482
Diagraming [grammar]
  Sentence (Diagraming) S:304
Diaguita Indians
  Indian, American (Table of tribes) I:179
Dial
  Clock (Kinds of clocks) Ci:682g
  Sundial So:990 *with picture*
  Telephone (The dialing mechanism) T:99
Dial, The [magazine]
  Emerson, Ralph Waldo (His prose works) E:259
  Magazine (History) M:43-45
Dial tone
  Telephone (How a telephone works) T:98
Dialect [language] D:180
  Chinese language C:510
  Cockney Ci:745
  England (Language) E:294-296
  German language (German dialects) G:138
  Grammar (Grammar and usage) G:304
  Greek language (Development of ancient Greek) G:376
  Hispanic Americans (Who are the Hispanic Americans?) H:245
  Italian literature (The Middle Ages) I:494
  Language L:64
  Pronunciation P:820
  Speech So:772
Dialectic [philosophy]
  Hegel, G. W. F. (Hegel's dialectic) H:165
  Philosophy (Terms used in philosophy) P:384; (Modern philosophy) P:387-389

Socrates (The Socratic method) So:568
Dialectical materialism [philosophy]
  Materialism M:300b
  Marx, Karl (Marx's theories) M:237
  Philosophy (Modern philosophy) P:387-389
Dialogs of the Dead [work by Fénelon]
  Fénelon, François de Salignac de la Mothe- F:71
Dialogue [book by Catherine of Siena]
  Catherine of Siena, Saint C:303
Dialogue [literature]
  Drama (Other parts of drama) D:325
  Greek literature (Philosophical literature) G:378
  Plato (The dialogues) P:567
Dialogue CAI
  Teaching machine (Computers) T:72
Dialogue Concerning the Two Chief World Systems [book by Galileo]
  Galileo (Galileo and the Roman Catholic Church) G:11-12
Dialogues Concerning Natural Religion [book by Hume]
  Hume, David (Hume's life) H:432
Dialysis machine
  Kidney (Kidney diseases) K:312-313
  Nephritis N:128
  Uremia U:245
Diamagnetism [physics]
  Magnetism (Magnetism in atoms) M:60b
Diameter [geometry] D:180
  Circle (Parts of a circle) Ci:558 *with diagram*
  Sphere So:779 *with diagram*
Diamond [baseball]
  Baseball (Baseball terms) B:124
Diamond [gem] D:180 *with pictures*
  Arkansas (Places to visit) A:704
  Carbon (Forms of pure carbon) C:205; (Properties and uses) C:205
  Gem (Crystal shape) G:77 *with picture;* (Index of refraction) G:77; (Sources of gems) G:77-79; (Cutting and polishing) G:79
Diamond [road]
  Road (Intersections) R:359
Diamond [suit]
  Card game (History) C:209
Diamond-ring effect [eclipse]
  Baily's beads B:31
Diamond Head [volcano, Hawaii]
  Hawaii *picture on* H:88
  Honolulu (The city) H:320 *with picture*
Diamond Match Company
  Match (The first matches) M:300-300a
  Ohio (Interesting facts) O:681
Diamond point nail
  Nail (The parts of a nail) N:3 *with picture*
Diamond Shoals [region, Atlantic]
  Cape Hatteras C:188
Diamond Sutra [book]
  Book (The development of printed books) B:478 *with picture*
  Tang dynasty T:25
Diamondback rattlesnake
  Rattlesnake R:149
  Snake *picture on* S:533
Diamondback terrapin [turtle]
  Terrapin T:176 *with picture*
Diamonds Are Forever [book by Fleming]
  Fleming, Ian Lancaster F:233
Diana [Roman mythology] D:183
  See also Artemis *in this index*
  Moon (Mythology) M:793
  Mythology (table) M:980
Diana, La [book by Montemayor]
  Spanish literature (The 1500's) So:758-759
Diana, Princess of Wales [wife of Prince Charles]
  Charles, Prince C:382
  Elizabeth II *picture on* E:241
Diana in Love [book by Polo]
  Spanish literature (The 1500's) So:758-759
Diana of the Crossways [book by Meredith]
  Meredith, George M:417
Dianthus [botany]
  Pink P:473
Diapause [entomology]
  Hibernation (Other kinds of dormancy) H:221
  Metamorphosis (The pupa) M:428-429
  Moth (Migration) M:839

Worksheet 60

GEOGRAPHY

Atlases

OBJECTIVES

1. To review the contents of a standard atlas: maps, gazetteer, world statistical tables, time zone map, special sections, index
2. To discuss copyright dates in relation to atlases
3. To present a historical atlas
4. To explain and compare gazetteer and index entries
5. To present examples of your school library's reference and circulating atlases

MATERIALS

1. If available, an atlas with a recent copyright date
2. If available, a historical atlas
3. Examples of your school library's atlas collection. Include reference and circulating copies of various sizes.
4. A chalkboard, chalk, and eraser

PREPARATIONS

1. In a standard atlas, use bookmarks to designate the following:
   a. The copyright page
   b. The table of contents
   c The gazetteer
   d. A political map, a physical map, and any other maps you wish to present
   e. A table of world statistics

    f. A time zone map, if available

    g. Special sections

    h. An index on a map page, if there is one, and an index in the back of the book

    i. Any special inclusions, such as flags, and so forth

2. In a historical atlas, use bookmarks to designate several maps of interest

3. Put the following on the chalkboard:

Gazetteer

Country	Page	Index Ref.	Sq. Miles	Population
Iceland	63	B2	39,768	228,785

Index

Country	Pop.	Key	Page
Iceland	228,785	B2	63

(When you put the following on the board, enlarge it.)

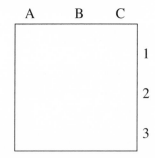

4. Record the call numbers of your school library's reference and circulating atlases.

LESSON

If you want to locate a particular place on a map, for example, Iceland, what kind of book would you refer to? (atlas, encyclopedia)

    If someone responds to the question by suggesting the use of an encyclopedia, agree that an encyclopedia could be used. Then try to elicit "atlas" from the class.

An atlas would be a good source.

What is an atlas? (a book of maps)

Let's look at a standard atlas.

    Hold up the atlas that you've chosen to present in detail.

First let's check the copyright date.

    Open the atlas to the copyright date.

The copyright date of this atlas is _____.

The copyright date is especially important in atlases. Many changes are happening in the world. Boundaries of countries are changing. New highways have been constructed. Populations have changed.

This doesn't mean that older atlases aren't of any value. Many areas of the world are unchanged geographically. However, if you are seeking information about an area that has been changed, look at a current atlas.

When using an atlas, read the table of contents to see what's included.

Show your atlas's table of contents, and read part of it.

This atlas has a gazetteer.

What's a gazetteer? (a geographical dictionary or index)

Show a page or two.

I've put an example on the board.

Point to the gazetteer information as you discuss it.

The entry is for Iceland. We are told that a map can be found on page 63. The coordinates for locating Iceland are B2. Iceland is 39,768 square miles in size. The population is 228,785.

I've drawn a square on the board to represent the outside edges of a map.

Point to the square.

The index reference lists B2 as the key to finding Iceland on page 63.

Point to B with the index finger of one hand and to 2 with the index finger of the other hand. Proceed from the coordinates until your fingers meet.

Iceland will be found where the coordinates B and 2 meet.

Point to the gazetteer population figures on the board.

What does the word population mean? (the number of people in a country or region)

You're probably familiar with political maps.

Turn to a political map, and show it to the students.

Political maps show man-made boundaries of countries, states, cities, and so forth.

Turn to a physical map, and show it to the students.

Physical maps show the earth's surface: oceans, rivers, mountains, deserts, plains.

There are other types of maps, such as rainfall, temperature, vegetation, and road maps.

If you want to show any other types of maps, do so now.

Atlases usually contain world statistical tables. Such tables list major mountains, rivers, islands, and lakes of the world in order of size.

Show a table of world statistics. Read a few entries.

Some atlases contain time zone maps.

Show an example.

By looking at a time zone map, you can find out what time it is any place in the world. You'll see that when it's 4 P.M. in California, it's 7 P.M. in Florida. When it's Friday evening in the United States, it's Saturday in China.

Atlases often include special sections.

If you want to mention and show some specials sections, do so now.

In some atlases, an index to a map may appear on the same page as a map.

Show an example, if you have one.

In the back of an atlas, you'll find an index to all of the maps.

Turn to the back of the atlas, and show the index.

Point to the index example you wrote on the board.

Here's an index entry for Iceland.

What's Iceland's population? (228,785)

What's the key to locating Iceland on the map? (B2)

On which page will the map of Iceland be found? (63)

Compare the gazetteer information to the index information. How are they alike? (They both include the page number, the key, and the population figures.)

How do the differ? (The gazetteer gives the number of square miles in Iceland.)

Present any special features, such as the inclusion of flags.

Some atlases contain only historical maps: maps that depict a region or country at various times in history.

If you have a historical atlas, show a couple of maps, and tell what they illustrate.

If you don't have a historical atlas, tell the students about the kinds of maps that can be found in one, for example, maps of the United States throughout its history.

Introduce examples of your school library's atlases. Tell the students whether the atlases can be found in the reference or circulating sections, or in both. Write the call number(s) on the board.

The call number(s) for atlases in our library is/are _____.

Point to the board.

Atlases are found in the reference and in the circulating sections of most libraries.

Leave the atlases on the table so students can examine them.

SUGGESTION

Teacher. You may want to have a learning center devoted to map skills. If so, put a copy of *Essential Map Skills* (a book of skills for levels 7–12, Hammond, updated 1993) and/or a copy of *Intermediate World Atlas* (an atlas for serious students, levels 7–8, Hammond, updated 1993) on a table for use by those who finish assignments early, for advanced students, and for extra work.

To request a Hammond Education catalog, write Hammond, 515 Valley St., Maplewood, N.J. 07040. (Telephone: 1-800-526-4953)

NOTE

This lesson is designed to be a complete presentation for librarians or an overview for teachers. An in-depth study of atlases can be taught in the classroom.

Webster's New Geographical Dictionary

Webster's New Geographical Dictionary. Springfield, Mass., Merriam-Webster, 1988. 1,408 p.
A pronouncing dictionary of current and historical geographical names.

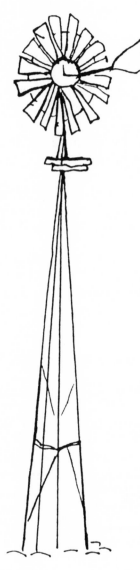

OBJECTIVES

1. To introduce *Webster's New Geographical Dictionary*
2. To give students practice in locating, reading, and interpreting geographical entries

MATERIALS

1. If available, *Webster's New Geographical Dictionary*
2. A chalkboard, chalk, and eraser
3. Back-to-back reproductions of two sample pages from *Webster's New Geographical Dictionary,* worksheets 61 and 62

PREPARATIONS

1. Copy these on the chalkboard:

   word by word   **letter by letter**

   Mud Lake   Mudki
   Mudki   Mud Lake

2. Copy the following on the board:
   ⊗ county seat
   ✪ capital

3. *Teacher.* Find out if your school library has a copy of *Webster's New Geographical Dictionary.*

227

LESSON

Does anyone know where Mud Lake is located?

Since we don't know in which state it can be found or even in which country, how can we find it?

   If students suggest looking in an encyclopedia, agree that that's a possibility. Explain, however, that Mud Lake may be too small to be listed.

Let's start with what we know. We know that Mud Lake is a geographical name. If we look in a book that covers geographical names, we'll find an answer.

   If you have a copy of *Webster's New Geographical Dictionary,* hold it up.

Webster's New Geographical Dictionary covers more than 47,000 current and historical geographical names. It covers all countries. Very small places may not be included. For example, if you look up a tiny town named Weed, you won't find it listed.

I'm going to distribute back-to-back reproductions of two pages from *Webster's New Geographical Dictionary.* As soon as you receive a copy, look on Worksheet 61, find Mud Lake, and be ready to read the entry.

   Distribute back-to-back reproductions of Worksheets 61 and 62.

Who would like to read the information about Mud Lake?

   Call on someone.

   The entry should be read as follows: Intermittent lake. East Washoe County, Nevada.

What does intermittent mean? (stops and starts or disappears and reappears)

Notice that the name Mud Lake is followed by its pronunciation.

Look at the information that appears at the end of the right column. What do we call that information? (a pronunciation key)

Use the key when you need it.

The entry before Mud Lake is Mudki. (See worksheet entry for pronunciation.)

   Point to the board, where you have written the entries Mud Lake and Mudki.

There are two ways of alphabetizing: word by word and letter by letter.

   Point to the first column on the board.

Mud Lake comes before Mudki according to word-by-word alphabetizing. However, *Web-*

ster's New Geographical Dictionary is not alphabetized word by word, but letter by letter. Therefore, Mud Lake is alphabetized as if it were written together.

Erase Mud Lake under the letter by letter entry on the board, and write: MudLake.

Note that the letter k comes before the letter L. If you are used to word-by-word alphabetizing, this can be confusing. When looking for an entry, it may be better to look through all the words with M-u-d, since you won't know which form of alphabetizing is being used unless you read the explanatory note in the front of the book.

Names are usually entered at the significant part of the full name. In other words, if you're going to look up Cape Horn, look under Horn. If you're going to look up Lake Michigan, look under Michigan.

The explanatory notes in the front of *Webster's New Geographical Dictionary* explain the method of alphabetizing and the abbreviations and symbols that are used. I've copied two symbols and their meanings on the board.

Point to county seat and capital.

The first symbol is used to designate a county seat. The second symbol is used to designate a capital.

Turn your paper over to Worksheet 62.

Find Carson at the bottom of the left column.

How many different listings are included in that entry? (four)

Who would like to read the first entry? (1. River, rising in Alpine County, East California, and flowing North and East into Carson Sink, North Churchill County, West Nevada, about 170 miles long.)

The second one? (2. County in Texas. See table at Texas.)

The third one? (3. Urban community [unincorporated], Los Angeles County, California, SE of Los Angeles, population [1980 census] 81,221.)

The last one? (4. Village, county seat of Grant County, S. North Dakota, population [1980 census] 469.)

So there are four Carsons: a river, a county, an urban community, and a village.

Find Carson City.

Who'd like to read the entry? (Carson City, capital of Nevada. . . .)

Who would like to read the information about Carson Peak?

The information about Carson Sink?

Who'd like to read the information about Carson Lake?

The information about Carrot?

   Write Carrot on the board.

Who'd like to read the entry for Carrum?

   Write Carrum on the board.

Is *Webster's New Geographical Dictionary* limited to the United States? (no)

What kinds of geographical places and features does it cover? (towns, counties, rivers, states, villages, mountains, countries, etc.)

When might you want to refer to *Webster's New Geographical Dictionary?* (when you want to identify or find information about a geographical name)

Webster's New Geographical Dictionary is a standard reference book found in most libraries. Our library has/doesn't have a copy.

As you know, reference books can't be checked out; they must be used in the library.

   If someone suggested earlier that Mud Lake could be found in an encyclopedia, ask for a volunteer to look it up. Ask how the volunteer will proceed. If the volunteer says he or she will look under Mud Lake, discuss the fact that there may not be a direct entry. Explain that it may be necessary to use the encyclopedia's index. Have the researcher report his or her findings to the class.

FOLLOW-UP

Have a student helper write a different geographical name, from the list on the next page, on a half sheet of lined paper for each student in the class. Distribute the papers. Have students write their names at the top. Instruct the students to look up the geographical names in *Webster's New Geographical Dictionary* and to copy the information they find.

   If you have a copy of *Webster's New Geographical Dictionary,* put it on a learning center table. If the book is not available, tell the students they will have to do their research in the library. Announce the date on which the papers will be due.

Geographical Names (Total: 36)

Angel Island
Truth or Consequences
Red Wing
Thief River Falls
Sugar Creek
Red Cloud

Broken Bow
Pocahontas
Hiawatha
Tell City
Opportunity
Broken Arrow
Freedom
Mustang
Medicine Bow
Sunday
Black Diamond
Belly
Oldman
Wildcat Mountain
Cochise
Gold Beach
Bath
Battle Mountain
Ruby Lake
Story
Burnt Mountain
Whitehouse Mountain
Pyramid Lake
Medicine Hat
Sunflower
Friendly Islands
Friday Harbor
Tombstone
Tom Green
Timbuktu

You may want to have the students present their information orally, too.

Staple the students' papers together, and put them on a table so everyone can read them.

Mu·dan·ya \mü-'dän-yə\. Town on Gemlik Gulf, an inlet of the Sea of Marmara, Bursa prov., NW Turkey, Asia; port of Bursa.

Mud·dus National Park \'müt-əs-\. National park, N Sweden; 195 sq. m.; coniferous woodland, bogs; established 1942.

Mud·dy \'məd-ē\. River, SE Nevada; ab. 80 m. long; rises in Lincoln co., flows S into Virgin river.

Muddy Bog·gy Creek \-'bäg-ē-, -'bȯg-\. River, SE Oklahoma; ab. 100 m. long; rises in Pontotoc co., flows SE into Red river in S Choctaw co.

Muddy Pass. Mountain pass, Jackson and Grand cos., N Colorado, in Park Range of the Rocky Mts.; 8710 ft.; highway.

Mu·dhol \'müd-ˌȯl\. 1 Former Indian state, now part of Mysore state, W India; 350 sq. m.
2 Town, its ✳, 70 m. SE of Kolhapur; pop. (1961c) 12,100.

Mud·ki \'müd-kē\. Village, Punjab state, NW India, 18 m. SE of Firozpur; scene of British victory Dec. 11, 1845 by Sir Hugh Gough over Sikhs.

Mud Lake \'məd-\. Intermittent lake, E Washoe co., Nevada.

Mud Mountain Dam. See UNITED STATES, *Dams and Reservoirs.*

Mudros. See MOUDROS.

Mu·fu·li·ra \ˌmü-fə-'lir-ə\. Town, Zambia, 21 m. NNE of Kitwe; pop. (1980p) 149,778.

Mufumbiro Mountains. See VIRUNGA MOUNTAINS.

Mug·gia \'mü-jə\. Seaport, Trieste prov., Fruili-Venezia Giulia, NE Italy, on bay in Gulf of Trieste at N end of Adriatic Sea 4 m. SW of Trieste; pop. (1981p) 13,875; 15th cent. cathedral; 9th cent. basilica.

Muğ·la *or* **Mugh·la** \mü(g)-'lä\. 1 Province of SW Turkey. See table at TURKEY.
2 Town, its ✳, near coast; pop. (1980p) 27,162; center of medieval emirate noted for piracy.

Mu·gu, Point \-mə-'gü\. Cape, Ventura co., SW California, SE of Oxnard; site of Point Mugu Naval Air Missile Test Center.

Mu·ham·mad, Ra's \ˌräs-mə-'ham-əd\. Cape, S end of Sinai Penin., NE Egypt, extending S into Red Sea; Sinai Penin. occupied by Israel 1967–1982.

Mu·har·raq \mü-'här-ək\ *also* **Mo·ha·rek** \mō-\. 1 Island in Bahrain, Persian Gulf, ab. 1½ m. NE of Bahrain I.; 4 m. long by 1 m. wide.
2 Town, on Muharraq I.; pop. (1981c) 46,061. See MANAMA.

Mühl·berg \'m(y)ül-ˌbe(ə)rg\. Town, East Germany, on the Elbe ab. 37 m. E of Leipzig; scene of battle Apr. 24, 1547 in which the Elector John Frederick of Saxony was defeated by Emperor Charles V; in World War II taken by U.S.S.R. Apr. 23, 1945.

Mühl·dorf \'m(y)ül-ˌdȯrf\. Town, Bavaria, West Germany, on the Inn river 45 m. E of Munich; pop. (1980c) 14,598; in World War II had subterranean jet plane factory built 1944 by 5000 slave laborers.

Muh·len·berg \'myü-lən-ˌbərg\. County in Kentucky. See table at KENTUCKY.

Muh·len·fels Point \'myü-lən-ˌfelz-\. Cape on S coast of St. Thomas I., Virgin Is. of U.S., West Indies.

Mühl·hau·sen in Thü·ring·en \m(y)ül-'haüz-ᵊn-in-'tür-iŋ-ən\. Industrial city, Erfurt dist., East Germany, 29 m. NW of Erfurt; pop. (1970e) 45,385; textiles, leather, wood and metal products; 13th cent. town hall. First mentioned 775 A.D.; became city c. 1200; to Prussia 1802, to kingdom of Westphalia 1807, again to Prussia 1815.

Mühl·heim am Main \'m(y)ül-ˌhīm-äm-'mīn\. City, Hesse, West Germany, 8 m. E of Frankfurt am Main; pop. (1980c) 24,490; metalworking, leather, rubber, concrete products.

Mu·hu \'mü-(ˌ)hü\ *or Ger.* **Moon** \'mōn\ *or Russ.* **Mu·khu** \'mü-(ˌ)kü\. Island in Baltic Sea bet. Saaremaa I. and the mainland; 80 sq. m.; attached to Estonian S.S.R., U.S.S.R.

Muichdhui, Ben. See BEN MACDHUI.

Muil·rea *or* **Mweel·rea** \mwēl-'rä\. Mountain in SW co. Mayo, W Eire; highest point 2688 ft.

Muir, Mount \-'myü(ə)r\. Peak in Sierra Nevada, E Tulare co., S cen. California; 14,015 ft.

Muir Glacier. Glacier in Glacier Bay National Monument, SE Alaska; covers ab. 350 sq. m.; crossed by 59°N, 136°W. See UNITED STATES, *National Monuments.*

Muir Pass. Mountain pass, Fresno co., S cen. California; in N part of Kings Canyon National Park on the John Muir Trail which extends from Yosemite National Park to Sequoia National Park; 12,059 ft.

Muir Woods National Monument. See UNITED STATES, *National Monuments.*

Mui·zen·berg \'māz-ᵊn-ˌbərg, 'mȯi-zən-\. Town, SW Cape Province, S Rep. of South Africa, on NW shore of False Bay 14 m. SSE of Cape Town; now included in municipality of Cape Town; summer resort; cottage in which Cecil Rhodes died 1902.

Mu·je·res \mü-'her-əs\. An island belonging to Mexico in the Caribbean Sea off NE coast of Yucatán penin.

Mu·ka·che·vo *or Czech* **Mu·ka·če·vo** \'mük-ə-ˌchev-(ˌ)ȯ\ *or Hung.* **Mun·kács** \'müŋ-käch\. Town, Transcarpathian Oblast, W Ukrainian S.S.R., U.S.S.R., formerly in Carpathian Ruthenia, E Czechoslovakia; pop. (1969e) 61,000; tobacco, beer and spirits, furniture; flour mills. Transferred to Hungary 1938, to U.S.S.R. July 29, 1945.

Mu·kah \'mü-(ˌ)kä\. Coastal town, W Sarawak, Malaysia, on island of Borneo, just NE of the Rajang delta; pop. (1980p) 35,831.

Mu·kal·la \mü-'kal-ə\. Seaport and chief town of Hadhramaut, Yemen (✳ Aden), S Arabian Penin., 320 m. NE of Aden; pop. (1976e) 45,000; exports gums, hides, and coffee.

Mu·kā·wir \mü-'kä-wir\. Town, Jordan, E of Dead Sea; site of fortified village (**Ma·chae·rus** \mə-'kir-əs\) of anc. Moab, place where John the Baptist was beheaded.

Muk·den *also* **Mouk·den** \'mük-dən, 'mək-; mük-'den\ *or Chin.* **Shen·yang** \'shən-'yäŋ\ *or formerly* **Feng·tien** \'fəŋ-tē-'en\. Industrial city, Liaoning prov., NE China; pop. (1970e) 3,750,000; strategically located on the Hun for control over N to S routes in S Manchurian plain; one of China's leading industrial cities, producing machinery, transformers, wires and cables, machine tools, flour, textiles, soap, paper, and chemicals; trades in agricultural and forest products. Divided into three major parts: old walled city, ab. 4 m. in circumference; new town, orig. Japanese concession; Teihsi district, center of modern heavy industries. Educational and cultural center; has notable palaces, mausoleums, and monuments.

History: Capital of Kin Tatars in 12th cent.; base for Manchu conquest of China in 17th cent. and site of royal tombs and treasury during rule of Manchu dynasty 1644–1912; in Russo-Japanese War scene of major battle Feb. 19–Mar 10, 1945 when it fell to Japanese; seat of important warlord Chang Tso-Lin during civil war 1924–1928; occupied by Japanese 1931–1945; scene of heavy fighting in Chinese civil war 1947–48; occupied by Communist forces Nov. 1, 1948.

Mukhā. See MOCHA 2.

Mukhmas. See MICHMASH.

Mukhu. See MUHU.

Mu·ko·shi·ma \ˌmük-ə-'shē-mə\. One of the Bonin Is., Japan.

Mu·la \'mü-lə\. Commune, Murcia prov., SE Spain, 18 m. WNW of Murcia; pop. (1970c) 9168; thermal springs and baths; ruins of ancient castle.

Mulahacen. See MULHACÉN.

Mulange, Mount. See MLANJE, MOUNT.

\ə\ abut	\ᵊ\ kitten, Fr table	\ər\ further	\a\ ash	\ā\ ace
\ä\ cot, cart	\à\ Fr bac	\aü\ out	\ch\ chin	\e\ bet	\ē\ easy
\g\ go	\i\ hit	\ī\ ice	\j\ job	\k\ Ger ich, Buch	\ⁿ\ Fr vin
\ŋ\ sing	\ō\ go	\ȯ\ law	\œ\ Fr bœuf	\œ̄\ Fr feu	\ȯi\ boy
\th\ thin	\th\ this	\ü\ loot	\ù\ foot	\ue\ Ger füllen	\ūe\ Fr rue
\y\ yet	\ᵞ\ Fr digne \dēnᵞ\, nuit \nwᵞē\	\yü\ few	\yù\ fury	\zh\ vision

Car·rick·fer·gus \ˌkar-ik-ˈfər-gəs\. **1** Administrative county, E Northern Ireland; estab. 1974. See table at IRELAND, NORTHERN.

2 Municipal borough, its ⊗, co. Antrim, NE Northern Ireland, on N shore of Belfast Lough 9½ m. NE of Belfast; pop. (1981c) 17,633; seaport; historic settlement of Scottish Protestants.

Car·rick·ma·cross \ˌkar-ik-mə-ˈkräs\. Town, co. Monaghan, NE Eire; pop. (1981c) 1768.

Car·rick on Shan·non \ˈkar-ik . . . ˈshan-ən\. Town, ⊗ of co. Leitrim, N Eire, 28 m. SE of Sligo; pop. (1981c) 360.

Carrick on Suir \-ˈshü(ə)r\. Urban district, SE co. Tipperary, S Eire, 18 m. WNW of Waterford; pop. (1981c) 5566; slate quarrying; 14th cent. castle; at nearby Carrickbeg are ruins of a 14th cent. abbey.

Car·ri·er Mills \ˌkar-ē-ər-ˈmilz\ *also* **Car·ri·ers Mills** \-ərz-\. Village, Saline co., SE Illinois; pop. (1980c) 2268.

Car·ring·ton \ˈkar-iŋ-ˌtən\. City, ⊗ of Foster co., E cen. North Dakota, NNW of Jamestown; pop. (1980c) 2641; dairy products.

Carr Inlet \ˈkär-\. Inlet, S end of Puget Sound, W of Tacoma, Washington.

Car·ri·zal \ˌkär-ə-ˈsäl\. Village, Chihuahua state, Mexico, ab. 85 m. S of Ciudad Juárez; scene of skirmish June 21, 1916 in which Mexican government troops defeated Pershing's forces who were in pursuit of Villa.

Car·ri·zo Springs \kə-ˌrē-zō-\. City, ⊗ of Dimmit co., S Texas, 47 m. S of Uvalde; pop. (1980c) 6886; fruit packing, oil refining.

Car·ri·zo·zo \ˌkär-ə-ˈzō-(ˌ)zō\. Town, ⊗ of Lincoln co., cen. New Mexico, 75 m. W of Roswell; pop. (1980c) 1222.

Car·roll \ˈkar-əl\. **1** Name of counties in thirteen states of the U.S. See tables at ARKANSAS, GEORGIA, ILLINOIS, INDIANA, IOWA, KENTUCKY, MARYLAND, MISSISSIPPI, MISSOURI, NEW HAMPSHIRE, OHIO, TENNESSEE, VIRGINIA. For parishes of Louisiana, see *East Carroll* and *West Carroll* in table at LOUISIANA.

2 City, ⊗ of Carroll co., W cen. Iowa, 47 m. SW of Fort Dodge; pop. (1980c) 9705; poultry processing; beans, oats.

Car·roll·ton \ˈkar-əl-tən\. **1** Town, ⊗ of Pickens co., W Alabama; pop. (1980c) 1104; cotton gin; lumber.

2 City, ⊗ of Carroll co., W Georgia, 40 m. WSW of Atlanta; pop. (1980c) 14,078; wire cable; cotton; West Georgia Coll. (1933); incorp. 1856.

3 City, ⊗ of Greene co., W Illinois, 33 m. NNW of Alton; pop. (1980c) 2816; settled 1818, incorp. as city 1853.

4 City, ⊗ of Carroll co., N Kentucky, on Ohio river 37 m. N of Frankfort; pop. (1980c) 3967; livestock, tobacco.

5 Town, a ⊗ of Carroll co., cen. Mississippi; pop. (1980c) 338.

6 City, ⊗ of Carroll co., NW cen. Missouri, 30 m. S of Chillicothe; pop. (1980c) 4700; dairy products.

7 Village, ⊗ of Carroll co., E Ohio, 21 m. SE of Canton; pop. (1980c) 3065; coal mines nearby.

8 City, Dallas and Denton cos., N Texas, 15 m. NNW of Dallas; pop. (1980c) 40,595; wheat farming.

Car·ron \ˈkar-ən\. **1** River, Central region, S cen. Scotland; 20 m. long; flows E into the Firth of Forth.

2 Village, Central region, Scotland, on Carron river ab. 2 m. NW of Falkirk; noted for ironworks, established 1760.

Car·rot \ˈkar-ət\. River, cen. Saskatchewan, Canada; 250 m. long; flows ENE across Manitoba border into Saskatchewan river.

Car·rum \ˈkar-əm\. Town, Victoria, SE Australia, on E shore of Port Phillip Bay.

Carso. See KRAS.

Car·son \ˈkärs-ᵊn\. **1** River, rising in Alpine co., E California, and flowing N and E into Carson Sink, N Churchill co., W Nevada; ab. 170 m. long.

2 County in Texas. See table at TEXAS.

3 Urban community (unincorporated), Los Angeles co., California, SE of Los Angeles; pop. (1980c) 81,221.

4 Village, ⊗ of Grant co., S North Dakota; pop. (1980c) 469.

Carson City. City, ✳ of Nevada, near Lake Tahoe and Carson river 30 m. S of Reno; pop. (1980c) 32,022; alt. 4678 ft.; in agricultural region; tourism; surrounding region formerly important for silver production; site of branch of U.S. mint 1870–93; settled 1858 and named for Kit Carson; became ✳ 1861; made an independent city 1969.

Carson Lake. Lake, SW Churchill co., W Nevada, in S part of Carson Sink; ab. 12 m. long; no outlet.

Carson Pass. Mountain pass, Alpine co., E California, in main range of the Sierra Nevada Mts.; elev. 8634 ft.; discovered during winter 1834–44 by Capt. John Frémont and Kit Carson; used by the forty-niners.

Carson Peak. Mountain, Hinsdale co., SW Colorado; 13,600 ft.

Carson Sink. Shallow marshy region in N Churchill co., W Nevada. See CARSON LAKE.

Carstensz, Mount. See DJAJA, MOUNT.

Car·ta·ge·na \ˌkärt-ə-ˈgä-nə, -ˈjē-, -ˈhä-\. **1** Seaport, ✳ of Bolívar dept., on NW coast of Colombia, 60 m. SW of Barranquilla; pop. (1973p) 292,512; textiles, leather goods; has good harbor with narrow entrance; Colombia's principal oil port; univ. (1824); founded 1533, became one of the most important cities of Spanish America; in 17th cent. second only to Mexico City in W hemisphere; strongly fortified in Spanish times; often attacked by the French and English (Drake in 1585 and Vernon in 1741); Spanish until 1815 when it was taken by Bolívar but soon lost, retaken 1821.

2 *or anc.* **Car·tha·go No·va** \ˌkär-ˌtäg-ō-ˈnō-və\. Seaport city, Murcia prov., SE Spain, on Mediterranean 28 m. ESE of Murcia; pop. (1981c) 167,936; naval arsenal; lead, iron, zinc, copper mines; medieval Gothic cathedral; ancient castle.

History: Founded by Carthaginians under Hasdrubal 227 B.C.; captured by Scipio Africanus 209 B.C. and made a Roman colony; sacked by Goths 425 A.D.; taken by Byzantines 534 and Visigoths 624; held by Moors from 711 until freed by James I of Aragon 1269; sacked by Sir Francis Drake 1585; occupied by duke of Berwick 1707; site of communistic revolt 1873–74.

Car·ta·go \kär-ˈtäg-(ˌ)ō\. **1** Town, Valle dept., W Colombia, 125 m. W of Bogotá; pop. (1973p) 69,154.

2 Province of cen. Costa Rica. See table at COSTA RICA.

3 City, ✳ of Cartago prov., Costa Rica, at foot of Mt. Irazú 14 m. SE of San José; pop. (1973c) 21,753; alt. 4765 ft.; in agricultural region; former capital of Costa Rica; founded 1563; destroyed by earthquakes 1841 and 1910.

Car·te·ia \kär-ˈtē-(y)ə\. Ancient town and port on S coast of Spain (Hispania), at head of bay bordered on E by Mt. Calpe (*or mod.* Gibraltar); founded by Phoenicians; colonized 170 B.C. by Roman soldiers.

Car·ter \ˈkärt-ər\. Name of counties in five states of the U.S. See tables at KENTUCKY, MISSOURI, MONTANA, OKLAHOMA, TENNESSEE.

Carter, Mount. Peak in Glacier National Park, NW Montana; 9834 ft.

Carter Dome \-ˈdōm\. Peak, SE Coos co., N New Hampshire, E of **Carter Notch**; 4860 ft.

Car·ter·et \ˌkärt-ə-ˈret\. **1** County in North Carolina. See table at NORTH CAROLINA.

2 Borough, Middlesex co., cen. New Jersey, 6 m. NNE of Perth Amboy near Staten I.; pop. (1980c) 20,598; metal and oil refining; manufactures steel, tobacco, chemicals.

Car·te·ret \ˌkärt-ə-ˈrā\. Village, W coast of Manche dept., NW France, 20 m. SW of Cherbourg; pop. (1962c) 754, small port. When reached by Allied forces June 18, 1944, N part of Cotentin Penin. (*q.v.*) was cut off; important point in battle of Normandy.

Cart·ers Dam and **Carters Reservoir** \ˈkärt-ərz-\. See UNITED STATES, *Dams and Reservoirs*.

Car·ters·ville \ˈkärt-ərz-ˌvil\. City, ⊗ of Bartow co., NW Georgia, 35 m. NW of Atlanta; pop. (1980c) 9508; cotton; iron ore deposits nearby.

Familiar Quotations

Bartlett, John. *Familiar Quotations*. 16th ed., Justin Kaplan, general editor. Boston: Little, Brown, 1992. 1,405 p.

13 ed. 1955, 14th ed. 1968, 15th ed. 1980, 16th ed. 1992.

Standard collection of passages, phrases, and proverbs traced to their sources in ancient and modern literature. Arranged chronologically by authors.

OBJECTIVES

1. To introduce quotation books in general and *Familiar Quotations* in particular
2. To present a sample page from *Familiar Quotations*
3. To teach students how to use *Familiar Quotations*

MATERIALS

1. If available, a copy of *Familiar Quotations*
2. All of your library's quotation books
3. A chalkboard, chalk, and eraser
4. Reproductions of a sample page from *Familiar Quotations,* Worksheet 63
5. If you plan to assign Worksheet 64, make reproductions. (To do the worksheet, your students will need to have access to a copy of the 13th, 14th, 15th or 16th edition of *Familiar Quotations.*)

PREPARATIONS

Put the following items on the board.
Leave some space between them.

1. c. 2650–2600 B.C.
2. "If you want to be happy, be."
3. Index, 15th edition
   Happy a man as any in world, 309:21
       as kings, 668:14
       ending, 653:6
       if you want to be h. be, 561:6
4. Index, 14th edition
   If you want to be h. be, 684b
5. ib., ibid., ibidem

If you have any other quotation books, look them over and if there is something you want to bring out about any of them, make a note of it.

Teacher. Find out if your school library has a copy of *Familiar Quotations*.

LESSON

Here's a famous quotation: "Nothing can bring you peace but yourself."

   Pause and let the students think quietly for a few moments.

Do you know who said that? (A reply isn't expected.)

Here's another: "If a man does not keep pace with his companions, perhaps it is because he hears a different drummer."

Do you know who said that?

How can you find out?

You can look in a book of quotations to get the answer.

What's a quotation? (a reproduction of something someone has said or written)

There are a number of quotation books. One of the best-known is *Familiar Quotations* by John Bartlett. It's often referred to as Bartlett's *Familiar Quotations*.

   Hold up a copy, if available.

Familiar Quotations is arranged chronologically by authors.

What does chronologically mean? (by time)

The first entry in the 15th edition of *Familiar Quotations* dates back to the time I've written on the board.

   Point to the board to "c. 2650–2600 B.C."

What does the "c" stand for? (circa)

What does circa mean? (about)

What does B.C. stand for? (Before Christ)

Pause.

Point to the information again.

The entry reads "about 2650–2600 years before Christ."

Notice that the latest date is first. We count backwards from the birth of Christ. For example, we'd say one year before Christ, two years before Christ, and so forth.

The first entry in *Familiar Quotations* dates back to about 2650–2600 years before Christ.

Familiar Quotations starts with quotations from the earliest periods of history and progresses down through the years.

Remember, I said the book is arranged chronologically by authors. That means that it's arranged first by date. Then it's arranged by authors. When you get to the year when a particular author was born, you'll find all of his or her quotations listed together.

When you come to 1732, you'll find quotations from George Washington. Abraham Lincoln's quotations are found under 1809. Quotations from Mark Twain are found in the 1835s.

There are basically three ways to locate a selection in *Familiar Quotations*.

If you want a selection representative of a particular time, for example, the 1920s, look in the main body of the book under the date you have in mind.

If you want a quotation from a particular person, for example, Mark Twain, you can look in the author index under Twain, and you'll be referred to Twain's quotations.

If you want to know the author of a particular quotation, look in the word index under one of the quotation's significant words.

Perhaps you want to know who said "If you want to be happy, be."

Point to the quotation on the board.

The most significant word in this quotation is the word "happy."

When you look in the index under "happy," you'll find hundreds of listings. I've put a few on the board.

Point to "happy" in the quotation. Then point to "Happy" in the 15th edition index entry: *Happy* a man as any in world, 309:21.

The word happy is the entry word. The first reference to a quotation containing the word reads "Happy a man as any in world, [page] 309, [quotation] 21."

Point to the index entry word "Happy." Then point to "as kings, 668:14" as you read the following from the board.

"Happy as kings, [page] 668, [quotation] 14."

Point to the index entry word "Happy," and then point to "ending, 653:6."

"Happy ending, [page] 653, [quotation] 6."

Point to the index entry word "Happy."

In the last reference, the subject is "happy," but the word "happy" appears towards the end of the quotation.

Point to "if you want to be h. be" in the 15th edition index listing.

In the entry, notice that happy is abbreviated: "if you want to be h. [happy] be, [page] 561, [quotation] 6."

Notice that all of the entries are alphabetized.

Point to the first word of each index entry for "Happy": a, as, ending, if.

The first words listed, "a, as, ending, if" are in alphabetical order.

Some editions of *Familiar Quotations* give the page and quotation number like the examples you've just seen.

Other editions use a slightly different method. They refer you to the page and column number.

Point to the index listing for the 14th edition: "If you want to be h. be, 684b."

"If you want to be happy, be, [page] 684 [column] b."

The first column on a page is indexed as column "a," and the second is indexed as column "b."

The quotation "If you want to be happy, be" is found in the 14th and 15th editions of *Familiar Quotations*. It's not found in the 13th or 16th editions.

Sometimes a quotation has several significant words. If so, you may find the quotation by looking under any of them.

The author of "If you want to be happy, be" is Alexi Konstantinovich Tolstoi, who lived between 1817 and 1875.

Familiar Quotations has two indexes: an author index and a significant word index. The location of the indexes varies with editions. Sometimes one index may be in the front and the other in the back. Other times they may both be in the back. You can locate the indexes when you look at a copy of the book.

Why might you want to look up a quotation? (to find the exact words of a particular quotation; to determine the author of a passage; because you need quotations on a particular subject or for a particular time)

I'm going to distribute a reproduction of a page from *Familiar Quotations*.

Distribute reproductions of Worksheet 63.

At the top of the page you see the guide words Geronimo and Brown. The first quotation on the page is from Geronimo. The last is from Brown.

Look at the quotation from Geronimo. What does the "c" in front of 1829 mean? (circa: about)

It is believed that Geronimo was born about 1829.

When did Geronimo die? (1909)

Who'd like to read the quotation and its source?

Who'd like to read the third quotation from Carl Schurz?

If the source wasn't read, ask the student to read it.

Who'd like to read the first quotation listed under Charles Dudley Warner?

Call on a student.

If the quotation's source wasn't read, ask the student to read it.

Who wants to read the second quotation from Charles Dudley Warner?

Did you notice the letters "I-b." at the end? Does anyone know what they mean?

"Ib." is an abbreviation for the Latin word ibidem (i-bī′ dem), which means "the same." "Ibid." is another way of saying the same thing.

Point to the board to "ib., ibid., ibidem."

There could be numerous quotations from a source. Instead of naming the source over and over again, the abbreviation "ib." or "ibid." is used.

Charles Dudley Warner's second quotation is from the same source as the first one. It's from *My Summer in a Garden,* which was published in 1870. The quotation is located in the Preliminary of the book.

Look at the third quotation from Charles Dudley Warner.

Who wants to read it?

What is the source? (*My Summer in a Garden,* Third Week)

"Ib." means "the same," so we need to go back up the page until we find a source listed. Under the first entry we see *My Summer in a Garden.*

The first quotation was from the Preliminary part of the book. The third quotation is from the part called "Third Week."

All of Warner's quotations except the first and last have the abbreviation "ib." after them.

Check to see if that is right.

Wait.

The first eight quotations from Warner are from *My Summer in a Garden*. However, they are from different parts. The book has a preliminary, and then it's divided by weeks. One quotation is from the part titled "Third Week," another is from the "Thirteenth Week," and so forth.

Who wants to read the last quotation listed for Charles Dudley Warner?

To summarize, you can find a passage in *Familiar Quotations* by looking under one of the quotation's significant words in the word index or by looking under the author's name in the author index. If you want a quotation representative of a certain time, you can look in the main body of the book under the date you have in mind.

Familiar Quotations is arranged chronologically by authors. Other quotation books have different arrangements.

Quotation books are usually reference books. However, there may be some that circulate, too.

You'll find *Familiar Quotations* in most college, public, junior high school, and senior high school libraries.

Our school library has/doesn't have a copy of *Familiar Quotations*.

The first quotation I read today, "Nothing can bring you peace but yourself," was quoted from Ralph Waldo Emerson.

The second quotation, "If a man does not keep pace with his companions, perhaps it is because he hears a different drummer," was quoted from Henry David Thoreau.

Introduce any quotation books your library has. If you have something particular you wish to say about one or more of the books, say it. Otherwise, just hold each book up, and read its title.

Collect the papers.

FOLLOW-UP

The librarian or teacher may want to use one or more of the following ideas.

1. Have students look up the quotations listed on Worksheet 64. Put a copy of the 13th, 14th, 15th or 16th edition of *Familiar Quotations* at a learning center.

2. Write a quotation from Worksheet 64 on the board. Ask for a volunteer to find out the name of the author. Leave the quotation on the board until the volunteer reports the findings to the class. Continue, if desired.
3. Use Worksheet 64 as an extra credit assignment.
4. Ask students to find quotations from specific authors, for example, Benjamin Franklin, Henry David Thoreau, or Mark Twain. Have the students record the quotations, their sources, and the authors' names and dates.
5. Teachers may want to ask students to include an appropriate quotation with an oral or written report.
6. Assign students to find several quotations on a particular subject.
7. Have students check the accuracy of one or more quotations.

NOTES

1. The quotations listed on Worksheet 64 are all in the 13th, 14th, 15th and 16th editions of *Familiar Quotations*.
2. *Librarian.* A new edition of a quotation book doesn't necessarily mean a better edition. Some of the best quotations in the older editions do not appear in the new ones. Keep your old editions even if you buy new ones. They can be used for reference, for circulation, or for loan to classrooms.

Geronimo[1]
c. 1829–1909

1 It [Arizona] is my land, my home, my father's land, to which I now ask to be allowed to return. I want to spend my last days there, and be buried among those mountains. If this could be I might die in peace, feeling that my people, placed in their native homes, would increase in numbers, rather than diminish as at present, and that our name would not become extinct.

To President Grant from the reservation at Fort Sill, Oklahoma, after surrender [1877]

Carl Schurz
1829–1906

2 Ideals are like stars; you will not succeed in touching them with your hands. But like the seafaring man on the desert of waters, you choose them as your guides, and following them you will reach your destiny.[2]

Address, Faneuil Hall, Boston [April 18, 1859]

3 I will make a prophecy that may now sound peculiar. In fifty years Lincoln's name will be inscribed close to Washington's on this Republic's roll of honor.

Letter to Theodore Petrasch [October 12, 1864]

4 Our country, right or wrong.[3] When right, to be kept right; when wrong, to be put right.

Address, Anti-Imperialistic Conference, Chicago [October 17, 1899]

Ivan Mikhailovich Sechenov
1829–1905

5 All psychical acts without exception, if they are not complicated by elements of emotion . . . develop by way of reflex. Hence, all conscious movements resulting from these acts and usually described as voluntary, are reflex movements in the strict sense of the term.

Reflexes of the Brain [1863],[4] ch. 2

6 The initial cause of any action always lies in external sensory stimulation, because without this thought is inconceivable.

Ib.

---

[1] Goyathlay, Apache chief.
[2] See Emerson, 499:9.
[3] See Charles Churchill, 375:13; John Quincy Adams, 417:17; and Decatur, 445:19.
[4] Translated by S. Belsky.

Charles Dudley Warner[5]
1829–1900

7 To own a bit of ground, to scratch it with a hoe, to plant seeds, and watch the renewal of life—this is the commonest delight of the race, the most satisfactory thing a man can do.

My Summer in a Garden [1870]. Preliminary

8 No man but feels more of a man in the world if he have a bit of ground that he can call his own. However small it is on the surface, it is four thousand miles deep; and that is a very handsome property. *Ib.*

9 What a man needs in gardening is a cast-iron back, with a hinge in it.

Ib. Third Week

10 The toad, without which no garden would be complete. *Ib. Thirteenth Week*

11 Politics makes strange bedfellows.

Ib. Fifteenth Week

12 What small potatoes we all are, compared with what we might be! *Ib.*

13 Public opinion is stronger than the legislature, and nearly as strong as the Ten Commandments. *Ib. Sixteenth Week*

14 The thing generally raised on city land is taxes. *Ib.*

15 Everybody talks about the weather, but nobody does anything about it.[6]

Editorial, Hartford Courant [August 24, 1897]

Charlotte Alington Barnard
[Claribel]
1830–1869

16 I cannot sing the old songs I sang long years ago. *I Cannot Sing the Old Songs[7]*

Thomas Edward Brown
1830–1897

17 A Garden is a lovesome thing, God wot!

My Garden

---

[5] Warner collaborated with Mark Twain on *The Gilded Age.* See 622:8.
[6] The phrase is commonly attributed to Mark Twain, but the *Hartford Courant* has the exact statement in the aforementioned editorial, which is of course unsigned. Warner was associate editor of the paper [1867–1900]. See Mark Twain, 622:18.
[7] I cannot sing the old songs now! / It is not that I deem them low; / 'Tis that I can't remember how / They go. — C. S. CALVERLEY [1831–1884], *Changed*

FAMILIAR QUOTATIONS

Write the name of the author, his date of birth and death, and the source of each of the following quotations.

1. "No race can prosper till it learns that there is as much dignity in tilling a field as in writing a poem." _____

_____

_____

2. "The reports of my death are greatly exaggerated." _____

_____

_____

3. "I can resist everything but temptation." _____

_____

_____

4. "There is no substitute for hard work." _____

_____

_____

5. "Remember that time is money." _____

_____

_____

6. "There is no duty we so much underrate as the duty of being happy." _____

_____

_____

The Columbia Granger's Index to Poetry

The Columbia Granger's Index to Poetry. 10th ed., completely revised, indexing anthologies published through June 3, 1993. Edited by Edith H. Hazen. New York: Columbia University Press, 1994. 2,150 p.

Index to standard and popular poetry collections. Inclusion varies.

   1st ed. 1904; 2d ed. 1918; 3d ed. 1940; 4th ed. 1953; 5th ed. 1962; 6th ed. 1973; 7th ed. 1982; 8th ed. 1986; 9th ed. 1990; 10th ed. 1994, with intervening supplements.

OBJECTIVES

1. To introduce *The Columbia Granger's Index to Poetry*
2. To teach students how to use a poetry index

MATERIALS

1. If available, a copy of *The Columbia Granger's Index to Poetry* or a copy of the book under its previous title: *Granger's Index to Poetry*
2. Back-to-back reproductions of two pages from *The Columbia Granger's Index to Poetry:* a page of sample entries, Worksheet 65; and a List of Anthologies, Worksheet 66
3. Reproductions of the follow-up paper, Worksheet 67

PREPARATION

Teacher. Find out if your school library has *The Columbia Granger's Index to Poetry* or a copy of the book under its previous title: *Granger's Index to Poetry.*

LESSON

I'm going to read the beginning of a famous poem. Listen and see if you know the title.

The wind was a torrent of darkness among the gusty trees,
The moon was a ghostly galleon tossed upon cloudy seas,
The road was a ribbon of moonlight over the purple moor,
And the highwayman came riding—
Riding—riding—
The highwayman came riding, up to the old inn-door.

Who knows the title? ("The Highwayman")

> If no one knows the answer, don't supply it. If someone does know, ask who wrote the poem and proceed from that line.

How can we find out?

We can refer to an index to poetry.

> If a copy of *The Columbia Granger's Index to Poetry* or the book under its previous title, *Granger's Index to Poetry,* is available, hold it up.

If you know the author, title, subject, or first line of a poem, you can usually locate it by referring to *The Columbia Granger's Index to Poetry* or to the index under its previous title, *Granger's Index to Poetry.* In the 10th edition, you can even locate some poems by their last lines.

What do you know about the poem that I read that would enable you to find its title? (the first line; the subject, possibly)

> If a student says "subject," agree, then say there is something else the students know that would give more information and which you'd like to try first.

> Read the first line and pause. Someone should respond with the fact that the first line is known.

You don't know the title, and you don't know the name of the author, but you do know something that would help you locate the poem. You know the first line: "The wind was a torrent of darkness among the gusty trees."

I'm going to distribute some excerpts from *The Columbia Granger's Index to Poetry.*

> Distribute back-to-back reproductions of Worksheets 65 and 66.

Look at Worksheet 65.

The 10th edition of *The Columbia Granger's Index to Poetry* has three indexes: a Title, First Line, and Last Line Index; an Author Index; and a Subject Index. The inclusion of indexing by last lines is new with this edition. Not all of the poems included are indexed by last line, only 12,500 of them.

On Worksheet 65, two examples of the Title, First Line, and Last Line Index have been presented. Two were necessary because we will need to look two places: in the w's for the first line and in the h's for the title.

Look at the top of the paper. The first excerpts are from page 1517 of the Title, First Line, and Last Line Index. The guide word on the right is "Window." The last entry on the page will end with that word. We don't have the full page so we can't see that. The guide word on the left can't be seen because it's on the facing page, which we don't have.

There are three entries in the first excerpt. I'll read the first one to you. Follow as I read.

"Wind tapped like a tired man, The." Poem titles or their last lines aren't entered under "a," "an," or "the." However, if they start with one of those articles, the article is tacked onto the end. This should be read "*The* wind tapped like a tired man!" Notice that only the first word, Wind or The, is capitalized. This isn't a title, it's the first or last line.

Next we read "The Wind's Visit." All three words are capitalized. This is the title.

Emily Dickinson is the poem's author.

The poem can be found in two anthologies, which this index abbreviates as AnAmPo and MeMAP.

What is an anthology? (a collection of poems or stories)

We will see how to decode the abbreviations of anthologies later.

Do you see the first line of the poem I was reading to you when we started this lesson? Who wants to read the poem's first line? ("*The* wind was a torrent of darkness among the gusty trees")

What is the title of the poem? ("The Highwayman")

What is a highwayman? (a robber who preys on travelers)

Who wrote the poem? (Alfred Noyes)

What are the letters following the poet's name? (abbreviations of the anthologies in which the poem can be found)

Notice the sixth abbreviation: FaPON and the letters "abr." What does "abr." mean? (abridged)

What does abridged mean? (shortened)

Yes, in the book designated FaPON, there's an abridged, a shortened version of the poem.

At the beginning, if we had known the title instead of the first line, we could have looked under the title. The second excerpt is from the Title, First Line, and Last Line Index, too, but it's from the h's. Notice the page number, 495, at the left. On the right is the guide word: Hippolytus. Look at the three entries and find "The Highwayman."

Who is the author? (Alfred Noyes)

What are all the letters after the author's name? (abbreviations of the anthologies in which the poem will be found)

Compare the abbreviations under the title with those under the first line. Are they the same? (yes)

　　You may need to hold up Worksheet 65 and point to excerpts 1 and 2.

Turn your paper over to the List of Anthologies. We don't have a complete list. We have only one page, which contains some anthologies in the a's and b's. The actual list is several pages long.

What is the first anthology listed for "The Highwayman" on your Title, First Line, and Last Line Index? (BeLS)

Look at the list of anthologies on Worksheet 66 and tell me what those letters stand for. (*Best Loved Story Poems*)

What would you do if our library didn't have *Best Loved Story Poems?* (Look at the Title, First Line, and Last Line Index again and decode the second symbol. Then check to see if that anthology is available. If not, continue the process until an anthology is found.)

Look at Worksheet 65. Find the Author Index.

On the left is a guide word: Noll. On the right is the page number: 1796.

After Noyes' name, you see his dates: 1880–1958. The inclusion of the author's dates is new with this edition. Underneath Noyes' name you see a list of his poems, which has been abridged on the worksheet.

Can you find the name of an anthology in the Author Index? (no)

You can select a title—perhaps "The Highwayman"—and look it up in the Title, First Line, and Last Line Index. Then you'll be told where the poem can be found.

Look at the next entry: "A Salute from the Fleet." What does "Sels." mean? (Selections)

Perhaps you want to find a poem by subject. Let's say you want a poem about highwaymen. You'd look in the Subject Index, wouldn't you?

On Worksheet 65, look at the Subject Index.

At the left, you see the guide words: Hero and Leander. At the right, you see the page number: 2014.

Put your finger on the subject highwaymen. How many poems are listed about that subject? (six)

Who wants to read the first title listed? ("Brennan on the Moor")

What does the word unknown refer to? (the author)

The fourth listing is "The Highwayman." What information are you given about it? (the author's last name)

So by looking under a subject, we will find a list of poems and the author's last name, but we aren't told in which books/anthologies those poems can be found.

In which index can we look to find a list of anthologies that contain "The Highwayman"? (the Title, First Line, and Last Line Index)

Look at the top of Worksheet 65 again. Follow as I read part of the third entry on the page: "A window cleaner's life is grand! The Window Cleaner."

How can you distinguish between the first or last line and the title? (Titles are capitalized.)

So what is the title of the entry I just read? ("The Window Cleaner")

What is *The Columbia Granger's Index to Poetry?* (an index to poetry)

What information can you have about a poem that will enable you to start searching for it in *The Columbia Granger's Index to Poetry?* (the title, first line, last line, author, or subject)

The 10th edition of *The Columbia Granger's Index to Poetry* has two new features: indexing of last lines and author dating.

Our school library has/doesn't have a copy of *The Columbia Granger's Index to Poetry.*

I'm going to distribute a paper for you to do. Refer to the two worksheets you have for the answers.

Distribute reproductions of Worksheet 67.

NOTE

Librarian. Don't discard old editions of *The Columbia Granger's Index to Poetry,* previously titled *Granger's Index to Poetry.* The inclusion of poems varies, and all editions are useful. Also, if there is more than one edition, loans can be made to classrooms.

Wind tapped like a tired man, The. The Wind's Visit. Emily Dickinson. AnAmPo; MeMAP

Wind was a torrent of darkness among the gusty trees, The. The Highwayman. Alfred Noyes. BeLS; EBEvV; EBNV; FaBV; FaPON, abr.; NTP; OBNV; OBSP; PoLF

Window cleaner's life is grand! A. The Window Cleaner. Elizabeth Fleming. BoTP

Highway to Glory Song. W. H. Auden. Fr. Man of La Mancha. AnAn

Highwayman, The. Alfred Noyes. BeLS; EBEvV; EBNV; FaBV; FaPON, abr.; NTP; OBNV; OBSP; PoLF

Hills are white, but not with snow, The. An Orchard at Avignon. Agnes Mary Frances Robinson. NOBVV; OBTV

Noyes, Alfred (1880–1958)

    Barrel-Organ, The
    Daddy Fell into the Pond
    Highwayman, The
    Salute from the Fleet, A. Sels.
    Search-Lights, The
    Song of Sherwood, A.

Highwaymen

    Brennan on the Moor. Unknown
    Death of Morgan, The. Unknown
    Execution of Luke Hutton, The. Unknown
    Highwayman, The. Noyes
    Mulberry Mountain. Unknown
    Rambling Boy, The. Unknown

XIV

ArOW	Articles of War; a Collection of American Poetry about World War II. *Leon Stokesbury, ed.* (1990) University of Arkansas Press
ArPe	†Arabic & Persian Poems in English. *Omar S. Pound, comp.* (1970) New Directions
AS	American Songbag, The. *Carl Sandburg, comp.* (1927) Harcourt, Brace & Company
ASW	Anglo-Saxon World, The; an Anthology. *Kevin Crossley-Holland, ed. and tr.* (1991) Oxford University Press
AWP	Anthology of World Poetry, An. *Mark Van Doren, ed.* (Rev. and enl. ed., 1936) Reynal & Hitchcock
BAP-89	Best American Poetry, 1989. *Donald Hall, ed.* (1989) Macmillan Publishing Company
BAP-90	Best American Poetry, 1990, The. *Mark Strand, ed.* (1990)Collier Books
BAP-91	Best American Poetry, 1991, The. *Mark Strand, ed.* (1991) Collier Books
BCF	Before Columbus Foundation Poetry, The; Selections from the American Book Awards, 1980–1990. *J. J. Phillips, Ishmael Reed, Gundars Strads, and Shawn Wong, eds.* (1992) W. W. Norton & Company
BeJo	Ben Jonson and the Cavalier Poets; *Hugh Maclean, ed.* (1974) W. W. Norton & Company
BeLS	Best Loved Story Poems. *Walter E. Thwing, ed.* (1941) Garden City Publishing Company
BiHa	Bitter Harvest; an Anthology of Contemporary Irish Verse. *John Montague, ed.* (1989) Charles Scribner's Sons
BIrV	Book of Irish Verse, The; an Anthology of Irish Poetry from the Sixth Century to the Present. *John Montague, ed.* (1974) Macmillian Publishing Company (Also published as The Faber Book of Irish Verse)
BLPA	**Best Loved Poems of the American People, The. *Hazel Felleman, ed.* (1936) Doubleday & Company
BLPL	Best-Loved Poems in Large Print. *Virginia S. Reiser, ed.* (1983) G. K. Hall & Company
BLRP	Best Loved Religious Poems, The. *James Gilchrist Lawson, comp.* (1933) Fleming H. Revell Company
BlSi	Black Sister; Poetry by Black American Women, 1746–1980. *Erlene Stetson, ed.* (1981) Indiana University Press
BOEP	Book of English Poetry, A: Chaucer to Rossetti. *G. B. Harrison, ed.* (New, enl. ed., 1950) Penguin Books
BoLoP	Book of Love Poetry, A. *Jon Stallworthy, ed.* (1974) Oxford University Press (Published in Great Britain as The Penguin Book of Love Poetry)
BoNaP	Book of Nature Poems, A. *William Cole, comp.* (1969) The Viking Press
BoTP	Book of a Thousand Poems, The; a Family Treasury. *J. Murray Macbain, ed.* (1983) Peter Bedrick Books
BoWoP	*Book of Women Poets from Antiquity to Now, A. *Aliki Barnstone and Willis Barnstone, eds.* (1980) Schocken Books
BPo	**Black Poets, The. *Dudley Randall, ed.* (1971) Bantam Books

THE COLUMBIA GRANGER'S INDEX TO POETRY

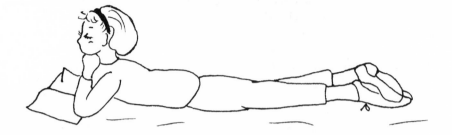

To find the answers to these questions, refer to Worksheets 65 and 66.

1. What is the title of the poem that starts or ends like this: "The hills are white, but not with snow"? _____

2. What is the guide word for page 1517 of *The Columbia Granger's Index to Poetry?*

   _____

3. To which anthology do the letters "AS" refer? _____

   _____

4. What is the title of the poem that starts or ends like this: "The wind tapped like a tired man"? _____

5. Who wrote the "Highway to Glory Song"? _____

6. Which letters represent the anthology in which it can be found? _____

7. Name a poem by Alfred Noyes other than "The Highwayman." _____

8. To which anthology do the letters BeLS refer? _____

   _____

9. What is the guide word on page 495? _____

10. What is the subject heading under which "The Highwayman" can be found? (Look carefully at how the heading is spelled.) _____

    _____

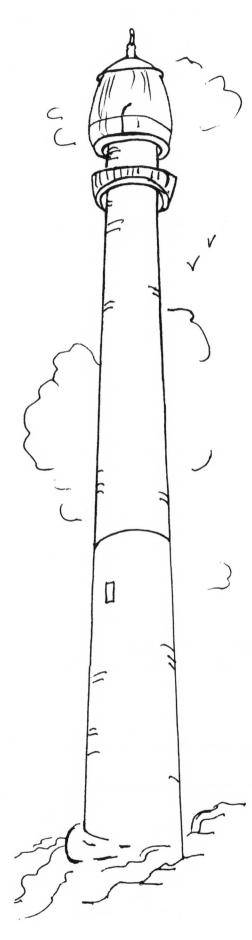

The Junior Authors and Illustrators Series

The Junior Book of Authors. Edited by Stanley J. Kunitz and Howard Haycraft. New York: H. W. Wilson, 1951. 309 p.

Biographical and autobiographical sketches of 289 pioneers of juvenile literature.

More Junior Authors. Edited by Muriel Fuller. New York: H. W. Wilson, 1963. 235 p.

Biographical and autobiographical sketches of 268 young people's authors and illustrators, most of whom came to prominence after the 1951 publication of *The Junior Book of Authors*.

Third Book of Junior Authors. Edited by Doris de Montreville and Donna Hill. New York: H. W. Wilson, 1972. 320 p.

Contains 255 autobiographical or biographical profiles of young people's authors and illustrators, who achieved recognition after the 1963 publication of *More Junior Authors*.

Fourth Book of Junior Authors and Illustrators. Edited by Doris de Montreville and Elizabeth D. Crawford. New York: H. W. Wilson, 1978. 370 p.

Biographical and autobiographical sketches of nearly 250 authors and illustrators of young people's books, most of whom came into prominence after the *Third Book of Authors* was published in 1972.

Fifth Book of Junior Authors and Illustrators. Edited by Sally Holmes Holtze. New York: H. W. Wilson, 1983. 357 p.

Contains information about 243 creators of young people's literature who have achieved distinction between 1978 and 1983.

Sixth Book of Junior Authors and Illustrators. Edited by Sally Holmes Holtze. New York: H. W. Wilson, 1989. 356 p.

Biographical or autobiographical sketches of nearly

250 authors and illustrators who have come into prominence in the field of children's books since the *Fifth Book* was published in 1983.

OBJECTIVES

1. To introduce *The Junior Authors and Illustrators Series*
2. To present sample pages from the *Sixth Book of Junior Authors and Illustrators*
3. To familiarize students with the format, coverage, and indexing of books in the series

MATERIALS

1. If available, one or more volumes of *The Junior Authors and Illustrators Series,* preferably the *Sixth Book*
2. A copy of *Where the Red Fern Grows,* if available
3. Reproductions of Wilson Rawls's biography from the *Sixth Book of Junior Authors and Illustrators,* Worksheets 68a, 68b, 68c
4. Reproductions of the follow-up paper, Worksheet 69

PREPARATION

Teacher. Find out which volume of *The Junior Authors and Illustrators Series* your library owns.

LESSON

Hold up a copy of *Where the Red Fern Grows,* if available.

You may have read *Where the Red Fern Grows.* If you have, you probably liked it very much. If you're interested in reading about the book's author, Wilson Rawls, you can find his biography in the *Sixth Book of Junior Authors and Illustrators.*

If available, hold up a copy of the *Sixth Book of Junior Authors and Illustrators.*

There are about 250 biographies and autobiographies of young people's authors and illustrators in this book.

What is a biography? (a story of someone's life, written by another person)

What is an autobiography? (the story of a person's life, written by oneself)

If you have copies of the following books, hold them up as you mention them.

The Junior Book of Authors and Illustrators Series is a six-volume set. The titles of the volumes are *The Junior Book of Authors, More Junior Authors, Third Book of Junior Authors,*

Fourth Book of Junior Authors and Illustrators, Fifth Book of Junior Authors and Illustrators, and *Sixth Book of Junior Authors and Illustrators.*

Tell the students which of the books can be found in your school library.

Each volume in the series has a cumulative index to all of the previous volumes. That means the index for Volume Two indexes Volumes One and Two. The index for Volume Three indexes Volumes One, Two, and Three. The index for Volume Four indexes Volumes One, Two, Three, and Four. The index for Volume Five indexes Volumes One through Five. The index for Volume Six indexes all six volumes.

If you need to find a particular author or illustrator, to which volume's index would you refer? (the sixth, which indexes all six volumes)

I mentioned that the *Sixth Book of Junior Authors and Illustrators* has a biographical sketch of Wilson Rawls, the author of *Where the Red Fern Grows.* I'm going to distribute copies of that sketch.

Distribute reproductions of Worksheet 68a, 68b, 68c.

Notice that the author's name appears at the top of the page on the left.

His biography starts toward the end of the second column.

When was Wilson Rawls born? (September 24, 1913)

When did he die? (December 16, 1984)

Name one book that he wrote. (*Where the Red Fern Grows; Summer of the Monkeys*)

I'm going to distribute a worksheet. Read it, and then read the sketch. Answer the questions on the worksheet.

Distribute Worksheet 69.

After the students are finished, collect the worksheets.

Leave any copies of *The Junior Authors and Illustrators Series* on a table so the students can examine them.

FOLLOW-UP

For extra credit, assign a written or oral report about an author or illustrator covered in one of the series' books.

FLORENCE ENGEL RANDALL

four years old, Randall's brother gave an old typewriter to the family. She greeted the gift with joy and set it up in the family laundry room, where she produced her first novel, *Hedgerow*, a book for adults that was published in 1967. Her method of writing consists of an attempt to produce three pages a day, working five or six hours a day. Randall also paints and plays the piano, and enjoys gardening.

The Almost Year began as an attempt to write a supernatural story, and Randall did a great deal of research into Ouija boards, seances, and other manifestations of the occult. She studied poltergeists, and conceived the idea of an angry, unhappy girl moving into a family's house. This idea coincided with the introduction of busing into the community where Randall lives, and it took two years for her to complete the story of a fifteen-year-old black girl who comes to stay with a white family in an affluent suburb after the death of her mother. The book was named a 1971 Best Book for Young Adults by the American Library Association.

The Watcher in the Woods is a suspense story of a visitor from another planet that is spying on a girl who has moved into a

new house. *All the Sky Together* is the first-person story of a lonely, idealistic girl who ignores the advice of those who warn her away from her relationships with two wealthy, attractive, but uncaring teenagers, whose actions lead to tragedy. Nancy B. Hammond, writing in *The Horn Book Magazine*, called the protagonist's "struggle for independence . . . poignant and credible."

Randall's stories have appeared in magazines like *Harper's*, *Good Housekeeping*, *Redbook*, *Cosmopolitan*, *Seventeen*, and others. In addition to *Hedgerow*, she has written two other books for adults, *The Place of Sapphires* and *Haldane Station*. She has written several articles for *The Writer* describing the process of writing.

A Watcher in the Woods was made into a film by Walt Disney Productions.

SELECTED WORKS: The Almost Year, 1971; The Watcher in the Woods, 1976; All the Sky Together, 1983.

ABOUT: Contemporary Authors (First Revision), Vol. 41; The International Authors and Writers Who's Who, 1980; Something About the Author, Vol. 5; Who's Who of American Women, 1981-1982; The Writer March 1968; January 1972; The Writers Directory 1988-90.

WILSON RAWLS

September 24, 1913–December 16, 1984

AUTHOR OF *Where the Red Fern Grows*, etc.

Biographical sketch of Woodrow Wilson Rawls by Sophie Rawls:

WILSON RAWLS was born in 1913 in Scraper, Oklahoma. He grew up on the farm he described in his novels. Because there were no schools in that area when he was growing up, his mother taught her children how to read and write. Wilson's grandmother would order books for his mother and she would read the stories to them. She taught them to read by having

WILSON RAWLS

each of them take turns reading from the books after she had first read the stories to them.

Wilson Rawls was still quite young when his grandmother ordered *The Call of the Wild*. When they were finished with the book, his mother gave it to him. It was his first "very own" book. He loved it so much, he carried it with him wherever he went and read a page or two every chance he had.

One day he got the idea that it would be wonderful if he could write a story like *Call of the Wild*. He was about ten years old at the time. From that day for the rest of his life, he knew he wanted to be a writer. He told his father of his dream and asked him if he thought Wilson could be one. His father said he didn't know anything about writing, but told him that if that was what he wanted and he didn't give up, he could do it. His father added that he thought he would need an education to be a writer.

Because he had very little schooling, Rawls decided to get an education by reading books he got from the library. He developed a great appetite for every kind of subject from his reading. His love of reading stayed with him throughout his life.

Wilson started his writing by trying to describe the sounds he heard, and the places and things around his home. His first writing was in the dust of the country road and the sand banks along the river.

The family moved from the farm to Tahlequah, Oklahoma, when Wilson was about fifteen years old. Soon afterward, the Depression hit the country. He left home and crisscrossed the country looking for work. His family also left Oklahoma for California, but their old car broke down just outside of Albuquerque. His father got a job to pay for repairs. They liked the place and ended up settling there.

Wilson kept writing no matter where he traveled. Because he was ashamed of his spelling, grammar, and punctuation, he did not show his writing to anyone. However, he did not throw anything away—he saved his stories in an old trunk in his father's workshop.

Just before we got married, Wilson made a trip to his mother's home (his father had died a few years earlier) and destroyed all his manuscripts. He had decided that he would forget his dream of being a writer. He returned to Idaho Falls, Idaho, and we were married on August 23, 1958. Later that year, he found he couldn't put aside his dream. He told me that he had always wanted to be a writer. I encouraged him to rewrite one of his stories. I told him I could help him with his spelling, grammar, and punctuation.

The story Wilson decided to rewrite was the one based on his boyhood life. He named it "The Secret of the Red Fern." After a year of work on it, he sent it to *The Saturday Evening Post*. They rejected it. I then sent it to *The Ladies' Home Journal*. The *Journal* editors decided it didn't suit their magazine and asked for permission to send it to *The Saturday Evening Post*. This time, the *Post* accepted it and published the story as a three-part serial under the title "The Hounds of Youth." They published it again in 1986.

The novel was published in hardcover in

1961 by Doubleday as *Where the Red Fern Grows*. His second book, *Summer of the Monkeys*, was published by Doubleday in 1976. Both books have won numerous awards, particularly awards voted upon by children. *Summer of the Monkeys* won the 1979 William Allen White Award, and *Where the Red Fern Grows* was a Literary Guild selection. That book was also made into a motion picture by Doty-Dayton Productions and released in March 1974.

After the publication of his first novel, Wilson started to visit schools, speaking to the children, telling them about his childhood. He encouraged them to hang on to their dreams, that they could come true. His dreams did, and so could theirs, if they didn't give up, no matter how tough it may be.

Wilson continued the visits until he became ill in the fall of 1983. During those years, his trips took him to schools in twenty-two states, mostly in the West and South. He was a featured speaker at many teacher and librarian conventions as well.

Wilson Rawls was a member of the Authors Guild. His papers were donated to the Cherokee National Historical Society in Tahlequah, Oklahoma, in 1986. An exhibit of memorabilia and other materials, "The Wilson Rawls Collection," was held there in Spring 1987.

We had no children, but Wilson felt he had many children in the fans who loved his novels. He had one regret, that he couldn't take a copy of his book to his father and say, "It took a long time, Dad, but I made it."

SELECTED WORKS: Where the Red Fern Grows, 1961; Summer of the Monkeys, 1976.

ABOUT: Contemporary Authors, Vol. 1; (New Revision Series), Vol. 5; The International Authors and Writers Who's Who, 1982; Library Journal February 1961; Salt Lake City Tribune April 7, 1974; Something About the Author, Vol. 22; Who's Who in the West, 1965.

DEBORAH KOGAN RAY

August 31, 1940–

AUTHOR AND ILLUSTRATOR OF *My Dog, Trip*, etc.

Autobiographical sketch of Deborah Raphaela Kogan, who writes under the pen name "Deborah Kogan Ray":

PEOPLE stayed to their own streets where I grew up in Philadelphia. When I was a little girl, Carpenter Street was my whole world. There were lots of children on our block. We played alley games behind the long rows of houses. There was always a "Baby in the Air" or stickball game to join. I was good at games, but I felt like an outsider. Mostly, I loved to read and draw pictures.

The summer I was eight, I heard about an arts and crafts program at the playground in the park that was two blocks away. I begged my mother to let me go.

The first day I went to the playground, I was teased about my small size and pushed off the jungle gym, and my dime for water ice was taken. I ran home crying, but I returned the next day. By the end of the summer I had finished several potholders and a lariat keychain, and had been accepted as one of the playground group because of my bravery in leaping off the swings when hitting the "bumps."

It was pure stubborness that kept me returning to the playground that summer. Now I'm glad I did.

From the playground I explored further into Cobbs Creek Park. The park became my special place. I sat by the creek for hours. I followed its path beyond the park to where the city ended. When I was older, I rode my bike up back roads into marshlands where egret and heron lived in reedy grass. In that city park I first learned to love the natural world. Things of nature have remained the subject of my work as an artist.

As long as I can remember, I saw my thoughts in pictures. When I was twelve, I decided I would become an aritst. I took ex-

SIXTH BOOK OF JUNIOR AUTHORS AND ILLUSTRATORS

To answer the following questions, refer to Worksheets
68a, 68b, 68c.

1. Where was Wilson Rawls born? _____

   _____

   _____

2. What was his full name? _____

   _____

3. Name Wilson Rawls first "very own" book. ____

   _____

4. How old was Wilson Rawls when he knew he wanted to be a writer? _____

5. Who published Wilson Rawls's story under the title "The Hounds of Youth"? ____

   _____

6. What title did Doubleday give to "The Hounds of Youth"? _____

   _____

7. What is the title of Rawls's second book? _____

   _____

8. Which book was made into a movie?_____

   _____

9. What was Rawls's one regret? _____

   _____

   _____

10. What relationship was Sophie to Wilson Rawls? _____

The Random House Thesaurus

The Random House Thesaurus. College Edition. N.Y.: Random House, 1992. 812 p.

An A-to-Z thesaurus. Includes synonyms, antonyms, and one or more example sentences for each main entry.

OBJECTIVES

1. To introduce thesauruses
2. To present a sample page from *The Random House Thesaurus*
3. To teach students how to use a thesaurus, and to give them practice using one
4. To check mastery with a follow-up ditto

MATERIALS

1. Your school library's thesauruses
2. A chalkboard, chalk, and eraser
3. Reproductions of a sample page from *The Random House Thesaurus,* Worksheet 70
4. Reproductions of the follow-up, Worksheet 71. (The two worksheets should not be put back-to-back.)

PREPARATION

Teacher. Find out if your school library's thesauruses are shelved in the reference section, in nonfiction, or in both.

LESSON

Do you ever find yourself using the same words over and over?

Maybe you use the word *good* all the time. You may make remarks like these. Mr. Smith is a *good* man. Johnny is a *good* skater. My little brother was a *good* boy today. My mother bakes *good* cakes. Vitamins are *good* for you. I had a *good* time at the dance. I wore my *good* suit.

Let's see if you can think of another word that means good, that can be used in each of those sentences.

Listen to each sentence. Raise your hand if you know a word that can be used to replace the word good. The meaning of the word you supply should be the same, or almost the same, as that of the word good.

Mr. Smith is a *good* man.

Who can think of a word to replace the word good? (kind, honest, honorable, etc.)

    State the sentence again, this time using the replacement word that the student supplied.

    You may want to suggest several other words that could be used.

    Repeat these two steps, or at least the first one, after each of the following sentences in which a substitute for the word good is to be supplied.

Who can replace the word good in each of these sentences?

Johnny is a *good* skater. (skilled, excellent, first-class)

My little brother was a *good* boy today. (obedient, well-mannered, etc.)

My mother bakes *good* cakes. (delicious, wonderful, excellent, etc.)

Vitamins are *good* for you. (healthful, beneficial, etc.)

    Modify sentences when necessary. Example: Vitamins are healthful.

I had a *good* time at the dance. (pleasant, enjoyable, etc.)

I wore my *good* suit. (best, newest, most stylish, expensive, etc.)

The words you've substituted had the same meaning, or almost the same, as the word good.

What do we call words which have the same, or almost the same, meaning? (synonyms)

What do we call words that have the opposite meaning? (antonyms)

Let's see if you can supply antonyms for these sentences.

Mr. Smith is a *good* man. (wicked, evil, mean, cruel, unkind, immoral, etc.)

Johnny is a *good* skater. (awful, unskilled, horrible)

My little brother was a *good* boy today. (naughty, mischievous, disobedient, ill-mannered, etc.)

My mother bakes *good* cakes. (awful, etc.)

Vitamins are *good* for you. (unhealthful, etc.)

I had a *good* time at the dance. (boring, awful, unpleasant, etc.)

I wore my *good* suit. (worst, oldest, etc.)

What do we call words which have opposite meanings of other words? (antonyms)

Write the following on the chalkboard:

antonym
anti

Point to the first three letters of antonym.

The letters "a-n-t" in the word antonym come from "anti," which means opposite. An antonym is a word whose meaning is the opposite of another word.

You hear many words in the news that start with the prefix anti: anti-government, anti-pollution, anti-war.

You can remember that antonyms mean the opposite of other words by remembering the prefix anti. Anti means opposite or against.

We discussed the fact that you may find yourself using the same word over and over. If you want to be more colorful, vigorous, and precise in your language, you'll need to replace some of the tired, overused words in your vocabulary.

A book that can help you do that is a thesaurus.

A thesaurus is a book of synonyms and antonyms.

The plural of thesaurus is thesauri (-rī) / thesauruses (-iz).

You'll want to refer to a thesaurus if you can't think of just the right word you need or if you find yourself using the same words over and over.

I'm going to distribute reproductions of a page from *The Random House Thesaurus*.

Distribute Worksheet 70.

At the top of the worksheet you see two guide words: bidding and billet.

How do guide words help you? (By looking at the two guide words, which represent the first and last words on the page, you can determine whether the word you are seeking will be found between them. If the word you are seeking is not on the page, you can use the guide words to determine whether you should turn forwards or backwards in the book.)

The entry words are in boldface, which means they're in a heavy, dark type. Notice that the entry words start one space to the left of the other lines.

How many entry words are on the page? (12)

Most of us overuse the word big. We speak of a *big* country, a *big* movie star, *big* talk, a *big* heart, a *big* boy.

Let's see if we can find some more precise and colorful words.

Find the word big on your worksheet.

After the word you see the letters "a-d-j." What do those letters mean? (adjective)

What's an adjective? (a word that limits or qualifies a noun)

To be an effective speaker or writer, we should use precise, colorful, and vigorous words.

People judge you by your ability to express yourself—by your language.

Don't you find yourself making instant judgments about people when you hear them speak?

If you were watching television and you saw a gorgeous, graceful woman wearing a dazzling evening dress and she said, "I ain't got no diamonds to wear with this here get-up," wouldn't you make an instant judgment about her educational background and possibly her intelligence?

What if she'd said, "I don't have any jewelry to complement my attire"? Would you have gotten a different impression?

Look at your ditto.

The meaning of big is illustrated in sentences. Follow me as I read them. "Brazil is a *big* country. Farmers expect a *big* corn crop this year. Wrestlers have to be *big*."

The synonyms of *big* are listed next.

   Read the synonyms for meaning number one (large through massive).

Those synonyms all refer to being large in size.

You need to choose synonyms carefully. You can replace the word big with abundant in the sentence "Farmers expect a *big* crop this year." It would then be "Farmers expect an *abundant* crop this year." The word abundant wouldn't be a good choice to replace the word big in the sentence "Wrestlers have to be *big*." You wouldn't want to say "Wrestlers have to be *abundant*." You could say "Wrestlers have to be *large*."

A thesaurus supplies synonyms: words that have the same meaning, but you have to be selective in using them.

Look at the second meaning of big. It's designated by the number two.

Follow as I read.

"The president has a *big* decision to make." "Clark Gable was a *big* star in his day."

Follow while I read the synonyms.

   Read the synonyms for meaning number two (important through high).

Which synonym can we use for big in this sentence: "The president has a *big* decision to make"? (important, etc.)

In this sentence: "Clark Gable was a *big* star in his day"? (major, etc.)

Look at meaning number three.

"No one likes his *big* talk."

In this context, big means pretentious, arrogant, pompous, boastful, conceited, bragging, haughty.

Any of those synonyms for big can be used. Here are two examples. "No one likes his *pretentious* talk." "No one likes his *bragging*."

Look at meaning number four.

"Your charitable contribution shows that you have a *big* heart." "It takes a *big* man to admit his mistakes."

Follow as I read synonyms that express the meaning of the word big as used in the context of those two sentences.

Read the synonyms ("generous" through "great").

Look at meaning number five.

The example sentence is "You're a *big* boy now." The meaning of big in that context is "mature, grown, grown-up, adult."

You can replace big with grown-up: "You're *grown-up* now."

See the letters "A-n-t." in boldface. "A-n-t." is an abbreviation for antonyms.

What are antonyms? (words that mean the opposite of other words)

If you want to find some words that mean the opposite of big, you can look under antonyms.

See the number "1" listed after "Ant." The words following the "1" are antonyms of the synonyms designated "1."

Look at the synonyms. Find number one. The first sentence reads "Brazil is a *big* country." If you want to replace the word big with an antonym, look under Antonyms, number 1. The antonym little can be used. "Brazil is a *little* country."

Look at the second meaning of big. The first sentence is "The president has a *big* decision to make." Big in this context means important. "The president has an *important* decision to make." If we want to replace big or important with its opposite, we can look at number two under antonyms.

Unimportant would be a suitable antonym. "The president has an *unimportant* decision to make."

How many different meanings of the word big are given? (five)

There's a list of antonyms for each of the five meanings of big.

Find the entry "big shot."

What does "n." mean? (noun)

What's a noun? (a word naming a person, place, or thing)

The sentence used to convey the meaning of big shot is "The board of directors is composed of *big shots* from the world of business."

Next you see the word slang. All of the synonyms up to the semicolon are slang: language that's outside of standard usage.

Slang expressions for big shot are "wheel, big gun, big deal, wheeler-dealer, bigwig, big cheese, fat cat, VIP, high-muck-a-muck."

See the semicolon. It designates an end to slang.

Now you have a list of synonyms that are used in standard language. The synonyms are "mogul, nabob, magnate, dignitary, tycoon, somebody, name, personage."

Antonyms of big shots—opposites of big shot—are "nobody, nothing, cipher, nebbish, underling, minion, follower."

The Random House Thesaurus, which we are studying, gives sentences to illustrate the meanings of synonyms. Not all thesauruses do that. Some just give the entry word, for example, big, and then list some synonyms. They don't distinguish between the five different meanings of big: large, important, pretentious, generous, and mature. You have to determine the different shades of meaning yourself.

Does a thesaurus replace a dictionary? (no)

Why not? (A thesaurus doesn't give pronunciations, definitions, origins.)

What is a thesaurus? (a book of synonyms and antonyms)

What's a synonym? (a word that has the same, or almost the same, meaning as another word)

What's an antonym? (a word that has the opposite meaning of another word)

Why would you use a thesaurus? (to find a synonym or antonym)

Why would you want to replace words you overuse? (to express yourself more effectively, colorfully, precisely)

> Introduce your school library's thesauruses, one by one. (Reading the title of each book will be sufficient.)

> Tell the students where the thesauruses are shelved. (Are they shelved in the reference section, in nonfiction, or in both?)

I'm going to distribute a paper for you to do. You'll need to refer to the sample page from *The Random House Thesaurus* for the answers.

> Distribute Worksheet 71.

> Leave the thesauruses on a table. Students may wish to examine them.

posal, bidding; invitation. **5** *McGovern's bid for the presidency failed:* try, attempt, effort, endeavor.
Ant. 1 forbid, prohibit, disallow, ban, bar.

bidding *n.* **1** *The dog came at his master's bidding:* command, order, request, behest, demand, direction, charge, injunction, instruction, mandate, dictate; summons, summoning, invitation, bid, call, beck. **2** *The bidding at the auction reached $500 for one antique chair:* offer, offering, offers, proffering, tendering, proposal.

bide *v.* **1** *Bide with us awhile:* remain, wait, stay, tarry, linger, abide, dwell. **2** *Aunt Mary could never bide children:* endure, put up with, suffer, tolerate, stand.
Ant. 1 go, depart, leave. **2** resist, rebel against, abominate.

big *adj.* **1** *Brazil is a big country. Farmers expect a big corn crop this year. Wrestlers have to be big:* large, huge, enormous, vast, immense, gigantic, mammoth, great, colossal, monumental, grandiose; considerable, sizable, substantial, abundant, ample, prodigious; strapping, husky, bulky, hulking, heavy, massive. **2** *The president has a big decision to make. Clark Gable was a big star in his day:* important, vital, major, consequential, significant, momentous, weighty; prominent, leading, eminent, notable, top, great, chief, main, prime, head, high. **3** *No one likes his big talk:* pretentious, arrogant, pompous, boastful, conceited, bragging, haughty. **4** *Your charitable contribution shows that you have a big heart. It takes a big man to admit his mistakes:* generous, magnanimous, benevolent, liberal, gracious, kind; noble, humane, honorable, just, princely, high-minded, chivalrous, heroic, great. **5** *You're a big boy now:* mature, grown, grown-up, adult.
Ant. 1 little, small, diminutive, microscopic, wee, tiny, petite, minute, miniature, bantam, pygmy, dwarf, pocket-sized, teeny, teeny-weeny, itsy-bitsy. **2** unimportant, insignificant, inconsequential, minor; low-ranking, subordinate, unknown. **3** ordinary, commonplace, modest, humble, unassuming, meek, unpretentious, mild, unpresuming, reserved, restrained, diffident. **4** stingy, cheap, petty, dishonorable, unjust, unchivalrous; ignoble, inhumane, unkind, cruel. **5** little, young, immature.

big-hearted *adj.* *The concert season looked hopeless, but a big-hearted donor came to our rescue:* generous, unselfish, liberal, open-handed, free-handed, benevolent, unstinting, magnanimous, charitable, beneficent, open-hearted; bounteous, bountiful, lavish, prodigal, princely, handsome.
Ant. miserly, niggardly, stingy, tight-fisted, penny-pinching.

bigoted *adj.* *Bigoted people can never bring themselves to admit that the other fellow might be right, too:* prejudiced, intolerant, biased, narrow-minded, closed-minded.
Ant. unbigoted, unprejudiced, tolerant, unbiased, broad-minded, open-minded.

bigotry *n.* *At one time or another, every race and religion has been the object of bigotry:* prejudice, intolerance, bias, narrow-mindedness, closed-mindedness; racism, discrimination, unfairness.
Ant. tolerance, open-mindedness, broad-mindedness.

big shot *n.* *The board of directors is composed of big shots from the world of business:* Slang wheel, big gun, big deal, wheeler-dealer, bigwig, big cheese, fat cat, VIP, high-muck-a-muck; mogul, nabob, magnate, dignitary, tycoon, somebody, name, personage.
Ant. nobody, nothing, cipher, nebbish, underling, minion, follower.

bilious *adj.* **1** *That hot dog gave me a bilious feeling:* sick, queasy, nauseous, green at the gills, sickly, sickening; greenish, bilelike. **2** *The boss was in a bilious mood today:* irritable, peevish, ill-tempered, ill-humored, angry, grumpy, nasty, cranky, crabby, cross, grouchy, petulant, testy, touchy, snappish, short-tempered, cantankerous, huffy, out of sorts.
Ant. 1 good, fine, healthy; attractive. **2** happy, pleasant, good-tempered, amicable, genial, cordial, gentle, mild, warm; agreeable, sympathetic, compliant, winsome.

bilge *n.* *His speech was full of the same old bilge about big government gobbling up the little fellow:* nonsense, drivel, rubbish, stuff and nonsense, foolishness, gibberish, jabber; Slang bosh, bull, hogwash, twaddle, jabberwocky, balderdash, tosh, hooey, bunk, malarkey, piffle, humbug, baloney, rot, horsefeathers, tripe.

bilk *v.* *The lad was bilked out of his inheritance:* swindle, cheat, defraud, victimize, trick, dupe, deceive, bamboozle, hoodwink, fleece, gyp, rook, gull, cozen, Slang take, rip off.

bill *n.* **1** *Did you pay the phone bill?:* statement, invoice, account, chit, charge, charges, fee, reckoning, tally. **2** *A dollar bill doesn't buy much nowadays:* banknote, treasury note, treasury bill, greenback, silver certificate. **3** *How many bills are before Congress this session?:* piece of legislation, proposal; measure, act; law, statute, regulation, ordinance, decree. **4** *On the wall was a sign reading "Post no bills":* poster, placard, advertisement, bulletin; handbill, leaflet, circular, brochure. **5** *The Palace Theater used to have the best vaudeville bill. The waiter brought us a bill of fare:* program, schedule, list, agenda, card, roster, calendar, catalog, inventory, ticket, register, docket.

billet *n.* **1** *The town fathers agreed to find billets for the soldiers:* quarters, lodging, lodgment, residence, dwelling, Slang digs. **2** *He found a billet as a typist at the auto factory:* job, post, situation, berth, position, office, place, appointment. —*v.* **3** *Headquarters said to bil-*

86

THE RANDOM HOUSE THESAURUS

Write a synonym for each of the underlined words below. Designate which of the five meanings applies (meaning 1, 2, 3, 4, or 5). Refer to the sample page from *The Random House Thesaurus*.

1. It takes a <u>big</u> person to dedicate his or her life to helping others.

    _____

    Meaning _____

2. New York City is <u>big.</u> _____

    Meaning _____

3. He's full of <u>big</u> talk. _____

    Meaning _____

4. I'm no longer a child; I'm <u>big</u> now. _____

    Meaning _____

5. I have a <u>big</u> assignment to do. _____

    Meaning _____

Write an *antonym* for each of the words underlined below. Designate which of the five meanings applies.

1. The parade is a <u>big</u> event. _____

    Meaning _____

2. Fido is no longer a puppy; he's <u>big</u> now. _____

    Meaning _____

3. He lives near a <u>big</u> waterfall. _____

    Meaning _____

4. His <u>big</u> talk costs him a lot of friends. _____

    Meaning _____

5. The poor man's donation of his last dime shows that he has a <u>big</u> heart. _____

    Meaning _____

Something About the Author

Something About the Author. Edited by Anne Commire.
Detroit: Gale Research, 1971–. Volume 76, 1994.
A reference series of facts and pictures about early and
contemporary authors and illustrators of books for
young people.

OBJECTIVES

1. To acquaint students with *Something About the Author*
2. To give students an opportunity to examine three sample pages from *Something About the Author*
3. To discuss the Author Index, the Illustrations Index, and the Character Index
4. To present some examples of illustrators' work

PRESENTATIONS

Basic

The basic lesson consists of a presentation which covers each of the objectives listed above.

Enrichment

In addition to the basic lesson, an enrichment presentation may be made. In the enrichment presentation, a volume of *Something About the Author* and back-to-back reproductions of Worksheets 73a and 73b are distributed to each student. Time is allowed for students to write reports on an author or illustrator of their choice from the volumes they receive.

Considerations

1. Are there enough volumes of *Something About the Author* for each student to have one?
2. If not, are there enough volumes for half of the class? If so, the activity can be rotated.
3. Although personal examination of the volumes is of the greatest value, consider how many classes and students will be having this lesson. Ask yourself if the books can withstand the planned amount of handling.

Homework or Extra Credit Assignment

This is an alternative to the enrichment presentation. Use Worksheets 73a and 73b as a homework or extra credit assignment.

MATERIALS

Basic Presentation

1. If available, Volume 49 of *Something About the Author*. Alternative: Any volume of *Something About the Author*
2. If available, some volumes with pictures representative of the kinds included in the series. Suggestions:
   a. A portrait of popular author Judy Blume, Vol. 31, p. 28
   b. A two-page illustration from *Black Beauty,* illustrated by Susan Jeffers, Vol. 50, p. 135
   c. A portrait of writer-producer George Lucas, author of *Star Wars,* Vol. 56, p. 94
      (1) A photograph from the movie *Star Wars,* Vol. 56, p. 97
      (2) A picture of the *Raiders of the Lost Ark* movie poster, Vol. 56, p. 102 (George Lucas wrote the screenplay for *Raiders of the Lost Ark* and was executive producer of the movie.)
3. A chalkboard, chalk, and eraser
4. Back-to-back reproductions of three sample pages from *Something About the Author,* Worksheets 72a, 72b, 72c
5. Reproductions of the first page of the follow-up, Worksheet 73a, items 1–14

Enrichment Presentation

1. One volume of *Something About the Author* for each of your students. If the library doesn't have enough volumes, borrow what is available and have some students use the books while others work on other assignments. Rotate the activities.
2. Back-to-back reproductions of Worksheets 73a and 73b

Homework or Extra Credit Assignment

1. A set, or partial set, of *Something About the Author*
2. Reproductions of Worksheets 73a. If the enrichment lesson wasn't presented, reproduce Worksheets 73a and 73b back-to-back instead.

PREPARATIONS

1. Select an interesting biography. Example: Dick Tracy creator Chester Gould, Vol. 49, pp. 110–118
2. Put the following on the chalkboard:

3. If presenting examples of illustrators' art, use bookmarks to designate the pages you want to present.

BASIC PRESENTATION

If you aren't using Chester Gould as an example, modify the following accordingly.

If you don't have a volume of *Something About the Author,* adapt the lesson to that fact, and present the series verbally and with the excerpts on Worksheets 72a, 72b, 72c.

Would you like to know something about the writer who created Dick Tracy? If so, you can refer to *Something About the Author*.

Hold up Volume 49 and show the cover. Open the book to page 110 and turn it to face the class.

Something About the Author has approximately eight pages about Chester Gould, the creator of Dick Tracy.

With the pages turned toward the students, show all of those related to Gould. This will arouse the students' interest plus demonstrate the abundance of illustrations characteristic of *Something About the Author*. Lay the volume down.

Something About the Author features authors and illustrators of books for young people.

The series began in 1971 with Volume 1. Volume 76 came out in 1994.

How do you think a person can locate a biography of a particular person in *Something About the Author* without looking through 76 or more volumes? (Look in the index)

The Author Index and the Illustrations Index cover the volume in which they appear plus preceding volumes in the series.

If you need to refer to an index, should you look in Volume 1's index, the last volume's index, or some other one? (the last volume's index)

Why? (It'll index all the volumes.)

If you look in Volume 1's index, you'll find an index to only that one volume. If you look in Volume 76's index, you'll find the indexing for 76 volumes.

Here's an example of the information you'll find in the Author Index.

Point to the chalkboard examples as you discuss them.

Gould, Chester 1900–1985. . . 49

Notice that the author is entered in the index under his last name.

What do you think 1900–1985 means? (Gould was born in 1900 and died in 1985.)

The number 49 refers to the volume in which Chester Gould's biography appears.

Obituary. . . 43

What's an obituary? (a notice of death)

Chester Gould's obituary appears in Volume 43.

Gould's obituary appeared before his biography was featured. The popular interest in Dick Tracy necessitated the recent inclusion of the author-illustrator.

Let's look at some examples of the Illustrations Index.

   Point to the chalkboard information you recorded about Robert Lawson.

These numbers refer to where pictures by Robert Lawson can be found.

Notice that Robert Lawson is entered in the index under his last name. The number of the volume in which his work appears is placed before the colon, and the page on which it appears is placed after the colon. Let's see if you can read this information.

Raise your hand if you want to read the specific item to which I'm pointing.

   Point to the following, one at a time.

   5:26 (Volume 5, page 26)
   6:94 (Volume 6, page 94)
   13:39 (Volume 13, page 39)
   16:11 (Volume 16, page 11)
   20:100, 102, 103 (Volume 20, pages 100, 102, 103)

YABC refers to a two-volume book titled *Yesterday's Authors of Books for Children,* which was published by the same publisher who published *Something About the Author.*

Actually two books are being indexed: *Something About the Author* and *Yesterday's Authors of Books for Children.*

Who can read the YABC entry? (Volume 2, pages 222, 224–225, 227–235, 237–241)

Beginning with Volume 50 a Character Index was added to the series. Volumes containing a Character Index have this fact printed on their covers. If you need to locate a character—such as Injun Joe, Friday, or Bob Cratchit—check the Character Index in *Something About the Author.*

Sources: Injun Joe from *The Adventures of Tom Sawyer*. Friday from *Robinson Crusoe*. Bob Cratchit from *A Christmas Carol*.

Something About the Author contains portraits and biographies of authors and illustrators. It also contains examples of illustrators' work.

Here are some pictures representative of those found in the series.

Show some portraits of authors and or illustrators. Also show some illustrators' art. Some suggestions are given under Materials, Basic Presentation, 2.

Each volume of *Something About the Author* is arranged alphabetically.

The biographies range in length from a paragraph or two to eight or more pages.

I'm going to distribute a biographical entry.

Distribute reproductions of Worksheets 72a, 72b, 72c.

The biographee we're considering is Gene Perret (pronunciation rhymes with ferret).

When was Perret born? (April 3, 1937)

Is he still living? (yes)

How do you know? (After the birth date and hyphen, there's no death date.)

Let's see what's covered. Follow me as I read the main subheadings.

Personal
Addresses
Career
Awards, Honors
Writings
Work in Progress
Sidelights

Read the entire biography. Afterwards refer to it to answer the questions on the worksheet that will be distributed to you.

Distribute Worksheet 73a, items 1-14 only.

If you're going to cover only the basic presentation, conclude the lesson here.

ENRICHMENT PRESENTATION

I'm going to give a volume of *Something About the Author* to each of you. Find an author or illustrator about whom you'd like to report. Select someone who has a full biographical entry. Don't choose anyone who has a brief entry. I'll distribute a report form which you are to fill out. After you complete your work, browse through your volume until the class is finished.

Distribute the books and the report forms, Worksheets 73a, 73b.

At the end of the period you may want to collect the books in mixed order and assign a student to arrange them properly. Alternative: Call the volume numbers slowly, beginning with Volume 1, and let each student come forward and place his or her book in order on a table or cart and then line up.

HOMEWORK OR EXTRA CREDIT ASSIGNMENT

Ask students to find a biography about their favorite author or illustrator in *Something About the Author* and to report about him or her on Worksheet 73a. Review the fact that they'll want to use the index in the latest volume to locate an author or illustrator.

If the enrichment lesson was presented to the class, don't assign Worksheet 73b, the students will have done that page. Worksheet 73a can be used a second time without a sense of duplication.

If the enrichment lesson wasn't presented, assign Worksheets 73a and 73b.

Having students locate authors or illustrators of their choice is ideal. It gives students practice in locating specific biographies from the entire set of volumes.

get bored or lonely with the radio on while painting, but I find writing very difficult as it must be done in silence—and a blank sheet of writing paper is far more daunting than a white sheet of water-color board waiting for an image."

One of Penney's trademarks is that each of his picture's contain his wife's maiden name initials: C.A.W. "I hope to continue working on children's picture books," he says, "as I feel they are the very best expression of my work and the most exciting area of publishing in which to practice."

*   *   *

PERRET, Gene 1937-

■ Personal

Surname rhymes with "ferret"; born April 3, 1937, in Philadelphia, PA; son of Joseph H. (a shipping clerk) and Mary (a homemaker; maiden name, Martin) Perret; married Joanne Bonavitacola (a nurse), October 11, 1958; children: Joseph M., Terry, Carole, Linda. *Education:* Attended Drexel Institute of Technology, 1956-61.

■ Addresses

Home—San Marino, CA.

GENE PERRET

■ Career

Comedy writer for comedians and television programs, including *The Jim Nabors Hour,* 1969-70, *Laugh-In,* 1970, and *The Carol Burnett Show,* 1973-78; script supervisor, *The Bill Cosby Show,* 1972; television writer for Bob Hope, 1969-78, head writer, 1978—; producer for television programs, including *Welcome Back Kotter,* 1978, *Three's Company,* 1978, and *The Tim Conway Show,* 1979-80. Professional speaker, 1977—. *Member:* Writers Guild of America.

■ Awards, Honors

Emmy Awards for writing, National Association of Television Arts and Sciences, 1974, 1975, and 1978, and Writers Guild Award, 1974, all for *The Carol Burnett Show;* named outstanding discovery in the field of humor by the International Platform Association, 1983, for the speech "Laughing Matters."

■ Writings

FOR YOUNG READERS

How to Write and Sell Your Sense of Humor, Writer's Digest, 1982, published as *Comedy Writing Step by Step,* foreword by Carol Burnett, Samuel French, 1990.
Funny Comebacks to Rude Remarks, illustrated by Sanford Hoffman, Sterling, 1990.
Comedy Writing Workbook, Sterling, 1990.
Laugh-A-Minute Joke Book, illustrated by Hoffman, Sterling, 1991.
Super Funny School Jokes, illustrated by Hoffman, Sterling, 1991.
(With daughter, Terry Perret Martin) *Great One-liners,* illustrated by Myron Miller, Sterling, 1992.

OTHER

Hit or Miss Management: The World's First Organic, Natural, Holistic, Environmentally Sound Management Technique, Houghton, 1980.
How to Hold Your Audience with Humor: A Guide to More Effective Speaking, Writer's Digest, 1984.
Using Humor for Effective Business Speaking, Sterling, 1989.
(With daughter, Linda Perret) *Gene Perret's Funny Business: Speaker's Treasury of Business Humor for All Occasions,* Prentice-Hall, 1990.
(With L. Perret) *Bigshots, Pipsqueaks, and Windbags: Jokes, Stories, and One-liners about People, Power, and Politics,* Prentice-Hall, 1993.
Shift Your Writing Career into High Gear, Writer's Digest, 1993.

Contributor to *You Know You're a Workaholic If—,* by Mel Loftus, illustrations by Rick Penn-Kraus, Price, Stern, 1991.

From *Something About the Author,* Volume 76, page 173, edited by Diane Telgen. Copyright © 1994 by Gale Research Company. Reprinted by permission of the publisher.

■ Work in Progress

If Bob Hope Calls, Tell Him I'm Not Home, a reminiscence of working with Bob Hope; *Make Me Laugh or Else,* a novel.

■ Sidelights

Gene Perret told *SATA:* "My writing career was actually a hobby that got carried away. As a youngster in grade school, I was fascinated with comedy. I listened to Red Skelton on the radio, I enjoyed Abbot and Costello films, and I idolized Bob Hope, who was then both a radio and movie star. I loved to make people laugh. People now ask if I was the 'class clown.' I wasn't; that required courage. Getting in trouble with the teacher was too big a risk for me to take, so I behaved myself. However, I would sometimes tell the class clown what to say and do. As a professional comedy writer now, I suppose that's what I still do.

"Writing witty sayings became a hobby that I enjoyed through high school. I wrote a humorous column for the school paper. Even having to work for a living and go to night school at the same time didn't dampen my

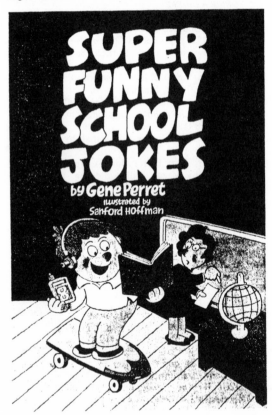

Perret shares his sense of humor with a schoolage audience in this book of wisecracks. (Cover illustration by Sanford Hoffman.)

comedy spirits. My coworkers enjoyed books of cartoons about our office that I drew and collections of photographs that I captioned. That eventually led to my writing career.

"My first supervisor retired, and our office planned a going-away party for him. Because I dabbled with comedy writing, they asked me to emcee his banquet and write a short 'roast'—sort of like a Johnny Carson or Jay Leno monologue about the guest of honor. The roast went over well. Not only the audience enjoyed it, but also the guest of honor and his family. It was important to me to do humor about this gentleman that kidded him, but didn't offend.

"The people I worked with then asked if I would do another retirement a few weeks later, then another a few weeks after that. Soon I was writing and delivering a new monologue about two or three times a month. I became the Bob Hope of our office.

"After a few years of this, I gained such a local reputation that people began to call me and ask to see my material. That's how I began to write material for Phyllis Diller. She asked to see some of my comedy writing. I sent it, and she sent back a check. After that assignment, Jim Nabors hired me to do his variety show. Then I worked on *Laugh-In, The New Bill Cosby Show,* and *The Carol Burnett Show.* After that, I produced *Welcome Back Kotter, Three's Company,* and *The Tim Conway Show.*

Association with Bob Hope Leads to World Travel

"In 1969 Bob Hope also asked me to write monologue material for his television specials and personal appearances. That became my first free-time assignment, working for Bob Hope when I wasn't working on the various television shows. In 1982, I began working exclusively for Bob Hope and am presently his head writer. My television writing career has been exciting and fun. In working with Bob Hope, I've travelled around the world several times. We've entertained the military in Beirut, the Persian Gulf, and Saudi Arabia. We've visited the Berlin Wall when it was being dismantled, and even did a show in Moscow. I've had the privilege of meeting many of the legendary entertainers and sports figures of our time.

"However, there is one drawback in writing television comedy—someone is always telling you what to write. That's the reason why books have such an appeal. When a person writes a book, he or she communicates directly to the audience, the readers. Also, television shows disappear after being shown on the screen. They're gone. A book you can hold in your hands, put on your shelf. You can leaf through a book from time to time. It's much more permanent.

"The collections of children's humor that I've written are especially rewarding because young people have a glorious sense of humor. They enjoy laughing. I enjoy

As a professional comedy writer, Perret now creates jokes for his childhood idol, Bob Hope.

making them laugh. The first book I did for school children was *Snappy Comebacks to Rude Remarks.* Through that book I relived my school yard duels of wits. Someone would kid me about something, and I'd try to 'get even.' Unfortunately, I didn't think of the clever retort until much later. So, I published a collection of snappy responses. Of course, I warned the young readers that the 'insults' were purely there for fun. I still believe, and think the readers should realize, that humor shouldn't be offensive.

"*The Laugh-A-Minute Joke Book* also was inspired by my own childhood—my own brothers and sisters, uncles and aunts, and many of the other things that I laughed at through my childhood. Youngsters can still laugh at these today, I thought, and so I wrote about them. *Super Funny School Jokes* seemed a natural since youngsters spend a good portion of their day in the classroom. It's their workplace and funny things happen there. I tried to capture some of that fun in the pages of this book.

Books Preserve Classic Humor for Today's Kids

"My goal in writing these books was to introduce a more sophisticated type of comedy to the younger readers. I wanted to write jokes they could enjoy, but also jokes that would help them develop a sense of humor. In the book *Great One-liners,* I've coupled some of my jokes with classic one-liners from legendary comics. The young readers of today can enjoy the wit of some of the funniest people of the past."

"I believe, too, that many young adults can learn to write comedy and might even be inspired to make it their career. That's why I've written two books about the craft of comedy writing: *Comedy Writing Step by Step,* which explains the process of writing a funny monologue, sketch, or television show from start to finish, from the blank pages to the completed manuscript. And to help develop the skills they'll need, I've written *Comedy Writing Workbook,* which contains almost one-hundred writing workouts and exercises.

"Comedy is a valuable, and often overlooked, resource in our lives. It helps us to think straight, it relieves stress. Doctors even tell us now that it aids the healing process. Through my books and my occasional lectures on humor, I want people, and especially youngsters, to learn that appropriate laughter is a reward in itself. It needn't be justified. Humor is not only fun, it serves a valid purpose for all of us.

"Bob Hope says of his travels that he's been welcomed with 'aloha,' 'willkommen,' 'shalom,' and even a twenty-one gun salute, which, he says, luckily missed. He says also, 'The most universal welcome I've received is the sound of laughter. It needs no translation. It means happiness and joy. Most important, it means freedom. In any country where liberty has been banished, the next thing to disappear is laughter.' He adds, 'The best way to communicate is with a chuckle.' That's what I'm trying to do with my writing."

*   *   *

PERRY, Steve 1947-

■ Personal

Born August 31, 1947, in Baton Rouge, LA; married Dianne Waller (a political expert and newspaper publisher); children: Dal, Stephani.

■ Addresses

Agent—Jean V. Naggar Literary Agency, Inc., 216 East 75th St., New York, NY 10021.

■ Career

Writer. Taught writing classes in the Portland and Washington County public school systems; has taught adult writing classes at the University of Washington in Seattle; briefly held a position as a staff writer for Ruby-Spears Productions, Hollywood, CA; worked variously as a swimming instructor and lifeguard, toy assembler, hotel gift shop clerk, aluminum salesperson, kung fu instructor, private detective, Licensed Practical Nurse, and Certified Physician's Assistant.

■ Writings

The Tularemia Gambit (mystery), Fawcett, 1981.
Civil War Secret Agent (young adult), Bantam, 1984.

From *Something About the Author,* Volume 76, page 175, edited by Diane Telgen. Copyright © 1994 by Gale Research Company. Reprinted by permission of the publisher.

Name _____ Date _____

SOMETHING ABOUT THE AUTHOR

Report on an author or illustrator whose biography appears in *Something About the Author*. Choose from full biographical entries, not from brief entries.

1. Author or illustrator _____

2. Date of birth _____

3. Place of birth _____

4. Parents _____

5. Married to _____

6. Children _____

7. Education _____

8. Address _____

_____

9. Career _____

_____

10. Awards/Honors _____

11. Writings/Art _____

_____

12. Work in Progress _____

13. Sidelights _____

14. Hobbies _____

15. What did you find particularly interesting about this author/illustrator? _____

_____

16. Find an obituary notice. Who is it about? _____

_____

17. Look in the Author Index. Name one author and list all of the references to him or her.

_____

_____

_____

18. Look in the Illustrations Index. Name one illustrator and list all of the references to

his or her work. _____

_____

_____

_____

19. Look in the Character Index. Name one character and list all of the references to him

or her. (If a volume contains a Character Index, the fact will be stated on the book's

cover. Two volumes that contain character indexes are Volumes 50 and 54.) _____

_____

_____

20. Evaluate *Something About the Author*. _____

_____

_____

_____

_____

_____

_____

_____

TWENTIETH CENTURY AUTHORS
(with Reference to Other Volumes of *The Wilson Author Series*)

Twentieth Century Authors. Edited by Stanley J. Kunitz and Howard Haycraft. New York: H. W. Wilson, 1942. 1,577 p.

Biographies and autobiographies of 1,850 authors of all nations whose work has been published in English and who flourished between 1900–1942. 1,700 portraits. Alphabetical arrangement.

Twentieth Century Authors, First Supplement. Edited by Stanley J. Kunitz. New York: H. W. Wilson, 1955. 1,123 p.

Provides updated biographical and bibliographical information on most of the authors covered in *Twentieth Century Authors* plus about 700 sketches of writers who flourished between 1942 and 1955. Supplement covers a total of 2,550 authors. Alphabetical arrangement.

Index to the Wilson Authors Series. Revised edition. New York: H. W. Wilson, 1991. 104 p.

Indexes the eleven-volume *Wilson Author Series*.

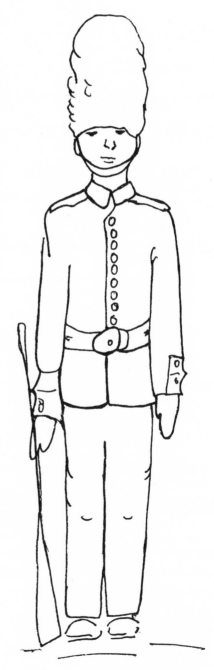

OBJECTIVES

1. To introduce *Twentieth Century Authors*
2. To familiarize students with *Twentieth Century Authors* by presenting a sample biography
3. To introduce the *First Supplement*, the *Index*, and the other volumes of *The Wilson Author Series*

MATERIALS

1. If available, *Twentieth Century Authors* and the *First Supplement*

2. Any other volumes of *The Wilson Authors Series: American Authors 1600–1900, European Authors 1000–1900, World Authors 1950–1970, World Authors 1970–1975, World Authors 1975–1980, World Authors 1980–1985, British Authors of the Nineteenth Century, British Authors Before 1800, Greek and Latin Authors 800 B.C.–A.D. 1000*
3. If available, the *Index to the Wilson Authors Series*
4. Reproductions of a sample biography from *Twentieth Century Authors,* Worksheet 74
5. Reproductions of the follow-up ditto, Worksheet 75
6. If assigning a report, make reproductions of the *Twentieth Century Authors* list on Worksheet 76 and the Author/Celebrity report form, Worksheet 29

LESSON

How many of you have heard of Tarzan?

Did you know that the first Tarzan story was written in 1912?

How many years ago was that?

    Call on a student to put the problem on the board. After solving the problem, let the student tell the class the answer.

The Tarzan stories were created by Edgar Rice Burroughs.

If we want to find some information about Mr. Burroughs, we can look in *Twentieth Century Authors.*

    Hold up a copy of *Twentieth Century Authors,* if one is available.

Twentieth Century Authors has 1,850 biographies or autobiographies of authors whose work flourished between 1900–1942. The volume covers authors from around the world whose work has been published in English.

There's a supplement to *Twentieth Century Authors.*

    Hold up a copy of the supplement, if one is available.

What's a supplement? (an addition)

Twentieth Century Authors covers the years 1900–1942. The supplement updates the information to 1955 on most of the authors covered in *Twentieth Century Authors.* It also covers about 700 new biographies of authors whose work was prominent from 1942–1955.

Altogether the supplement covers 2,550 authors. It was published in 1955.

Twentieth Century Authors and its supplement are alphabetically arranged.

Twentieth Century Authors and the *First Supplement* are two books of an eleven-volume series. Our library has _____.

There is an index to the series. Our library has/doesn't have a copy.

The eleven-volume *Wilson Author Series* is found in most public and college libraries. *Twentieth Century Authors* is found in many junior and senior high schools.

All of the volumes in the series are reference books.

I'm going to distribute a sample page from *Twentieth Century Authors*. It contains a biographical sketch of Edgar Rice Burroughs.

    Distribute reproductions of Worksheet 74.

Notice that the subject's last name appears at the top of the page.

Look at the left column. Mr. Burroughs' biography starts about two-thirds of the way down.

When was Mr. Burroughs born? (September 1, 1875)

Notice the asterisk before his name.

What's the purpose of asterisks? (to indicate footnotes)

See the footnote under column one. Who wants to read it? (died March 19, 1950)

Look at the bottom of column two at the part designated Principal Works.

Edgar Rice Burroughs' principal works and the dates they were published are listed there. Principal Works is concluded on the next page of *Twentieth Century Authors*. It's followed by a bibliography. You don't have that page.

What's a bibliography? (a list of sources of information about a particular subject)

I'm going to distribute a worksheet. Read it, and then read the article about Edgar Rice Burroughs. Answer the questions on the worksheet.

    Distribute Worksheet 75.

    When the students are finished, collect the worksheets.

FOLLOW-UP

Extra Credit Assignment

If your school library has a copy of *Twentieth Century Authors,* offer extra credit for a report on one of the biographees.

Preparations

1. Reproduce some copies of Worksheet 76, which lists some biographees of interest to students in grades 7–9.
2. Reproduce some copies of the Author/Celebrity Report form, Worksheet 29.

Presentation

1. Discuss the assignment and the report form.
2. Announce the date the report will be due.

there she produced a group of novels, which deal with the effect of English life on an American in a romantic, picturesque, and perhaps even humorous manner. Since 1925, four later stories have carried this romantic mood into new places, and have been followed by two biographies; while in editing Alice James' *Journal*, Mrs. Burr has brought it into the attention it deserves. Meanwhile, she lives in a new home in Bryn Mawr, Pa., surrounded by books and friends."

* * *

Mrs. Burr was born Anna Robeson Brown, the daughter of Henry Armitt Brown and Josephine Lea (Baker) Brown, and was educated in private schools. In 1899 she married Dr. Charles H. Burr. Both her biographies, of the banker James Stillman, and of the celebrated physician and novelist, S. Weir Mitchell, were based on long personal acquaintance. Her house, called "Scrivens," was near Bryn Mawr College and within easy commuting distance of Philadelphia, the region which, except for her years in England, was always her home. It was there that she died at the age of sixty-eight.

PRINCIPAL WORKS: *Novels*—The House on Charles Street, 1921; The House on Smith Square, 1923; The Wrong Move, 1923; The Great House in the Park, 1924; St. Helios, 1925; West of the Moon, 1926; Palludia, 1928; The Same Person, 1931; Wind in the East, 1933; The Bottom of the Matter, 1935; The Golden Quicksand, 1936. *Biographies*—Portrait of a Banker, 1927; Weir Mitchell: Life and Letters, 1931; Alice James: Her Journal, 1935. *Miscellaneous*—The Autobiography, 1909; The Religious Confession, 1914.

ABOUT: New York Times September 11, 1941.

*BURROUGHS, EDGAR RICE (September 1, 1875-   ), American novelist, creator of the "Tarzan" stories, was born in Chicago.

In his childhood his family was wealthy, and he was sent to a succession of private schools, ending at the Michigan Military Academy. He then enlisted in the army, but was soon discharged as under age. Fifteen years or more followed during which he was a cattle drover in Idaho, a worker on an Oregon gold dredge, a railroad policeman in Salt Lake City, and attempted a confusing number of minor business ventures, sometimes for others, sometimes for himself, and always unsuccessfully. In 1900

* Died March 19, 1950.

he married Emma Centennia Hulbert, and they had two sons and a daughter. In 1935 he married Florence Gilbert, who divorced him seven years later.

At thirty-six he was as complete a failure as could have been located among the "John Does" of any large city. The only recreation he could afford was a habit of daydreaming wild adventures, on other planets or in wild places of the earth. Happening on some pulp magazines, he, who had never written a word, decided he could do better than the stories he read there, by merely verbalizing his reveries. The result was a serial on life in Mars, which he sold to the Munsey publications. In 1912 he wrote his first "Tarzan" story, and his first book appeared in 1914.

The rest is history. Mr. Burroughs is not so much a writer as an institution. He has sold twenty-five million copies of Tarzan books in fifty-six languages. Tarzan is in the movies, the comic strips, on the radio, and has passed into the English language. Mr. Burroughs lives on a ranch in Southern California where the post office is called Tarzana. He dictates to a staff of secretaries, and he has incorporated himself. He has not yet seen Africa, where most of the Tarzan stories take place. The story of the English boy adopted and reared by apes—Tarzan himself is by now a grandfather—has some of the universality of folk-lore (and is more than a little reminiscent of Kipling). An editorial in *Commonweal* aptly called the stories "somewhat below Rider Haggard, somewhat above Trader Horn." Alva Johnston has called Mr. Burroughs "a master of the slaughter house branches of fiction," with "a certain galloping commonplaceness as one of his assets, but . . . pages of his books have the authentic flash and sting of story-telling genius." A big, bullet-headed man who looks like an army officer, he rides and golfs when he is not working on his giant industry. Probably few literate adults could read a Tarzan story with pleasure—but probably few of them failed to devour Tarzan stories in their earlier years. Burroughs' continuing series of books on Mars has never found the same vast public.

PRINCIPAL WORKS: Tarzan of the Apes, 1914; The Return of Tarzan, 1915; The Beasts of Tarzan, 1916; The Son of Tarzan, 1917; A Princess of Mars, 1917; Tarzan and the Jewels of Opar, 1918; The Gods of Mars, 1918; Jungle Tales of Tarzan, 1919; The Warlord of Mars, 1919; Tarzan the Untamed, 1920; Thuvia, Maid of Mars, 1920; Tarzan the Terrible, 1921; The Mucker, 1921; The Chessmen of Mars, 1922; At the Earth's Core, 1922; Tarzan and the Golden Lion, 1923; Pellucidar, 1923; The Girl From Hollywood, 1923;

227

Name _____ Date _____

TWENTIETH CENTURY AUTHORS

To complete the following, refer to Worksheet 74.

1. For what is Edgar Rice Burroughs remembered? _____

_____

2. Where was he born? _____

3. How old was he when he first started writing? _____

4. When did he write his first Tarzan story? _____

5. *Twentieth Century Authors* says that Edgar Rice Burroughs is not so much a writer as

an _____ .

6. In how many languages has Tarzan appeared? _____

7. Name two of Edgar Rice Burroughs' recreations. _____

_____

8. Name four mediums (forms) in which Tarzan has been presented to the public?____

_____

9. When was *The Return of Tarzan* published? _____

10. When did Edgar Rice Burroughs die?_____

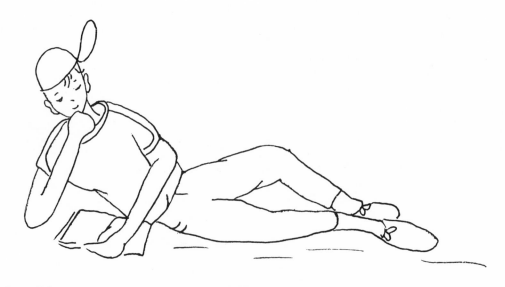

TWENTIETH CENTURY AUTHORS

AUTHORS	TITLES
Bess Streeter Aldrich	*A Lantern in Her Hand*
Joseph Alexander Altsheler	*The Wilderness Road*
Enid Bagnold	*"National Velvet"*
James Matthew Barrie	*Peter Pan*
Lyman Frank Baum	*The Wonderful Wizard of Oz*
Pearl Buck	*The Good Earth*
Willa Cather	*My Antonia*
Raymond Lee Ditmars	*Strange Animals I Have Known*
Arthur Conan Doyle	*The Adventures of Sherlock Holmes*
Daphne Du Maurier	*Rebecca*
Walter Dumaux Edmonds	*Drums Along the Mohawk; The Matchlock Gun*
Dorothea Frances (Canfield) Fisher	*Understood Betsy*
Esther Forbes	*Paul Revere and the World He Lived In*
James Hilton	*Goodbye, Mr. Chips*
Will James	*Smoky*
MacKinlay Kantor	*The Voice of Bugle Ann*
Rudyard Kipling	*Jungle Book; Kim*
Eric Knight	*Lassie Come Home*
Rose Wilder Lane	*Let the Hurricane Roar*
Jack London	*The Call of the Wild*
Charles Bernard Nordhoff	*Mutiny on the Bounty (co-authored)*
Sterling North	*Rascal*
George Orwell	*Animal Farm*
Marjorie Rawlings	*The Yearling*
Will Rogers	*The Autobiography of Will Rogers*
Antoine de St. Exupéry	*The Little Prince*
Felix Salten	*Bambi*
Ruth Sawyer	*Roller Skates*
Ernest Thompson Seton	*Wild Animals I Have Known*
Albert Payson Terhune	*Lad. A Dog*
John Roberts Tunis	*The Iron Duke*

POETS

Stephen Vincent Benét	Carl Sandburg
Robert Frost	Robert William Service
Vachel Lindsay	Sara Teasdale
Amy Lowell	Louis Untermeyer
Edwin Markham	Henry Van Dyke
John Masefield	Elinor Wylie
Edna St. Vincent Millay	William Butler Yates
Edwin Arlington Robinson	

SOCIAL SCIENCES

Occupational Outlook Handbook; Locating Career Books

U.S. Department of Labor. Bureau of Labor Statistics. *Occupational Outlook Handbook*. 1st. ed. Washington, D.C., 1949–. Biennial.

The 1994–1995 edition gives detailed descriptions of about 250 occupations. Coverage includes nature of the work; working conditions; employment; training, other qualifications, and advancement; job outlook; earnings; related occupations; and sources of additional information.

OBJECTIVES

1. To introduce *Occupational Outlook Handbook*
2. To familiarize students with *Occupational Outlook Handbook* by presenting a sample article
3. To teach students how to locate career books
4. To give students practice in locating information about a career

MATERIALS

1. If available, a copy of *Occupational Outlook Handbook*
2. Reproductions of the article "Police, Detectives, and Special Agents," Worksheet 77
3. Reproductions of the follow-up, Worksheet 78
4. If assigning a career report, reproductions of the Career Report form, Worksheet 79
5. If needed, reproductions of "How to Give an Oral Report," Worksheet 80

PREPARATIONS

Teacher. Find out if your school library has the following:
1. *Occupational Outlook Handbook*
2. A career pamphlet file

LESSON

It may be some time before you decide on your lifework, but in the meantime you should be exploring possibilities. Today we're going to consider a book that can help you learn about various careers. The name of that book is *Occupational Outlook Handbook*.

If a copy of *Occupational Outlook Handbook* is available, hold it up.

Occupational Outlook Handbook is published by the United States Government. Specifically it's from the U.S. Department of Labor, Bureau of Labor Statistics.

It's a biennial publication.

What does biennial mean?

Call on a student whose hand is raised. If no one responds, explain that a biennial publication is one that comes out every two years.

There are several reasons why *Occupational Outlook Handbook* is a valuable research tool.

The government has thoroughly researched the information. It has found out what the true employment picture is around the country, and it has presented that information for you to use.

Occupational Outlook Handbook describes in detail everything you'll need to know about an occupation.

Since the book is a biennial, the material is updated every two years.

The book describes about 250 occupations in detail. The 250 occupations include about 85 percent of all the jobs in the country.

A summary in the back of the book gives information on an additional 6 percent (77) of the country's occupations.

What percent of the country's occupations is covered to some degree in this book? (91%)

What percent of the jobs isn't covered? (9%)

You'll find *Occupational Outlook Handbook* in the reference section of junior high libraries, senior high libraries, college libraries, and public libraries. As you know, reference books can't be checked out. Some public libraries, besides having a reference copy, have older or duplicate copies that can be checked out.

Our library has/doesn't have *Occupational Outlook Handbook*.

Occupational Outlook Handbook is not meant to be read from cover to cover. It is to be referred to for specific career information.

Use the index to locate what you need. The articles aren't arranged alphabetically.

If you look "police" up in the index, you'll be directed to three pages of information. I'm going to pass out copies of those pages.

Distribute copies of "Police, Detectives, and Special Agents," Worksheets 77a, 77b, and 77c.

Who'd like to read the title of the article? ("Police, Detectives, and Special Agents")

To quickly determine what's covered, we can read the subheads.

What's the first subhead? (Nature of the Work)

The material under that heading tells what police, detectives, and special agents do.

What's the name of the next subhead? (Working Conditions)

The next one? (Employment)

The next? (Training, Other Qualifications, and Advancement)

The next? (Job Outlook)

Next? (Earnings)

Next? (Related Occupations)

And the last one? (Sources of Additional Information)

How do the subheads help you? (They help you locate the information you want.)

Under which heading would you look to find information about salaries? (Earnings)

Where would you look to find out what education or experience is required? (Training, Other Qualifications, and Advancement)

Where would you look to find out what the work is like? (Nature of the Work)

You'll have an opportunity to read the entire article later. Turn the pages over now so that a blank page is facing up.

Occupational Outlook Handbook is a useful book of career information. There are many other career books available, too.

If you don't want to assign a career report, adapt the following.

I'd like for each of you to choose a career and write a report about it.

If you plan to assign oral reports also, tell the students.

Explain that their written reports can be used as the basis of their oral presentations.

Where can you get the information you'll need for a report?

Elicit "in the library" and "from interviewing someone who's employed in the career field I'm considering."

It would be preferable to get information from both the library and from interviewing someone in the career field you've chosen. If you're unable to interview anyone, a report based solely on library research will be acceptable.

When you go to the library, how will you find the information you need? (Refer to the card or computer catalog.)

What subject headings will you look under? (You may receive the following answers: careers, occupations, vocations.)

Those sound like very appropriate headings; however, libraries use the subject heading "vocational guidance" for most career books. You may find a few books listed under "careers" and/or "occupations," but expect to find most listings under "vocational guidance."

If you look in the card catalog, thumb through all of the vocational guidance cards. You'll notice that most of them have the same Dewey Classification number. That number is the general number for career books. When you go to the shelves and find one book with that number, you have probably found the location of the basic career collection. It may not be necessary to refer to the card or computer catalog again. You can use your basic number to locate career books in both the nonfiction and the reference sections.

If your library has a career pamphlet file, tell your students.

The World Book Encyclopedia has an informative article on careers. You may want to refer to it. You'll find the article in the C–Ch Volume under "Careers."

I'm going to distribute a worksheet for you to do. Refer to the *Occupational Outlook Handbook* article "Police, Detectives, and Special Agents" for the answers.

Distribute reproductions of Worksheet 78.

Allow time for students to read the entire article on Worksheets 77a, 77b, and 77c.

If assigning a career report, distribute reproductions of Worksheet 79. If desired, require students to submit a career report in narrative form also.

If you assign an oral presentation, you may want to distribute copies of "How to Give an Oral Report," Worksheet 80.

SUGGESTIONS

1. If your library doesn't have *Occupational Outlook Handbook,* or if you'd like to have access to its information in your classroom, do one of the following:

a. Purchase a copy of *Occupational Outlook Handbook* for use in a learning center. Students can take turns visiting the center to research a career.
b. Order reprints of some *Occupational Outlook Handbook* sections. (See the back of *Occupational Outlook Handbook* for ordering information.)
c. Purchase a copy of *Occupational Outlook Handbook* to separate into individual articles. Tear or cut the articles from the book and staple them inside manila folders. Photocopy any page which overlaps with another article. Label the folders and file them in a box. Put the box in an accessible location.

NOTE

If worksheet pages reprinted from *Occupational Outlook Handbook,* or from any book, need to be enlarged to be more readable, please enlarge them.

Police, Detectives, and Special Agents

(A list of D.O.T. codes is available on request. See page 474.)

Nature of the Work

The safety of our Nation's cities, towns, and highways greatly depends on the work of police officers, detectives, and special agents, whose responsibilities range from controlling traffic to preventing and investigating crimes. In most jurisdictions, whether on or off duty, these officers are expected to exercise their authority whenever necessary.

As civilian police department employees and private security personnel increasingly assume routine police duties, police and detectives are able to spend more time fighting serious crime. Police and detectives are also becoming more involved in community relations—increasing public confidence in the police and mobilizing the public to help the police fight crime.

Police officers and detectives who work in small communities and rural areas have many duties. In the course of a day's work, they may direct traffic at the scene of a fire, investigate a burglary, or give first aid to an accident victim. In a large police department, by contrast, officers usually are assigned to a specific type of duty. Most officers are detailed either to patrol or to traffic duty; smaller numbers are assigned to special work such as accident prevention. Others are experts in chemical and microscopic analysis, firearms identification, and handwriting and fingerprint identification. In very large cities, a few officers may work with special units such as mounted and motorcycle police, harbor patrols, helicopter patrols, canine corps, mobile rescue teams, and youth aid services.

Sheriffs and deputy sheriffs generally enforce the law in rural areas or those places where there is no local police department. Bailiffs are responsible for keeping order in the courtroom. U.S. marshals serve civil writs and criminal warrants issued by Federal judges and are responsible for the safety and transportation of jurors and prisoners.

Detectives and special agents are plainclothes investigators who gather facts and collect evidence for criminal cases. They conduct interviews, examine records, observe the activities of suspects, and participate in raids or arrests.

Federal Bureau of Investigation (FBI) special agents investigate violations of Federal laws in connection with bank robberies, theft of Government property, organized crime, espionage, sabotage, kidnapping, and terrorism. Agents with specialized training usually work on cases related to their background. For example, agents with an accounting background may investigate white-collar crimes such as bank embezzlements or fraudulent bankruptcies and land deals. Frequently, agents must testify in court about cases that they investigate.

Special agents employed by the U.S. Department of Treasury work for the U.S. Customs Service; the Bureau of Alcohol, Tobacco, and Firearms; the U.S. Secret Service; and the Internal Revenue Service. Customs agents enforce laws to prevent smuggling of goods across U.S. borders. Alcohol, Tobacco, and Firearms agents might investigate suspected illegal sales of guns or the underpayment of taxes by a liquor or cigarette manufacturer. U.S. Secret Service agents protect the President, Vice President, and their immediate families, Presidential candidates, ex-Presidents, and foreign dignitaries visiting the United States. Secret Service agents also investigate counterfeiting, the forgery of Government checks or bonds, and the fraudulent use of credit cards. Internal Revenue Service special agents collect evidence against individuals and companies that are evading the payment of Federal taxes.

Federal drug enforcement agents conduct criminal investigations of illicit drug activity. They compile evidence and arrest individuals who violate Federal drug laws. They may prepare reports that are used in criminal proceedings, give testimony in court, and develop evidence that justifies the seizure of financial assets gained from illegal activity.

State police officers (sometimes called State troopers or highway patrol officers) patrol highways and enforce laws and regulations that govern their use. They issue traffic citations to motorists who violate the law. At the scene of an accident, they direct traffic, give first aid, and call for emergency equipment including ambulances. They also write reports that may be used to determine the cause of the accident. In addition, State police officers provide services to motorists on the highways. For example, they may radio for road service for drivers with mechanical trouble, direct tourists to their destination, or give information about lodging, restaurants, and tourist attractions.

State police officers also provide traffic assistance and control during road repairs, fires, and other emergencies, as well as during special occurrences such as parades and sports events. They sometimes check the weight of commercial vehicles, conduct driver examinations, and give information on highway safety to the public.

In addition to highway responsibilities, State police in the majority of States also enforce criminal laws. In communities and counties that do not have a local police force or a large sheriff's department, the State police are the primary law enforcement agency, investigating crimes such as burglary or assault. They also may help city or county police catch lawbreakers and control civil disturbances.

Most new police recruits begin on patrol duty, riding in a police vehicle or walking on "foot" patrol. They work alone or with experienced officers in such varied areas as congested business districts or outlying residential neighborhoods. Officers attempt to become thoroughly familiar with conditions throughout their area and, while on patrol, remain alert for anything unusual. They note suspicious circumstances, such as open windows or lights in vacant buildings, as well as hazards to public safety such as burned-out street lights or fallen trees. Officers enforce traffic regulations and also watch for stolen vehicles. At regular intervals, officers report to police headquarters from call boxes, radios, or telephones.

Regardless of where they work, police, detectives, and special agents must write reports and maintain police records. They may be called to testify in court when their arrests result in legal action. Some officers, such as division or bureau chiefs, are responsible for training or certain kinds of criminal investigations, and those who command police operations in an assigned area have administrative and supervisory duties.

Working Conditions

Police, detectives, and special agents usually work 40 hours a week, but paid overtime work is common. Because police protection must

Responsibilities of police officers range from controlling traffic and preventing and investigating crimes.

Worksheet 77a   **294**

be provided around the clock in all but the smallest communities, some officers work weekends, holidays, and nights. Police officers, detectives, and special agents are subject to call any time their services are needed and may work overtime, particularly during criminal investigations.

The jobs of some special agents such as U.S. Secret Service agents require extensive travel.

Police, detectives, and special agents may have to work outdoors for long periods in all kinds of weather. The injury rate among these law officers is higher than in many occupations and reflects the risks taken in pursuing speeding motorists, apprehending criminals, and dealing with public disorders. Police work can be very dangerous, and this can be very stressful for the officer as well as for his or her family.

Employment

Police, detectives, and special agents held about 700,000 jobs in 1992. Most were employed by local governments, primarily in cities with more than 25,000 inhabitants. Some cities have very large police forces, while hundreds of small communities employ fewer than 25 officers each. State police agencies employed about 12 percent of all police, detectives, and special agents; various Federal agencies, particularly the Treasury Department and the Federal Bureau of Investigation, employed an additional 5 percent. There are about 17,000 State and local police departments in the Nation.

Training, Other Qualifications, and Advancement

Civil service regulations govern the appointment of police and detectives in practically all States and large cities and in many small ones. Candidates must be U.S. citizens, usually at least 20 years of age, and must meet rigorous physical and personal qualifications. Eligibility for appointment depends on performance in competitive written examinations as well as on education and experience. Physical examinations often include tests of vision, strength, and agility.

Because personal characteristics such as honesty, good judgment, and a sense of responsibility are especially important in police and detective work, candidates are interviewed by a senior officer at police headquarters, and their character traits and background are investigated. In some police departments, candidates also may be interviewed by a psychiatrist or a psychologist, or be given a personality test. Most applicants are subjected to lie detector examinations and drug testing. Some police departments subject police officers in sensitive positions to drug testing as a condition of continuing employment. Although police and detectives often work independently, they must perform their duties in accordance with laws and departmental rules. They should enjoy working with people and serving the public.

In large police departments, where most jobs are found, applicants usually must have a high school education. An increasing number of cities and States require some college training, and some hire law enforcement students as police interns; some departments require a college degree. A few police departments accept applicants as recruits who have less than a high school education, particularly if they have worked in a field related to law enforcement.

To be considered for appointment as an FBI special agent, an applicant either must be a graduate of an accredited law school; be a college graduate with a major in either accounting, engineering, or computer science; or be a college graduate with either fluency in a foreign language or 3 years of full-time work experience. Applicants must be U.S. citizens, between 23 and 35 years of age at the time of appointment, and willing to accept an assignment anywhere in the United States. They also must be in excellent physical condition with at least 20/200 vision corrected to 20/40 in one eye and 20/20 in the other eye. All new agents undergo 15 weeks of training at the FBI academy at the U.S. Marine Corps base in Quantico, Virginia.

Applicants for special agent jobs with the U.S. Department of Treasury must have a bachelor's degree, or a minimum of 3 years' work experience of which at least 2 are in criminal investigation.

Candidates must be in excellent physical condition and be less than 35 years of age at the time they enter duty. Treasury agents undergo 8 weeks of training at the Federal Law Enforcement Training Center in Glynco, Georgia, and another 8 weeks of specialized training with their particular bureau.

Applicants for special agent jobs with the U.S. Drug Enforcement Administration must have a college degree in any field and either 1 year of experience conducting criminal investigations or have achieved a record of scholastic excellence while in college. The minimum age for entry is 21 and the maximum age is 36. Drug enforcement agents undergo 14 weeks of specialized training at the FBI Academy in Quantico, Virginia.

More and more, police departments are encouraging applicants to take post-high school training in law enforcement. Many entrants to police and detective jobs have completed some formal postsecondary education and a significant number are college graduates. Many junior colleges, colleges, and universities offer programs in law enforcement or administration of justice. Other courses helpful in preparing for a police career include psychology, counseling, English, American history, public administration, public relations, sociology, business law, chemistry, and physics. Participation in physical education and sports is especially helpful in developing the stamina and agility needed for police work. Knowledge of a foreign language is an asset in areas that have concentrations of ethnic populations.

Some large cities hire high school graduates who are still in their teens as civilian police cadets or trainees. They do clerical work and attend classes and are appointed to the regular force at age 21 if qualified.

Before their first assignments, officers usually go through a period of training. In small communities, recruits work for a short time with experienced officers. In State and large city police departments, they get more formal training that may last a number of weeks or months. This training includes classroom instruction in constitutional law and civil rights, State laws and local ordinances, and accident investigation. Recruits also receive training and supervised experience in patrol, traffic control, use of firearms, self-defense, first aid, and handling emergencies.

Police officers usually become eligible for promotion after a probationary period ranging from 6 months to 3 years. In a large department, promotion may enable an officer to become a detective or specialize in one type of police work such as laboratory analysis of evidence, traffic control, communications, or working with juveniles. Promotions to sergeant, lieutenant, and captain usually are made according to a candidate's position on a promotion list, as determined by scores on a written examination and on-the-job performance.

Many types of training help police officers and detectives improve their job performance. Through training given at police department academies—required annually in many States—and colleges, officers keep abreast of crowd-control techniques, civil defense, legal developments that affect their work, and advances in law enforcement equipment. Many police departments pay all or part of the tuition for officers to work toward associate and bachelor's degrees in law enforcement, police science, administration of justice, or public administration, and pay higher salaries to those who earn a degree.

Job Outlook

Employment of police officers, detectives, and special agents is expected to increase more slowly than the average for all occupations through the year 2005. A more security-conscious society and growing concern about drug-related crimes should contribute to the increasing demand for police services. However, employment growth will be tempered somewhat by continuing budgetary constraints faced by law enforcement agencies. In addition, private security firms may increasingly assume some routine police duties such as crowd surveillance at airports and other public places. Although turnover in police, detective, and special agent jobs is among

Reproduced from *Occupational Outlook Handbook,* 1994–1995. Courtesy of U.S. Department of Labor, Bureau of Labor Statistics.

the lowest of all occupations, the need to replace workers who retire, transfer to other occupations, or stop working for other reasons will be the source of most job openings.

The opportunity for public service through police work is attractive to many. The job frequently is challenging and involves much responsibility. Furthermore, in many communities, police officers may retire with a pension to pursue a second career while still in their 40's. Because of attractive salaries and benefits, the number of qualified candidates generally exceeds the number of job openings in many Federal agencies and some State and local police departments—resulting in increased hiring standards and selectivity by employers. Competition is expected to remain keen for higher paying jobs in larger police departments. Persons having college training in law enforcement should have the best opportunities. Opportunities will be best in those communities whose departments are expanding and are having difficulty attracting an adequate supply of police officers. Competition is expected to be extremely keen for special agent positions with the FBI, Treasury Department, and Drug Enforcement Administration as these prestigious jobs tend to attract a far greater number of applicants than the number of job openings. Consequently, only the most highly qualified candidates will obtain jobs.

The level of government spending influences the employment of police officers, detectives, and special agents. The number of job opportunities, therefore, can vary from year to year and from place to place. Layoffs, on the other hand, are rare because early retirements enable most staffing cuts to be handled through attrition. Police officers who lose their jobs from budget cuts usually have little difficulty finding jobs with other police departments.

Earnings

In 1992, the median salary of nonsupervisory police officers and detectives was about $32,000 a year. The middle 50 percent earned between about $24,500 and $41,200; the lowest paid 10 percent were paid less than $18,400, while the highest paid 10 percent earned over $51,200 a year. Generally, salaries tend to be higher in larger, more urban jurisdictions that usually have bigger police departments.

Police officers and detectives in supervisory positions had a median salary of about $38,100 a year, also in 1992. The middle 50 percent earned between about $28,300 and $49,800; the lowest paid 10 percent were paid less than $23,200, while the highest paid 10 percent earned over $58,400 annually.

Sheriffs, bailiffs, and other law enforcement officers had a median annual salary of about $25,800 in 1992. The middle 50 percent earned between about $20,500 and $30,900; the lowest paid 10 percent were paid less than $15,600, while the highest paid 10 percent earned over $38,800.

In 1993, FBI agents started at about $30,600 a year, while Treasury Department agents started at about $18,300 or $22,700 a year, and DEA agents at either $22,700 or $27,800 a year, depending on their qualifications. Salaries of experienced FBI agents started at around $47,900, while supervisory agents started at around $56,600 a year. Salaries of experienced Treasury Department and DEA agents started at $40,200, while supervisory agents started at $47,900. Federal agents may, however, be eligible for a special law enforcement compensation and retirement plan; applicants should ask their recruiter for more information.

Total earnings frequently exceed the stated salary due to payments for overtime, which can be significant, especially during criminal investigations or when police are needed for crowd control during sporting events or political rallies. In addition to the common fringe benefits—paid vacation, sick leave, and medical and life insurance—most police departments and Federal agencies provide officers with special allowances for uniforms and furnish revolvers, nightsticks, handcuffs, and other required equipment. In addition, because police officers generally are covered by liberal pension plans, many retire at half-pay after 20 or 25 years of service.

Related Occupations

Police officers maintain law and order in the Nation's cities, towns, and rural areas. Workers in related law enforcement occupations include guards, bailiffs, correction officers, deputy sheriffs, fire marshals, fish and game wardens, and U.S. marshals.

Sources of Additional Information

Information about entrance requirements may be obtained from Federal, State, and local civil service commissions or police departments.

Contact any Office of Personnel Management Job Information Center for pamphlets providing general information and instructions for submitting an application for jobs as Treasury special agents, drug enforcement agents, FBI special agents, or U.S. marshals. Look under U.S. Government, Office of Personnel Management, in your telephone directory to obtain a local telephone number.

Information about law enforcement careers in general may be obtained from:
☆ International Union of Police Associations, 1016 Duke St., Alexandria, VA 22314.

Reproduced from *Occupational Outlook Handbook,* 1994–1995. Courtesy of U.S. Department of Labor, Bureau of Labor Statistics.

Worksheet 77c

Name _____ Date _____

OCCUPATIONAL OUTLOOK HANDBOOK

Complete the following by referring to the article "Police, Detectives, and Special Agents."

1. How many police, detectives, and special agents were employed in 1992? _____

2. How old must candidates be? _____

3. List three personal characteristics which are especially important in police and detective work. _____

    _____

    _____

4. What is the usual educational requirement for getting a job with a large police department? _____

5. What do customs agents do? _____

    _____

    _____

6. Police officers maintain law and order. Name workers in three related law enforcement occupations. (See subhead Related Occupations.)

    _____

7. In 1992, what was the median salary of nonsupervisory police officers and detectives? _____

8. Which agents protect the President and Vice President? _____

    _____

9. What do bailiffs do? _____

    _____

10. How much pay will a police officer probably receive if he or she retires in 20–25 years? _____

Name_____ Date _____

CAREER REPORT

_____
(Name of career)

1. Nature of the work (what the worker does)_____

   _____

   _____

2. Working conditions (hours, days, inside/outside, safe/dangerous,

   etc.) _____

   _____

   _____

3. Education and/or special abilities required _____

   _____

   _____

4. Age requirement, if any _____

5. Other requirements, if any _____

   _____

6. Employment outlook (Are many or few openings expected?)

   _____

   _____

7. Earnings _____

   _____

8. Job security _____

   _____

9. Chance of advancement _____

   _____

10. Related occupations _____

    _____

HOW TO GIVE AN ORAL REPORT

PREPARATION

1. Research your subject thoroughly.
2. Organize your notes in a clear, step-by-step order.
3. Obtain visual materials such as tables, charts, and pictures, if available.
4. If needed, make brief notes on 3″ × 5″ cards for reference during your presentation.
5. Study your notes, but don't memorize them.

PRESENTATION

1. Face the class.
2. Stand up tall.
3. Don't lean on anything.
4. Wait until you have everyone's attention before starting your report.
5. Speak in a natural voice that is loud enough for the students in the last row to hear.
6. Present your report.
7. Show any visual materials that you have.
8. Finish your report before starting to walk back to your seat.

Profiles of American Colleges

Profiles of American Colleges. 20th edition, 1964–. Hauppauge, N.Y.: Barron's Educational Series, 1994. *1,800 p.* Biennial.

Easy-to-read, comprehensive profiles of more than 1,550 colleges. Includes information on admissions, housing, programs of study, etc.

OBJECTIVES

1. To present *Profiles of American Colleges*
2. To read and explain a college profile
3. To make students aware of the fact that their future salaries will be directly related to their years of education
4. To inform students about the many types of educational directories and career books that are available

MATERIALS

1. *Profiles of American Colleges,* if available
2. Back-to-back reproductions of the Salary–Education Ratio, Worksheet 81, and the sample page from *Profiles of American Colleges,* Worksheet 82

PREPARATIONS

1. You may want to designate which of the college directories and career books listed in this lesson will be of most interest to your students. When reading the list, read only titles you've designated.
2. *Teacher.* Find out if your library has a copy of *Profiles of American Colleges.*

LESSON

Some of you are planning on going to college. Others aren't. That's fine. There are jobs for those who are going to college, and there are jobs for those who aren't.

Regarding education and jobs, there are some facts of which you should be aware.

Did you know that having a high school diploma doubles your chances of getting a job? It does.

If money is important to you, you should be aware of the fact that usually the more education you have, the more money you'll make. Let's look at a table that demonstrates this.

> Distribute back-to-back reproductions of Worksheet 81, the Salary-Education Ratio, and the sample page from *Profiles of American Colleges,* Worksheet 82.

Look at Worksheet 81, the Salary–Education Ratio.

The table shows the relationship between the salary one makes and the education one has.

The figures are based on mean salaries. See the definition of mean on the lower half of the page.

> Read and explain the worksheet definition of mean.

Let's compare the $909 monthly salary of whites who have some high school to the $3,248 monthly salary of whites who have Master's degrees. Find those two on your table.

> Pause.

The whites with Master's degrees make over three-and-a-half times as much as whites with only some high school.

The more education you have, the more money you'll make.

> If your school is predominantly black, compare the figures for blacks. If it's predominantly Hispanic, compare the Hispanic figures.

> Make any other desired comparisons.

Today we're going to consider a book that has information about more than 1,550 American colleges and universities. It's titled *Profiles of American Colleges.*

> If you have a copy, hold it up.

You can find this book in the reference section of many junior high, senior high, college, and public libraries.

It's divided into four parts.

> You may want to discuss only Part IV.

> Presentation of the following information is optional:

> Part I helps you evaluate your needs and interests, select a college, fill out an application, write the essay, prepare for an interview, find the money, and survive the freshman year.

Part II gives advice on selecting a major and a career. It has an Index to College Majors, which tells which colleges offer majors in which you may be interested.

Part III provides information about study in Canada and Mexico and abroad.

Part IV has information on competition you may encounter in applying for a particular school. It has a list of collegiate terms, a key to abbreviations and an explanation of entries. Detailed descriptions of more than 1,550 colleges are provided.

Part IV with its detailed description of more than 1,550 colleges is the section in which you will probably be particularly interested.

Turn your papers over to Worksheet 82.

This sample is a profile of the University of California at Los Angeles.

On line 2 at the right, you see this: C-5. That refers to a map code. On the first page of California profiles, there's a map of California. By using the coordinates C and 5 on the map, you will be able to pinpoint where UCLA is located on the map of California.

On the third line you find UCLA's address and telephone number.

Discuss the items in the block of information at the top. Here are some explanations.

Faculty: 1. The number rating of 1 is the highest given. This means the faculty is of the highest caliber. The +$ means the faculty's salary is higher than usual.

Tuition $3,549 ($11,248). The tuition for in-state students is $3,549. The tuition for out-of-state students is $11,248.

SAT I: Scholastic Aptitude Test

ACT: American College Testing Program

For other abbreviations or for vocabulary, see the page titled Abbreviations and Vocabulary at the end of this lesson.

Read and discuss the material under each of the subheads, one by one. Explain any words that may be new to the students.

In this directory colleges are arranged alphabetically by state.

Our library has/doesn't have a copy of *Profiles of American Colleges.*

There are a number of college directories and career books available. I'm going to read the titles of some that were found in a medium-sized library. Listen and see if one of these would be of interest to you.

If you have designated which of these titles will be of most interest to your students, you may wish to read only those.

Pause between titles.

Career Choices
Finding Money for College
Paying Less for College
Directory of Financial Aids for Minorities
Directory of Financial Aids for Women
Scholarships, Fellowships and Loans
Sports Scholarships
Insider's Guide to Colleges
Barron's 300 Best Buys in College Education
Colleges in the West
Peterson's Guide to Four-Year Colleges
Peterson's Guide to Two-Year Colleges
Lovejoy's College Guide
Choose a Christian College
America's Best Colleges
ACT American College Testing Program
Pass Key to the ACT
SAT (How to Prepare for the Scholastic Aptitude Test)
But What if I Don't Want to Go to College?
The Macmillan Guide to Correspondence Study
Peterson's Guide to Vocational and Technical Schools

Browse through the career section at the library. You'll be amazed at all of the helpful books available.

ABBREVIATIONS AND VOCABULARY

AACSB—American Assembly of Collegiate Schools of Business

ABET—Accreditation Board for Engineering & Technology

ACT—American College Testing Program

AP credits—advance placement credits

accreditation—certification that set standards have been met by a school, which makes graduation acceptable for admission to higher or more specialized institutions

alumni—plural of alumnus. Alumnus—a person who has attended or been graduated from a school, college, or university

anthropology—the study of mankind's races, physical and mental characteristics, distribution, customs, social relationships, etc.

astrophysics—the science of dealing with the properties, changes, and interaction pertaining to stars or celestial bodies

·B.A.—Bachelor of Arts degree

baccalaureate—the degree of bachelor of arts, bachelor of science, etc.

B.S.—Bachelor of Science degree

CSS—College Scholarship Service

CSWE—Council on Social Work Education

Carnegie units—units that are more advanced than regular high school credits

chemistry—the science dealing with the composition and properties of substances, and with the reactions by which substances are produced or converted into other substances

coeducational—having students of both sexes attend classes together

cognitive—having to do with cognition. Cognition—the process of knowing or perceiving

cybernetics—the study of human control functions and of mechanical and electronic systems designed to replace them

doctoral degree—a degree for the status of doctor conferred by a university

economics—the science that deals with the production, distribution and consumption of wealth and with the various related problems of labor, finance, taxation

elective—that may be chosen but is not required

engineering—the planning, designing, construction, or management of machinery, roads, bridges, buildings, fortifications, waterways, etc.

ethnomusicology—the study of folk and primitive music and their relationship to the people and cultures to which they belong

FAF—Financial Aid Form

FAFSA—the federal government's Free Application for Federal Student Aid

fraternity—a group of men joined together by common interests, for fellowship, etc.

freshman—a first-year student in a high school or college (sophomore—a student in the second year of college or high school; junior—relating to a third-year student or class in high school or college; senior—of or belonging to the graduating class in a high school or college)

GED—General Education Development (high school equivalency examination)

GPA—grade point average

geology—the science dealing with the structure of the earth's crust and the formation and development of its various layers

geophysics—the branch of geology that deals with the physics of the earth and its atmosphere

intercollegiate—between or among colleges and universities

interdisciplinary—interacting branches of learning

internship—the period of service as an intern (intern—a doctor serving as an assistant resident in a hospital generally just after graduating from medical school)

intramural—limited to the members of a particular school or college

linguistics—the science of language

Master's degree—a degree from a college or university denoting completion of a prescribed course of graduate study in some field and ranking above that of Bachelor and below that of Doctor.

meteorology—the study of weather and climate

NAAB—an accrediting board

NLN—National League for Nursing

National Merit finalists—those high school sophomores who, after taking a preliminary SAT test, were judged finalists by the National Merit Scholarship judges

paleontology—the branch of geology that deals with prehistoric forms of life through the study of plant and animal fossils

pavilion—a building or part of a building used for entertainment, exhibits, etc. Often open-air and highly ornamented

Phi Beta Kappa—honor society composed of American college students of high scholastic rank

philosophy—a study of the processes governing thought and conduct; theory or investigation of the principles or laws that regulate the universe and underlie all knowledge and reality

physics—the science dealing with the properties, changes, interaction, etc. of matter and energy

portfolio—examples of work

psychobiology—use of biological methods to study normal and abnormal emotional and cognitive processes psychology—the science dealing with the mind and mental processes, feelings, desires

SAT—Scholastic Aptitude Test

seismology—science and study of earthquakes and their phenomena

shuttle bus—a motorbus making short regular trips between an outlying district and some point on a main transportation line

sociology—the study of the history, development, organization, and problems of people living together as social groups

sorority—a club or organization composed of women or girls, as at many colleges

undergraduate—a student at a university or college who has not yet received the first, or bachelor's, degree

urban—characteristic of the city as distinguished from the country

work-study programs—programs that combine study and work

SALARY–EDUCATION RATIO
(based on mean monthly income figures)

Education	Whites	Blacks	Hispanics	Males	Females
Some high school	$909	652	760	1,116	579
High school graduate	1,405	1,009	1,092	1,853	943
Some college	1,595	1,204	1,298	2,002	1,115
Bachelor's degree	2,552	2,002	1,895	3,235	1,698
Master's degree	3,248	2,786	2,840	3,748	2,614
Doctorate	4,679	N.A.	N.A.	4,915	3,162

N.A. = Not available. There were too few black and Hispanic recipients of doctoral degrees to determine monthly income.

Definition

mean—average

The mean is obtained by adding up all the figures in a specific list and dividing by the number of figures.

Figures adapted from the Bureau of the Census, U.S. Dept. of Commerce. Education and Income, 1993.

Worksheet 81

UNIVERSITY OF CALIFORNIA AT LOS ANGELES

C-5

Los Angeles, CA 90024   (213) 825-3101

Full-time: 11,525 men, 11,367 women	Faculty: I, +$
Part-time: none	Ph.D.s: 100%
Graduate: 6406 men, 5149 women	Student/Faculty: 14 to 1
Year: quarters, summer session	Tuition: $3549 ($11,248)
Application Deadline: November 30	Room & Board: $5410
Freshman Class: 22,165 applied, 10,096 accepted, 3391 enrolled	
SAT I or ACT: required	**HIGHLY COMPETITIVE**

University of California at Los Angeles (UCLA), founded in 1919, is a public, coeducational institution offering undergraduate and graduate degrees in arts and sciences, engineering, applied science, nursing, and theater, film, and television. There are 5 undergraduate and 14 graduate schools. In addition to regional accreditation, UCLA has baccalaureate program accreditation with AACSB, ABET, ADA, CSWE, NAAB, and NLN. The 13 libraries contain 6,390,409 volumes, 5,432,043 microform items, and 150,603 audiovisual forms, and subscribe to 94,612 periodicals. Special learning facilities include a learning resource center, an art gallery, a natural history museum, and a radio station. The 419-acre campus is in an urban area. Including residence halls, there are 230 buildings on campus.

Student Life: About 94% of undergraduates are from California. Students come from 47 states, 100 foreign countries, and Canada. Eighty-three percent are from public schools; 17% from private. Forty-six percent are white; 28% Asian American; 15% Hispanic. The average age of freshmen is 18; all undergraduates, 21. Six percent drop out of their first year; 70% remain to graduate.

Housing: A total of 5750 students can be accommodated in college housing. College-sponsored living facilities include coed dormitories, off-campus apartments, and married-student housing. On-campus housing is guaranteed for the freshman year only and is available on a lottery system for upperclassmen. Seventy-five percent of students commute. Alcohol is not permitted.

Activities: About 13% of men belong to 2 local and 32 national fraternities; about 12% of women belong to 2 local and 17 national sororities. There are 700 groups on campus, including band, cheerleading, choir, chorale, chorus, computers, dance, drama, ethnic, film, gay, honors, international, literary magazine, marching band, newspaper, photography, political, professional, radio and TV, religious, social, social service, student government, and yearbook.

Sports: There are 10 intercollegiate sports for men and 8 for women, and 21 intramural sports for men and 17 for women. Athletic and recreation facilities include a pavilion, a stadium, a tennis center, and a recreation and sports center.

Disabled Students: The following facilities are available: wheelchair ramps, elevators, special parking, specially equipped rest rooms, special class scheduling, lowered drinking fountains, and lowered telephones.

Services: In addition to many counseling and information services, tutoring is available in most subjects. In addition, there is a reader service for the blind, and remedial math, reading, and writing.

Campus Safety and Security: Campus safety and security measures include escort service, shuttle buses, informal discussions, and pamphlets, posters, and films. In addition, there are lighted pathways and sidewalks.

Programs of Study: UCLA awards the B.A. and B.S. degrees. Master's and doctoral degrees also are awarded. Bachelor's degrees are awarded in BIOLOGICAL SCIENCE (biochemistry, biology/biological science, microbiology, neurosciences, and physiology), BUSINESS (international economics, labor studies, and organizational behavior), COMMUNICATIONS AND THE ARTS (African languages, Arabic, art, art history and appreciation, broadcasting, Chinese, classics, communications, dance, design, dramatic arts, English, film arts, fine arts, French, German, Greek, Hebrew, Italian, Japanese, Latin, linguistics, music, Portuguese, Scandinavian languages, Slavic languages, Spanish, and video), COMPUTER AND PHYSICAL SCIENCE (applied mathematics, astrophysics, atmospheric sciences and meteorology, chemistry, computer science, cybernetics, earth science, geology, geophysics and seismology, mathematics, paleontolo-

gy, and physics), ENGINEERING AND ENVIRONMENTAL DESIGN (aeronautical engineering, Aerospace Studies, chemical engineering, civil engineering, computer engineering, electrical/electronics engineering, engineering, materials engineering, materials science, and mechanical engineering), HEALTH PROFESSIONS (nursing), SOCIAL SCIENCE (African American studies, anthropology, classical/ancient civilization, cognitive science, crosscultural studies, developmental psychology, East Asian studies, economics, geography, history, human development, international relations, Judaic studies, Latin American studies, Mexican-American/Chicano studies, Near Eastern studies, philosophy, political science/government, psychobiology, psychology, religion, Russian and Slavic studies, social studies, sociology, urban studies, and women's studies). Economics, psychology, political science, and engineering have the largest enrollments.

Required: Students must complete a minimum of 180 quarter units and maintain a minimum GPA of 2.0 in all courses. All students must demonstrate a proficiency in English composition, or take specific courses to achieve this proficiency, and must also meet course requirements in American history and institutions. Other requirements vary by major and college or school.

Special: Opportunities are provided for internships, work-study programs, study abroad in 33 countries, B.A.-B.S. degrees, student-designed majors, dual majors, and interdisciplinary majors, including chemistry/materials science, Chicana and Chicano studies, engineering geology, economics/systems science, ethnomusicology, and computer science and engineering. There is a Washington, D.C. program for 20 to 30 students selected each fall and spring. There is a freshman honors program on campus, as well as 4 national honor societies, including Phi Beta Kappa.

Faculty/Classroom: Eighty percent of faculty are male; 20%, female.

Admissions: About 46% of the 1993-94 applicants were accepted. The SAT scores for the 1993-94 freshman class were as follows: Verbal—38% below 500, 39% between 500 and 599, 21% between 600 and 700, and 2% above 700; Math—12% below 500, 24% between 500 and 599, 38% between 600 and 700, and 26% above 700. There were 74 National Merit finalists.

Requirements: UCLA requires applicants to be in the upper 12 1/2% of their class. The SAT I or ACT is required. Graduation from an accredited secondary school is required; a GED will be accepted. Applicants must submit a minimum of 15 Carnegie units, distributed as follows: 4 years of English, 3 of mathematics, 2 each of a foreign language and science, 1 of history, and the remainder from other academic electives. SAT II: Subject tests in writing, mathematics, and 1 subject of the student's choice are required. An essay is required, and a portfolio and audition are required for all majors in arts and theater and film and television. AP credits are accepted. Important factors used in the admissions decision are advanced placement or honor courses, evidence of special talent, leadership record, recommendations by school officials, and recommendations by alumni.

Procedure: Freshmen are admitted in the fall. Entrance exams should be taken preferably in the junior year, but no later than December of the senior year. Applications should be filed by November 30 for fall entry, along with an application fee of $40. Notification is sent March 15.

Transfer: About 1800 transfer students were enrolled in an earlier year. Transfer students must have earned a minimum of 84 quarter units at the previous college and have maintained a minimum GPA of 2.4. Most students selected present a GPA of 3.0 or better. A total of 68 quarter units out of 180 must be completed at UCLA.

Visiting: There are regularly scheduled orientations for prospective students, including campus tours led by current UCLA students offered weekdays at 10:15 and 2:15. Reservations are required. Visitors may sit in on classes. To arrange for a visit, contact Tours in Undergraduate Admissions at (310) 825-8764.

Financial Aid: In a recent year, 82% of all current freshmen and 80% of continuing students received some form of financial aid. About 72% of freshmen and 60% of continuing students received need-based aid. The average freshman award was $3200. Of that total, scholarships or need-based grants averaged $758 ($4000 maximum); loans averaged $939 ($4300 maximum); and work contracts averaged $1503 ($3000 maximum). Thirty-five percent of undergraduate students work part-time. Average earnings from campus work for the school year are $2000. The average financial indebtedness of the 1992-93 graduate was $2200. UCLA is a member of CSS. The FAF, the college's own financial statement, and the FAFSA are required. The deadline for financial aid applications is March 2.

International Students: There are currently 1730 international students enrolled. Students must take the SAT I or the ACT and SAT II: Subject tests in writing, mathematics, and their choice of literature, foreign language, science, or social science.

Computers: The college provides computer facilities for student use. The mainframe is an IBM 3090 Model 600S. There are also IBM, HP, Zenith, and DEC VAX PCs available throughout the campus. All students may access the system. It may be used 24 hours a day, 7 days

Excerpted and adapted from *Profiles of American Colleges*, 20th Edition, Copyright 1994, Barron's Educational Series, Inc. Used by permission.

      Worksheet 82

The World Almanac

The World Almanac and Book of Facts, 1868–. Mahwah, N.J., Funk & Wagnalls, 1868–. v. 1–. Annual. Comprehensive almanac of miscellaneous information. Publisher varies.

OBJECTIVES

1. To introduce almanacs in general and *The World Almanac* in particular
2. To give students an overview of the kinds of information contained in almanacs
3. To teach students how to locate information in an almanac

MATERIALS

1. If available, a copy of *The World Almanac*
2. Reproductions of a sample page from *The World Almanac,* Worksheet 83
3. Optional. If students have access to a copy of *The World Almanac,* for example, in a learning center, you may want to assign Worksheet 84. If so, make reproductions.

PREPARATIONS

If a copy of *The World Almanac* is available, use bookmarks to designate an article, a table, a chart, and a chronology. Suggestions. Article: Code of Etiquette for Display and Use of the U.S. Flag (Flags, U.S.); Table: U.S. Crime Arrests (Crime—Arrests); Chart: United States Government (United States of America, Government); Chronology: United States History (United States of America, History). These may vary somewhat from year to year.

LESSON

You may have a lot of questions you'd like to have answered, such as:

Which baseball player had the greatest number of home runs in 1993?

What were the ten top news stories last year?

Which actress won the Academy Award in 1992? In 1928–1929?

What is the population of Mexico City?

If you have a copy of *The World Almanac,* hold it up.

The World Almanac answers all of those questions and many, many more.

It lists government offices, such as the President's cabinet, the White House staff, the Department of States' staff, and so forth.

What is an almanac?

Call on those who raise their hands.

The dictionary defines an almanac as a calendar with astronomical data, weather forecasts, and tables of information.

The World Almanac contains articles.

If you have a copy of *The World Almanac,* show an article to the students, and read its title.

It contains tables full of *numbers*.

Show a table, and read its title.

It contains charts full of *words*.

Show a chart, and read its title.

It contains chronologies.

Read a couple of examples.

What's a chronology? (a list of events in the order of their occurrence)

When people refer to *The World Almanac,* they rarely use its full name: *The World Almanac and Book of Facts*. That's unfortunate because "book of facts" is an excellent description.

The World Almanac and Book of Facts covers election returns, United States history, celebrities, nations, sports, awards, and so forth.

Scientific awards and discoveries of the year are included.

Obituaries for the previous year are listed.

What are obituaries? (notices of death)

The World Almanac is an annual. What does that mean? (It is published yearly.)

The World Almanac is not arranged alphabetically. It's arranged by subjects.

There are two indexes to help you locate the information you need: the general index, which is located in the front, and the quick reference index, which is located in the back.

As you know, indexes are usually in the back of books. *The World Almanac* is one of the few books that has its main index in the front.

I'm going to distribute a copy of an index page from *The World Almanac*. See if you can find out which pages we should refer to if we want to know how many home runs Babe Ruth made.

You can look under some subjects directly. Other subjects have to be looked up under large subject areas. Babe Ruth is not listed under his name. You'll need to look under a large subject area.

What subject will you look under to find out how many home runs Babe Ruth made? (baseball)

When you find the heading "Baseball," you'll find that there are a number of subheadings under it. Read down the list until you find the one you want.

   Distribute Worksheet 83.

Who can tell us to which pages we should refer to find out how many home runs Babe Ruth made? (936–937, 948, 949)

What subhead did you look under? (Home runs—Leaders)

See if you can find out what page we should refer to if we want to know the name of Boston's mayor.

Who has the answer? (page 629)

On what page will we find descriptive information about blizzards? (page 164)

What heading did you look under? (Blizzards)

What subhead did you refer to? (Descriptive)

On which pages will we find references to Alexander Graham Bell? (335, 440)

What did you look under? (Bell, Alexander Graham)

On which page would you look to find a list of Belgium's ambassadors? (837)

On which page will you look to find the winners of the Miss America award? (page 312)

What heading did you refer to? (Awards, prizes)

What subheading did you look under? (Miss America)

On which page can you find addresses of NBA teams—National Basketball Association teams? (page 886)

What heading did you refer to? (Basketball)

What subheading did you look under? (Addresses, NBA teams)

On which page will you find the population of Berlin, Germany? (page 829)

What heading did you look under? (Berlin, Germany)

What subheading did you look under? (population)

On what page would you find information about best selling books? (page 289)

What heading did you look under? (Books)

What subheading did you look under? (Best sellers)

The World Almanac truly is a book of facts, isn't it?

FOLLOW-UP

Alternatives

1. Set up a *World Almanac* learning center. Put a copy of *The World Almanac*, reproductions of Worksheet 84, and a copy of the answers to Worksheet 84 on a table.
2. Assign Worksheet 84 as an extra credit assignment.

NOTE

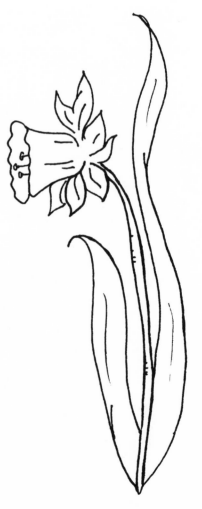

There are two *World Almanac* presentations you may want to use:

1. The lesson presented in this book
2. The video/cassette or the filmstrip/cassette "How to Use an Almanac"

Cost $22.50 each. Order toll free weekdays 8:30–5:00 (EST) 1-800-521-6600. In Ohio call collect, 216-621-7300.

Send mail orders to: World Almanac Education
1278 West Ninth Street
Cleveland, Ohio 44113

Ways to use the presentations:

1. Use one presentation as an introduction. The next year, use an alternate presentation as a review.
2. Use the lesson appropriate for each individual class.

THE WORLD ALMANAC

Refer to a copy of *The World Almanac* to find the answers to these questions.

1. When was the telephone invented? _____

2. Where was Tom Selleck born? _____

3. When was the University of Southern California founded? _____

   _____

4. Which city is the capital of Delaware? _____

5. How tall is the Statue of Liberty from the foundation of the pedestal to the torch? ____

6. What is the average depth of the Pacific Ocean? _____

7. How many lives were lost in the September 16, 1978, earthquake in Northeast Iran?

   _____

8. Who won the Miss America title in 1994? _____

9. What does the name Oklahoma mean? _____

10. What was the 1990 population of New York City? _____

REFERENCE BOOK ROUNDUP

OBJECTIVES

1. To have students examine the reference books they have been learning about
2. To culminate the lessons on reference books

PRESENTATIONS

Basic

In the basic presentation, a reference book is distributed to each student in the class. When the instructor gives a signal for the class to start, the students examine their books. After one minute, the instructor gives a signal for the students to pass their books to the right. This continues until everyone has seen each of the books.

Variation

The variation is similar to the basic presentation, with two exceptions. In the variation, the examination time is lengthened, and the students write a brief summary of each book.

MATERIALS

Basic Presentation

1. From the reference books you have taught and reviewed, select enough to give one to each student. If short of titles, precede the activity with several reviews of miscellaneous reference books or do the activity in groups and rotate.
2. A clock or watch with a second hand
3. If desired, reproductions of the Reference Book Test, Worksheet 85

Variation

1. The materials listed under Basic Presentation
2. Lined paper

3. A chalkboard, chalk, and eraser
4. If desired, reproductions of the Reference Book Test, Worksheet 85

PREPARATIONS

Basic Presentation

Before the class arrives, put one reference book out for each student.

Variation

1. Put the following on the chalkboard:

    Who's Who in America
    Biographies of living Americans

2. Before the class arrives, put one sheet of lined paper and one reference book out for each student.

LESSON

If the students have opened the reference books, ask them to close them for a few minutes.

You've been learning about reference books for quite some time. Today you're going to have the opportunity to examine the books you've been studying. Each of you has a reference book. When I say start, read the title of your book and examine the contents. When I say "change," pass your book to the person on your right.

Modify the direction of rotation according to the seating arrangement.

Point out the exact route the books are to be rotated. Be especially specific about rotation to different tables or rows.

You may want to reposition the tables or chairs for this activity.

If you are presenting the variation, have students record the title and a brief summary of each book on the paper that you provided. To summarize books, tell students to scan the title pages and the introduction, and then examine several entries.

Point to the example you've put on the board. Tell students that the title should be put on one line and that a brief summary should be put on the next line or two. Remind students that book titles should be underlined.

Start.

Jot down the number of students in the class and the time the activity is started. From this information, calculate when the activity will be completed.

After one/one-and-a-half/two minutes, give a signal for the students to change books.

Continue until all of the books have been examined.

SUGGESTIONS

1. The basic presentation may be appropriate for some classes, and the variation may be appropriate for others. You may even want to use both lessons with a class. If so, present the basic lesson first. On another day, present the variation.
2. Consider the students' attention span and needs, when setting the amount of time allowed for the activity. With the basic presentation, you may want to have the books rotated every minute. With the variation, you may need to allow one-and-a-half to two minutes. In the latter case, if you are unable to complete the lesson in one period, you can continue another time. To be able to proceed later, assign a number to each seat and have students note their numbers in the corners of their papers. Collect the papers. At the next visit, have students take the same seats as before. Distribute books according to the last book listed on each paper. If the students have summarized their last entry, you can rotate books and start.
3. If you use the variation, correct the papers or write a comment on each of them.
4. In rotating books, instead of saying "change," you may want to ring a bell.

FOLLOW-UP

You may want to give the Reference Book Test, Worksheet 85.

Name _____ Date _____

REFERENCE BOOK TEST

In which reference book will you find the answers to these questions? Write the letters of the answers on the lines provided below.

1. When was Adolph Hitler born?_____

2. Who said "Go west, young man"?   _____

3. Where is New River located?   _____

4. Who wrote the poem "The Barefoot Boy"? _____

5. What are the President's hobbies?   _____

6. Which words are synonyms of "beautiful"? _____

7. What are the educational requirements for the position of

   forest ranger?_____

8. What are Los Angeles State College's admission require-

   ments?   _____

9. Which books did Walter Farley write? _____

   _____

10. Who is the all-time home run leader?   _____

ANSWERS

a. *The Columbia Granger's Index to Poetry*
b. *Webster's New Biographical Dictionary*
c. *The Random House Thesaurus*
d. *The World Almanac and Book of Facts*
e. *Webster's New Geographical Dictionary*
f. *Occupational Outlook Handbook*
g. *Who's Who in America*
h. *Junior Book of Authors and Illustrators*
i. *Familiar Quotations*
j. *Profiles of American Colleges*

PART 3

REFERENCE BOOK REVIEWS

THE YOUNG READER'S COMPANION

The Young Reader's Companion. Edited by Gorton Carruth. New Providence, N.J.: Bowker, 1993. 681 p.

An illustrated A–Z literary encyclopedia for young people from the 5th grade through high school and beyond.

BOOKS TO REVIEW TOGETHER

You may want to review *The Young Reader's Companion* with *Books in Print.*

MATERIALS

If available, a copy of *The Young Reader's Companion.*

REVIEW

Would you like to find some information about a book? Perhaps the one titled *The Invisible Man?* Or maybe you'd like to know about an author, for example, Edgar Allan Poe? Or is there a literary character, such as Captain Hook, you'd like to know more about?

Hold up *The Young Reader's Companion,* if available.

The Young Reader's Companion is a literary encyclopedia that can give you information about all of those.

It contains information about 800 books—contemporary books as well as classics. For example, there are articles about

The Bible	*The Maltese Falcon*
The Koran	*The Sea Wolf*
The Talmud	*Robin Hood*
The Swiss Family Robinson	*North to Freedom*
The Treasure of Sierra Madre	*The Hobbit*

It also contains information about 750 authors. For example, there's information about

Jim Kjelgaard (pronounced Kel-guard)   Agatha Christie
Judy Blume   Robert Heinlein
Stephen King   Emily Bronte

Literary characters are covered. For example, there are articles about

Dorothy (of *The Wizard of Oz*)
Ichabod Crane
Tarzan
Doctor Dolittle

There are articles about 280 historical personages. For example, there's information about

Jesus
Michelangelo
Thomas Jefferson
Walt Disney

Two hundred mythological and legendary figures are covered. There's information about

King Midas
unicorn
Aladdin
goblins

There's a subject index in the back.

    You may want to read a few of the subject entries.

You remember that I said there's information about 800 books. I'm going to read one of the entries.

    Read the entry for one of the following books or choose an entry you'd like to share.

    North to Freedom (part or all)
    My Side of the Mountain
    The Longest Day

    Hold the book up with the title facing the students.

This is an attractive book and one that's fun to read. If you have a question about literature, refer to *The Young Reader's Companion*.

NOTE

Librarian. You'll want to have this book in your library.

BOOKS IN PRINT

Books in Print. New Providence, N.J.: Bowker, 1948–. Biennial.

An author and title index to books in print. The 1994–1995 edition has ten volumes: v. 1–4, Author Index; v. 5–8, Title Index; v. 9, O. P. (Out of Print)-O. S. I. (Out of Stock Indefinitely); v. 10, Publishers

Books in Print Supplement, N.J., Bowker. 3 v.

A mid-year supplement issued to list all the titles released since publication of *Books in Print.*

Subject Guide to Books in Print. 1957–. N.J., Bowker. Biennial. 5 v.

Vols. 1–4, subject arrangement of non-fiction titles listed in *Books in Print*. Vol. 5, subject guide to publishers, "thesaurus."

BOOKS TO REVIEW TOGETHER

You may want to review *Books in Print* with *The Young Reader's Companion.*

REVIEW

Do you know how many books are in print in the United States?

There are over one and a half million.

Do you know where you can find a list of them?

The public library has a set of volumes titled *Books in Print,* which lists the 1.6 million books currently being published. To locate a book in *Books in Print,* look under the book's title or author.

If your Aunt Mary wants a copy of *Wuthering Heights* for Christmas, look in the *Title Index* of *Books in Print* to find out if the book is available.

If your Uncle Henry wants a book by Louis L'Amour, look in the *Author Index* of *Books in Print* to find out which of L'Amour's books are currently in print.

By looking under a book's title or author, you'll find the name of the publisher and the cost of the book, if the book is in print. If you decide to order a book, look in the publisher's volume to get an address. If you prefer, have your local bookstore order the book for you.

To find out which nonfiction books are in print on a certain subject, you can refer to the *Subject Guide to Books in Print*.

Everyone should know about *Books in Print*. It's very useful.

WORLD ALMANAC OF THE U.S.A.

The World Almanac of the U.S.A. Mahwah, N.J.: World Almanac, 1993. 410 p.

   An in-depth profile of each state, including physical characteristics, historical milestones, contemporary facts, etc.

BOOKS TO REVIEW TOGETHER

You may want to review *The World Almanac of the U.S.A.* with *Lands and Peoples*.

MATERIALS

A copy of *The World Almanac of the U.S.A.,* if available

PREPARATION

Put a bookmark by each page you plan to read or show.

REVIEW

The World Almanac of the U.S.A. has an in-depth profile of each of the states. To find out what's covered, let's look at a particular state, for example, Montana (New York, your state, or any one).

   Turn to the state you've chosen. Read the subheads and any brief entries that sound interesting.

The coverage is quite complete, isn't it? For each state, we are told about the climate, environment, major cities, population, health, housing, and education.

The World Almanac of the U.S.A. also gives state capitals, official nicknames, mottoes, slogans, songs, symbols, and notable personalities.

Physical characteristics, historical milestones, and contemporary facts are given, too.

The 50 states, Washington, D.C., Puerto Rico, and U.S. associated regions are covered.

This book will answer questions you have about any of the states.

LANDS AND PEOPLES

Lands and Peoples. Danbury, Conn.: Grolier, 1993. 6 vols.
  A six-volume set of books covering the countries of the world, their lands and peoples.

Lands and Peoples Special Edition: Crisis in the Middle East. Danbury, Conn.: Grolier, 1992. 92 p.

Lands and Peoples Special Edition: Life after Communism. Danbury, Conn.: Grolier, 1993. 108 p.

BOOKS TO REVIEW TOGETHER

You may want to review *Lands and Peoples* with *The World Almanac of the U.S.A.*

MATERIALS

Volume One of *Lands and Peoples* and the two special editions: *Crisis in the Middle East* and *Life After Communism,* if available.

PREPARATIONS

Look Volume One over and be prepared to discuss the book up through page 13. See suggestions in this review.

REVIEW

If you were assigned to write a report about a particular country, to which books would you refer? (Possible answers: encyclopedias, books about the specific country assigned, etc.)

Yes, those are good sources.

There's another source of which you may not be aware. It's a six-volume set titled *Lands and Peoples.*

Hold up a volume, if available.

Lands and Peoples is organized by continents. Here's what appears in the six volumes:

Volume 1—Africa
Volume 2—Asia, Australia, New Zealand, Oceania
Volume 3—Europe
Volume 4—Europe
Volume 5—North America
Volume 6—Central and South America

Volume Six also has general statistical information and an index to the set.

Within each volume the countries of a particular continent are arranged geographically.

The set covers the geography, history, and economy of each country. Insights into the lives of people, lifestyles, beliefs, work, and play are given.

There are numerous colored photographs.

The first volume is about Africa.

Hold Volume One up, if available.

At the beginning of the book there are three pages of flags.

Show those three pages.

Next there's an introduction.

Show this.

The main text on Africa starts on page four.

Show page four. Read the captions under the illustrations on pages four and five.

On page six there's a map.

Show page six.

Page seven has facts and figures about Africa including location, area, population, and physical features.

"Countries and Territories of Africa" on page seven lists countries, square miles, populations, and capitals.

Show the illustrations on page 12 and 13.

After the six volumes of *Lands and Peoples* were published, events necessitated the publishing of two special editions: *Crisis in the Middle East* and *Life After Communism*.

If you have these, hold them up.

Lands and Peoples is a set of books you'll want to refer to.

THE WORLD ALMANAC INFOPEDIA

The World Almanac Infopedia: A Visual Encyclopedia for Students. New York: World Almanac, 1990. 382 p.

A one-volume, illustrated encyclopedia of concise articles for students of all ages, covering the universe, planet earth, countries of the world, history, the human body, animals, plants, science and technology, transport, communications, arts and entertainment, and sport.

BOOKS TO REVIEW TOGETHER

You may want to review *The World Almanac Infopedia* with *Guinness Book of Records.*

MATERIALS

A copy of *The World Almanac Infopedia,* if available.

PREPARATIONS

Place a bookmark by the Table of Contents.

If you plan to open the book to show specific examples, mark your places with bookmarks. See the examples in the review or choose some of your own.

REVIEW

Have you ever wondered how old the earth is? Or perhaps you've wondered which is the smallest animal in the world? Would you like to read about the results of the World Series?

If so, you can refer to *The World Almanac Infopedia.*

Hold the book up, if available.

The *Infopedia* is an illustrated encyclopedia of short articles for students of all ages.

Read the table of contents if you have the book. Otherwise, read or recite this list: "It covers the universe, planet earth, countries of the world, history, the human body, animals, plants, science and technology, transport, communication, arts and entertainment, sport."

There's an index in the back.

Open the book to illustrate each of the following or to illustrate examples you've chosen.

Here are some specific examples of the book's contents. The earth's vital statistics are covered: its age, diameter, circumference, area, height, etc.

The book has information about countries. For example, it covers North Korea by giving its location, its resources, and by telling what kind of work the people do.

It tells about important European monarchs: Napoleon, Queen Victoria, Henry VIII, and others.

There's a list of major wars.

A chronology of world history from c. 3500 B.C. is featured.

It lists the popes, tells facts about drugs, has a thumbnail article on AIDS.

The title gives you a good idea of its contents: Infopedia—info—information.

Look the book over. You'll find something that'll interest you.

THE GUINNESS BOOK OF RECORDS

The Guinness Book of Records. New York: Facts on File, 1956–. Annual. Publisher varies.

A book of records concerning the shortest, the tallest, the fastest, the deepest, etc., in relation to people, animals, sports, natural features, and so forth. Has a subject and name index. Formerly titled *The Guinness Book of World Records.*

BOOKS TO REVIEW TOGETHER

You may want to review *The Guinness Book of Records* with *The World Almanac Infopedia.*

MATERIALS

A copy of *The Guinness Book of Records,* if available.

PREPARATIONS

Teacher. Find out if your school library has reference and circulating copies of *The Guinness Book of Records.*

REVIEW

In which book can I find the answer to these questions?

Who is the richest woman in the world? How big is the biggest potato? Which statue is the tallest?

Hold up a copy of *The Guinness Book of Records,* if available.

The Guinness Book of Records gives information about superlatives—about the highest degrees, for example, the shortest, the tallest, the smallest, the biggest.

If you want to know which TV show ran longest, which breeds of dogs are most popular, who hit the longest home run, you can find the answers in *The Guinness Book of Records*.

The information is grouped into eleven subject divisions. Some examples are Human Beings, Arts and Entertainment, Sports and Games.

The book has a subject and name index.

It's an annual: it comes out yearly.

Tell the students whether their school library has reference copies and circulating copies.

If you want to know the highest temperature ever recorded, the oldest living person in the world, or the highest price ever paid for a book, look in *The Guinness Book of Records*.

GREAT ATHLETES

Great Athletes. Pasadena, Calif.: Salem Press, 1992. 20 vols.
  Compact, but detailed presentation of the careers, accomplishments, and unique personal qualities of 738 outstanding athletic champions.

The first set in a new series, *The Twentieth Century*.

BOOKS TO REVIEW TOGETHER

You may want to review *Great Athletes* with *Sports Almanac*.

MATERIALS

If available, one volume or a set of *Great Athletes*.

PREPARATION

Select one profile to show the students. Designate it with a bookmark.

REVIEW

How many of you are sports fans?

  Hold up a volume of *Great Athletes*.

Have you seen this wonderful set of books, *Great Athletes?*

There are 738 outstanding athletic champions—men and women, national and international—profiled in an easy-to-understand style.

  Open to the profile you've chosen to share. Hold the book up, and point out the section's subheads as you discuss them.

Each article is about four pages long and is divided into four sections, followed by a summary.

The first section, "Early Life," presents the athlete's place and date of birth and information about his or her's childhood, parents, brothers and sisters, and other family details.

The experiences and influences that shaped the athlete and propelled him or her to greatness are covered in "The Road to Excellence." Any obstacles the athlete had to overcome are considered here.

"The Emerging Champion" explains the characteristics and circumstances that made the athlete among the best in the world.

"Continuing the Story" covers the athlete's subsequent career development. Also considered is the athlete's life away from sports.

The "Summary" concludes the profile with a brief review of the athlete's life and career—the honors, awards, and human qualities that made him or her great.

Hold the book up and show the tabular material at the end of the profile you're presenting.

Each article contains tabular material such as career statistics, honors and awards, records set, etc.

Show the photograph that accompanies the profile under consideration.

A full-page photograph of the athlete is one of the most appealing features of the book.

There are three indexes at the end of each volume, which cover the entire set. The first index is arranged according to the athlete's last name, the second is organized by the type of sport, and the third is arranged by country. The indexes are arranged in alphabetical order and give the volume and page number.

Volume 20 features a time line and a glossary. The time line lists each athlete in chronological order by birth date. The glossary contains over 400 words and phrases found in the articles.

If you like sports, you'll like *Great Athletes*.

SPORTS ALMANAC

Sports Almanac. Edited by the editors of *Sports Illustrated.* Boston: Little, Brown, 1994. 800 p.

An annual covering all the sports, all the stars, all the sports statistics. Has a year-by-year record of each sport. Contains over 600 profiles of the world's greatest athletes. Features articles by *Sports Illustrated*'s top writers. Also has a color photo section.

BOOKS TO REVIEW TOGETHER

You may want to review *Sports Almanac* with *Great Athletes.*

MATERIALS

A copy of *Sports Almanac,* if available.

PREPARATION

Place bookmarks at the table of contents, the color section, and at any other pages you plan to show to the students.

REVIEW

Would you like to know who the NBA finals' most valuable player was in 1993, 1982, or 1969? Would you like to know the locations and dates of all the Olympic Games? Would you like a list of Super Bowl box scores?

You can find information about all of those in *Sports Almanac.*

Hold the book up, if available.

The table of contents lists the sports covered.

If you have a copy of the book, read the table of contents.

If you don't have a copy, read this:

"First there's Expanded Contents, Scorecard, and The Year in Sport. Then the sports are listed: Baseball, Pro Football, College Football, Pro Basketball, College Basketball, Hockey, Tennis, Golf, Boxing, Horse Racing, Motor Sports, Bowling, Soccer, NCAA Sports, Olympics, Track and Field, Swimming, Skiing, Figure Skating, Miscellaneous Sports. The table of contents ends with the Sports Market, Awards, Profiles, and Obituaries."

There are 600 brief profiles of the world's greatest athletes.

Turn to the next to last section and read a profile about one or more of the following athletes:

Bonnie Blair
Charles Barkley
Chris Evert
Michael Jordan
Peggy Fleming
Babe Ruth

There's a year-by-year record of each sport.

The feature articles that are included are by *Sports Illustrated*'s top writers.

There's a color photo section.

 Show one or more pictures.

If you're interested in sports, you'll be interested in this book, *Sports Almanac*.

ANNIVERSARIES AND HOLIDAYS

Gregory, Ruth W. *Anniversaries and Holidays*. 4th ed. Chicago: American Library Association, 1983. 262 p.
 Originated in 1928.
 Identifies notable anniversaries, holy days, holidays, and special events days. Bibliography.

BOOKS TO REVIEW TOGETHER

You may want to review *Anniversaries and Holidays* with *Famous First Facts*.

MATERIALS

A copy of *Anniversaries and Holidays,* if available.

REVIEW

Today is _____ (month and day).

Let's see what's special about it.

 Open a copy of *Anniversaries and Holidays* to Part 1, and locate today's month and day.

 State today's month and day again.

 Read the NAME of each entry listed.

Those are the anniversaries and special days listed for _____ (today's month and day). There's more information about each of them.

 Read one entry in its entirety.

The title of this book is *Anniversaries and Holidays*.

Anniversary means occurring on the same day every year.

Part One of this book is a Calendar of Fixed Days. By fixed days, the author means anniversaries and holidays which always occur on the same day, for example, Christmas. Christmas is always celebrated on December 25th.

Part Two is a Calendar of Movable Days. Some holidays are not celebrated on the same day every year. They're moved around on the calendar. An example is Easter. Easter isn't observed on a specific date each year. Easter is held on the first Sunday after the date of the first full moon that occurs on or after March 21st. In 1988 Easter fell on April 19th, but in 1989 it fell on March 26th.

Part Three is a bibliography related to anniversaries and holidays.

What is a bibliography? (a list of sources of information on a particular subject)

If you need to know which books have information about a particular holiday, for example, St. Patrick's Day, you can look in the bibliography.

You can also refer to the card/computer catalog under St. Patrick's Day. Holidays are entered in the catalogs as subjects, therefore, you can look directly under any major holiday: Christmas, Easter, Halloween, St. Patrick's Day, and so forth.

Anniversaries and Holidays has an index. If you want to know when Houdini Day, or Sadie Hawkins Day, or any other holiday occurs, look in the index.

If you need brief information about an anniversary, holiday, festival, or special events day, look in *Anniversaries and Holidays*.

FAMOUS FIRST FACTS

Kane, Joseph Nathan. *Famous First Facts*. 4th ed., expanded and rev. New York: H. W. Wilson, 1981. 1,350 pp.
   A record of inventions, discoveries, and first happenings in the United States.

BOOKS TO REVIEW TOGETHER

You may want to review *Famous First Facts* with *Anniversaries and Holidays*.

MATERIALS

A copy of *Famous First Facts,* if available.

REVIEW

If you want to find out about the first baseball game, the first automobile, the first dentist, the first hotel, the first pirate, or the first anything in American history, you can find it in *Famous First Facts*.

   Hold a copy up.

This book is easy to use because each event is listed in alphabetical order. If you want to find out about the first baseball game, look under "b" until you find baseball game.

There are four indexes. One index lists events according to the year in which they took place. If you want to know what significant first happenings, discoveries, and inventions took place in 1929, or in any other year, you can look in the index, which lists events by the year of occurrence.

One index lists events by the month and day of occurrence. If you want to find out what events happened on a particular day, for example, what happened on your birthday, June 12th, look under the month of June, the twelfth day.

Another index lists names of persons directly or indirectly involved with an event. If you're interested in Benjamin Franklin, you can look in this index under Franklin, and you'll be referred to all of the firsts associated with him.

One index lists events under the state and city where they took place. If you want to know which events first took place in our city, look under the state of _____, city of _____.

Famous First Facts is a book you'll want to refer to when you need to know about a first happening.

INFORMATION PLEASE ALMANAC

Information Please Almanac. 47th ed., 1994. Boston: Houghton Mifflin, 1947–. Annual.

    Publisher varies. Title varies.

    An almanac of miscellaneous information arranged by topics.

RELATED LESSON

Precede this review, on a different day, with the lesson on *The World Almanac.*

BOOKS TO REVIEW TOGETHER

You may want to review *Information Please Almanac* with the Abridged, Unabridged, Foreign Language, and Rhyming Dictionaries review.

MATERIALS

A copy of *Information Please Almanac,* if available.

REVIEW

We studied *The World Almanac* recently. Today we're going to consider a book which is similar in many ways. It's titled *Information Please Almanac.*

    Hold up a copy, if available.

The word almanac is defined as "a yearly calendar with astronomical data, weather forecasts, and tables of useful information." *The World Almanac* and *Information Please Almanac* both seem to extend far beyond that definition.

Like *The World Almanac, Information Please* is an annual.

What does the word annual mean? (published once a year)

Information Please Almanac is similar to *The World Almanac* in that both are almanacs, they're both annuals, they both cover miscellaneous information, and their indexes are in the front.

There are differences in the two almanacs. All of the material in *Information Please Almanac* is grouped into a few large subject areas. The subjects in *The World Almanac* are somewhat independent of each other.

Here are some examples of what's covered in *Information Please Almanac:* the environment, health, sports, history, religion, taxes, inventions and discoveries.

There is information about the Congress of the United States, the Constitution, crime statistics, great disasters, countries of the world, and so forth.

If you want to find a chronology of world events, you can find one in *Information Please Almanac*.

What's a chronology? (the arrangement of events in the order of occurrence)

The word chronology is derived from the word chronos, time. When you put something in chronological order, you put it in order by time.

The World Almanac has a chronology, too.

Information Please Almanac's chronology is titled Current Events, What Happened in 19__ (previous year).

Look at a copy of *The World Almanac* and *Information Please Almanac* together. Discover how they're alike and how they're different. Decide which features each has that make it particularly useful.

SUGGESTION

Librarian. Save your old copies of *Information Please Almanac*. They can be used in learning centers, for class study, or for circulation.

ABRIDGED, UNABRIDGED, FOREIGN LANGUAGE, AND RHYMING DICTIONARIES

BOOKS TO REVIEW TOGETHER

Your school library's abridged and unabridged English language dictionaries, its foreign language dictionaries, and its rhyming dictionaries.

You may also want to review *Information Please Almanac.*

MATERIALS

1. An abridged dictionary
2. An unabridged dictionary
3. One or more foreign-language dictionaries
4. A rhyming dictionary

PREPARATION

Teacher. Find out where the various dictionaries you are going to review are located. Note particularly whether there are reference and circulating copies.

REVIEW

If you need to find the definition of a word, where will you look? (in a dictionary)

   Hold up an abridged dictionary.

This dictionary is abridged.

What does abridged mean? (shortened)

The most-used words in the English language are probably contained in this dictionary. However, not all words are included.

If you look in this dictionary and can't find the word you need, where will you look? (in an unabridged dictionary)

   Hold up an unabridged dictionary.

This is an unabridged dictionary. Unabridged means not shortened. This dictionary defines the English language as currently spoken and written.

What kind of information is found in dictionaries? (information about words: definitions, pronunciations, spelling, parts of speech, synonyms, and so forth)

If you are looking up a common word, look in an abridged dictionary. If you need extensive information, or if the word you are looking up isn't in an abridged dictionary, refer to an unabridged dictionary.

   Announce where reference and circulating dictionaries are shelved.

Perhaps you need to translate something from one language to another. If so, you can refer to a foreign language dictionary.

   If you have a foreign language dictionary, hold it up and read its title. Explain its format and how to use it.

If you're a writer, a poet, or a rapper, perhaps you need a list of rhyming words. For example, maybe the only words you can think of to rhyme with June are moon and tune. If you refer to a rhyming dictionary, you'll be given some other words that rhyme.

   If you have a rhyming dictionary, hold it up and read its title.

What kind of dictionary would you refer to if you wanted to know the Spanish word for hello? (a foreign language dictionary; a Spanish-English dictionary)

What kind of dictionary would you refer to if you wanted to have access to all the words in the English language? (an unabridged dictionary)

What is an abridged dictionary? (a shortened dictionary)

What kind of dictionary would you refer to if you needed some words to rhyme with Mulligan stew? (a rhyming dictionary)

PART 4

WORKSHEET ANSWERS

Worksheets 2a and 2b

pages 13-14

1. binding
2. index
3. endpapers
4. frontispiece
5. glossary
6. bibliography
7. acknowledgments
8. title page
9. appendix
10. table of contents
11. text
12 introduction (preface; foreword)
13. half-title page
14. illustrations
15. dedication
16. flyleaves
17. copyright
18. author
19. publisher
20. illustrator
21. place of publication
22. title

Worksheet 5

page 38

1. books (literary works) that are not true
2. alphabetically by the authors' last names primarily (secondarily by the authors' first names)
3. fiction
4. easy books
5. story collection
6. a, an, the
7. Juvenile, Young Adult

1. Sanchez   *Surprise Visit*
   Sanders   *Night Train*
   Sutton   *Whispers*
2. Brown, Ed   *The Bridge*
   Brown, Ed   *An Island Afar*
   Jones, Pat   *A Trip East*
3. Jones, Ann   *The Crossing*
   Jones, Ann   *Sisters*
   Jones, Bill   *New Car*

Worksheet 11

page 50

1. 700
2. 500
3. 900
4. 200
5. 100
6. 600
7. 000
8. 800
9. 300
10. 400
11. 000
12. 500
13. 800
14. 700
15. 900
16. 200
17. 300
18. 400
19. 600
20. 100

Worksheet 12

page 59

1.	Class Numbers		Call Numbers
	926.3		—
	—		623 A
	—		423 Smi
	021		—
2a.	623	2b.	972
	623.15		973
	623.2		973.14
	623.73		973.2
	623.8		973.7

3. true
4. by numbers/subject
5a. true
5b. true
5c. true
5d. false
5e. true

Worksheet 13

page 66

1. FESTIVALS / FISH
2. FESTIVALS / FISH
3. F/FESTIVALS
4. FESTIVALS / FISH
5. FLOWERS / FORESTS
6. FLOWERS / FORESTS
7. FORESTS / FRONTIER
8. FLOWERS / FORESTS
9. FLOWERS / FORESTS
10. FISH / FLOWERS

Worksheet 14

page 67

1. subject   L-M
2. title   I-K
3. author   A-B
4. subject   Q-S
5. title   I-K
6. author   C-E
7. subject   Q-S
8. title   W-Z
9. author   N-P
10. subject   T-V

Worksheet 18a and 18b

page 78-79

1A. *Daniel Boone*
1B. *Rascal*
1C. *Island of the Blue Dolphins*
2A. Lawlor
2B. North
2C. O'Dell
3A. 921 B
3B. 599 N
3C. O'De
4A. A. Whitman
4B. E. P. Dutton & Company
4C. Houghton
5A. Bert Dodson
5B. John Schoenherr
5C. (none listed)
6A. 160 pages
6B. 189 pages
6C. 184 pages
7A. 1989
7B. 1963
7C. 1960
8A. title
8B. subject
8C. author

Worksheet 19

page 86

Set 1	Set 2	Set 3	Set 4
1	2	6	6
4	3	3	5
2	1	7	4
3	4	1	3
		5	1
		2	7
		4	2

1. author, title, subject
2. chronologically (alphabetized by country and given the subject heading HISTORY, then arranged chronologically)
3. a, an, the

Worksheet 27

page 114

(One, two, or three letters may be used after the number.)

1. 921 B
2. 920 D
3. 921 F
4. 920 B
5. 921 B
6. 920 R
7. 920 E
8. 921 C
9. 921 J
10. 920 R
11. 921 L
12. 920 H
13. 920 D
14. 921 F
15. 921 E

Worksheet 32

page 132

1. classics
2. historical fiction
3. fiction
4. autobiography
5. nonfiction
6. poetry
7. biography
8. science fiction
9. fantasy
10. fables
11. epics
12. fairy tales
13. myths
14. folk tales
15. prose

Worksheet 39

page 157

1. The next big one. . . .
2. network of underground faults crisscross southern California
3. Los Angeles earthquake, 1994
4. Earthquake prediction
5. Clint Eastwood: riding high
6. Ladies' Home Journal
7. 110
8. August 1993
9. 42+
10. G. Gibson

Worksheet 47

page 183

1. June 9, 1961
2. c/o NBC-TV, 3000 W. Alameda Ave., Burbank, CA 91523
3. energy, drive
4. *Family Ties*
5. He has "an incredible comic sensibility," "agile timing," and "infallible charm."
6. Andrew
7. Edmonton, Alberta, Canada
8. Bill and Phyllis Fox
9. *Back to the Future*
10. (answers will vary)

Worksheet 50

page 190

1. 1887
2. 1974
3. American
4. Philadelphia
5. *Craig's Wife*
6. George Kelly Barnes
7. 1895
8. 1954
9. Memphis, Tenn.
10. for a series of robberies and slayings in the Midwest

Worksheet 53

page 198

1. Santa Monica, California
2. George Francis and Gertrude Temple
3. Linda Susan, Charles Alden, Lori Alden
4. Westlake School for Girls
5. Czechoslovakia
6. 3½ years old
7. *Stand Up and Cheer*
8. Republican
9. Commonwealth of California
10. Care of Academy of Motion Picture Arts and Sciences, 8949 Wilshire Blvd., Beverly Hills, CA 90211

Worksheet 54

page 203

(Answers are included in the lesson.)

Worksheet 55

page 204

1. MOHAWK TRAIL
2. MILLION
3. JOHN MASEFIELD
4. MILITIA
5. —

1. N
2. G
3. S
4. A
5. B
6. C
7. S
8. T
9. T
10. B
11. V
12. B
13. C
14. T
15. S
16. L
17. S
18. E
19. R
20. H

Worksheet 56

page 207

(Answers are included in the lesson.)

Worksheet 57

page 208

These words should be circled:
1. Nobel Prize
2. Henry
3. Alamo
4. Olympic Games
5. robot
6. Titanic
7. Lindbergh
8. Mojave Desert
9. Scotland Yard
10. martial arts

These are the answers to the 10 items above:
1. Claude Simon
2. William Sydney Porter
3. San Antonio
4. Moscow, Russia
5. Czech
6. New York City
7. May 20–21, 1927
8. 25,000 square miles
9. London
10. the Orient (Asian countries)

Worksheet 64

page 243

1. Booker Taliaferro Washington, 1856–1915, *Up from Slavery*
2. Mark Twain, 1835–1910, Cable from London to the Associated Press
3. Oscar Fingal O'Flahertie Wills Wilde, 1854–1900, *Lady Windermere's Fan*, Act I
4. Thomas Alva Edison, 1847–1931, *Life*, Ch. 24
5. Benjamin Franklin, 1706–1790, *Advice to a Young Tradesman*
6. Robert Louis Stevenson, 1850–1894, Virginibus *Puerisque III, An Apology for Idlers*

Worksheet 67

page 252

1. "An Orchard at Avignon"
2. Window
3. *The American Songbag*
4. "The Wind's Visit"
5. W. H. Auden
6. AnAn
7. (Any one of these:)
   "The Barrel-Organ"
   "Daddy Fell into the Pond"
   "A Salute from the Fleet"
   "The Search Lights"
   "A Song of Sherwood"
8. *Best Loved Story Poems*
9. Hippolytus
10. Highwaym<u>e</u>n

Worksheet 69

page 259

1. Scraper, Oklahoma
2. Woodrow Wilson Rawls
3. *The Call of the Wild*
4. about ten years old
5. *The Saturday Evening Post*
6. *Where the Red Fern Grows*
7. *Summer of the Monkeys*
8. *Where the Red Fern Grows*
9. He regretted that he couldn't take a copy of his book to his father and say, "It took a long time, Dad, but I made it."
10. his wife

Worksheet 71

page 268

If students list the correct numbers for the meanings, the synonyms or antonyms are probably correct, too. Students may choose synonyms or antonyms other than those listed here.

1.	generous	4
2.	large	1
3.	pretentious	3
4.	mature	5
5.	important	2
1.	unimportant	2
2.	little (or young)	5
3.	little	1
4.	ordinary (meek)	3
5.	stingy (cheap)	4

Worksheet 75

page 286

1. for creating the "Tarzan" stories
2. Chicago
3. 36 years old
4. 1912
5. institution
6. 56 languages
7. horseback riding and golf
8. books, movies, comic strips, radio
9. 1915
10. March 19, 1950

Worksheet 78

page 297

1. about 700,000
2. usually at least 20 years of age
3. honesty, good judgment, and a sense of responsibility
4. a high school education
5. enforce laws to prevent smuggling of goods across U.S. borders
6. (Any three of these:) guards, bailiffs, correction officers, deputy sheriffs, fire marshals, fish and game wardens, and U.S. marshals
7. about $32,000 a year
8. U.S. Secret Service agent
9. keep order in the courtroom
10. half-pay

Worksheet 84

page 316

1. 1876
2. Detroit, Michigan
3. 1880
4. Dover
5. 305 ft. & 1 inch
6. 12,925 ft.
7. 25,000
8. Kimberley Aiken
9. red man
10. 7,322,564

Worksheet 85

page 320

1. b
2. i
3. e
4. a
5. g
6. c
7. f
8. j
9. h
10. d

INDEX

A, an, the, 33, 63, 70, 82
abridged, unabridged, foreign language and rhyming dictionaries, 345–46
acknowledgments, 8, 12, 20, 27
anniversaries and holidays, 339–40
annotated cards, 73
answers (worksheet), 347–53
appendix, 9, 12, 21, 22, 29; picture, 29
arrangement of shelves, 33
atlases, 221–25
author, 12, 17, 18
author/celebrity report (form), 117
autobiography, 109, 111–12, 121–22; worksheet, 114

bibliography, 9, 12, 21, 29, 210; picture, 29
binding, 5, 12, 16–17, 26; picture 26
biography, 109–17, 121, 122; report form, 115–16; worksheets, 114–17
book report (form), 43
book reviews (reference), 321–46
bookmarks, 1–2
Books in Print, 325–26
Burroughs, Edgar Rice, 282–283; biographical reprint, 285

call numbers, 56
card catalog, 61–91; arrangement of cards, 62, 69, 81–85;—, worksheet 86; author, title, subject cards, 71; catalog cards, pictures, 75–77 guide cards, 61–65, 88; —, pictures of 61, 66; worksheet 66; labels, drawer, 64; purpose, 88; worksheets, 66, 67, 75–79, 86, 91
career books, 289–99, 304
career report (form), 298
catalog cards. *See* card catalog
catalogs (types), 74
class numbers, 56
classics, 119, 122; list, 124
classified ads, 163
collective biography, 109, 111, 121; worksheet 114

Colleges. See *Profiles of American Colleges*
Columbia Granger's Index to Poetry, 245–52; worksheets, 250–52
compiler, 18
computer catalog, 93–107; worksheets, 102–7
copyright, 7, 12, 19; notice of, 7, 19; page, 12, 19, 27; picture, 27
cross references, 73; pictures, 77
Current Biography, 177–84; report form, 184; worksheet, 183

decimals, 53–55
dedication, 8, 12, 20, 27; picture, 27
Dewey Decimal Classification, 45–50; classification lists, 48–49; worksheet 50
dictionaries, 345–46

easy fiction, 35
editor, 18
editorial, 160–62; example, 167
editorial cartoon, 162; example, 168
encyclopedias, 199–219; arrangement, 199–201; cross references, 205; —,worksheets, 20; guide words, 201–202; —, worksheets, 203–4, 209; indexes, 215–28; —, worksheet, 219; key words, 206; —, worksheets, 207–8; special features, 218; study aids, 211; —, worksheet 214; subject location, 202; —, worksheets, 203–4; —, worksheets, 203, 204, 207, 208, 213–14, 219
endpapers, 5, 12, 17, 26; picture, 26
epics, 127, 129, 130

fables, 127–29
fairy tales, 127–30
Familiar Quotations, 235–43; worksheets, 242–43
Famous First Facts, 341–42
fantasy, 127, 129–30
feature story, 163; example, 166

ABOUT THE AUTHOR

Arden Druce has been a school librarian for twenty-one years, serving elementary, intermediate, junior, and senior high schools. She has also been a teacher of grades one through six.

She was formerly a librarian at:

Columbus Junior High School, Canoga Park, California
Antelope Union High School, Wellton, Arizona
Earlimart Elementary School, Earlimart, California
Earlimart Intermediate School, Earlimart, California

The author was formerly a teacher at:

Eton Elementary School, Canoga Park, California
Hart Street Elementary School, Canoga Park, California
Earlimart Elementary School, Earlimart, California
Sun Valley Private Elementary School, Sun Valley, California

Arden Druce is also the author of *Complete Library Skills Activities Program: Ready-to-Use Lessons for Grades K-6, Chalk Talk Stories,* and *Witch, Witch.*

The author lives in Camp Verde, Arizona, with her three dogs and six cats. She is currently devoting her time to writing, studying, and animal welfare.

ORDER FORM

Please ship the following book(s)

ISBN	Title	Price	Qty	Cost
0-8108-3100-7	Library Lessons for Grades 7–9	$55.00	_____	_____

Md. residents add 5% sales tax _____

Postage and Handling _____
($3.50/first book, 75¢ each add'l book)

Total* _____

*Make checks payable to Scarecrow Press

Examination copies: Examination copies are available for classroom adoption. The book's invoice will be canceled if ten or more copies are ordered for classroom use. Otherwise the examination copy may be purchased or returned (in saleable condition) within 60 days.

1. Call toll free: 1-800-462-6420 (local 301-459-3366)
2. Fax to: 301-459-2118
3. Mail to: Scarecrow Press, Inc.
                    4720 Boston Way
                    Lanham, Maryland 20706

- All orders from individuals must be prepaid
- Institutions with established accounts may attach a purchase order
- Prices subject to change without notice

Please check one of the following:

○ MasterCard
○ Visa
○ Purchase order
○ Check/Money Order enclosed
○ Exam copy

Card # _____

Exp. Date: _____   Signature _____

Name _____

Institution _____

Street _____

City _____ State _____ Zip _____